COLOR ME ENGLISH

Also by Caryl Phillips

In the Falling Snow

Foreigners

Dancing in the Dark

A Distant Shore

A New World Order

The Atlantic Sound

The Nature of Blood

Crossing the River

Cambridge

Higher Ground

The European Tribe

A State of Independence

The Final Passage

Caryl Phillips

Color Me English

Migration and Belonging
Before and After 9/11

THE NEW PRESS

NEW YORK
LONDON

Requests for permission to reproduce selections from this book should be mailed to:
Permissions Department, The New Press, 38 Greene Street, New York, NY 10013.

Grateful thanks to Dover Publications for permission to quote from
'If We Must Die' from Claude McKay's *Selected Poems* (1999)

Published in the United States by The New Press, New York, 2011
Published in Great Britain by Harvill Secker, London, 2011
Distributed by Perseus Distribution

LIBRARY OF CONGRESS CATALOGING-IN-PUBLICATION DATA
Phillips, Caryl.
Color me English : migration and belonging before and after 9/11 / Caryl Phillips.
p. cm.
ISBN 978-1-59558-650-6 (hc. : alk. paper)
I. Title.
PR9275.S263P47274 2011
824'.914--dc22

2011010274

The New Press was established in 1990 as a not-for-profit alternative to the large, commercial publishing houses currently dominating the book publishing industry. The New Press operates in the public interest rather than for private gain, and is committed to publishing, in innovative ways, works of educational, cultural, and community value that are often deemed insufficiently profitable.

www.thenewpress.com

Typeset in Centaur MT by Palimpsest Book Production Limited,
Falkirk, Stirlingshire

Printed in the United States of America

2 4 6 8 10 9 7 5 3 1

Acknowledgements

I am fortunate to have been guided and assisted by Sarah Burnes, Georgia Garrett, Geoff Mulligan, and Stuart Williams. I continue to be grateful for the support of Leon Wieseltier of the *New Republic*, but my greatest debt is to Annalena McAfee. During her time as editor of the *Guardian Review* she backed my ideas, practically and editorially, and enabled me to travel and reflect both at home and abroad. Without her generosity this would be an entirely different book.

For Tatiana

Table of Contents

Introduction

Color Me English

I was thirteen and entering my third year at Leeds Central High School, an all-boys grammar school in the centre of Leeds. This year marked a transition because for the first time I would no longer be the only black boy in the school. My brothers, Trevor and Malcolm, would be starting in the first year. Trevor was born at the start of September and Malcolm at the end of July and so, by a matter of a few days, they were both grouped together in the same school year. I remember feeling that my 'freedom' was about to be traduced by the arrival of my younger brothers, but it never occurred to me to advise them on how to cope with the somewhat lonely racial situation at the school. We had been the only black children at our primary school, and we remained the only black family on a tough, all-white working-class estate. All three of us were able to cope. We knew when to fight and we knew when to run. In fact, most of my childhood was spent either fighting or running, and my only refuge was reading, which I tried to conceal as a slightly shameful secret for it did not square with the rough, aggressive demeanour that I had to cultivate in order to survive. Naturally enough, both of my brothers knew full well how to fight and how to run, which meant that there was no need for a conversation on the topic of racial isolation. And so, as the black population of Leeds Central High School tripled, I settled down to the novelty of no longer being the only one in the school.

Two weeks into the term it happened. One morning as the teacher called out our names, there was an extra name, like an afterthought, tagged on the end of the register. 'Ali.' We all turned around and there, seated in the furthest corner, was a small moon-faced brown boy in a brand new school blazer that was clearly too big for him, and which served only to accentuate his diminutive stature. Ali looked terrified. Thirty pairs of eyes took in this oriental apparition and he began to blink furiously, as though he might at any moment burst into tears. The teacher did not bother to introduce the new boy, or explain why he was joining us two weeks into the term. He simply closed the register with a dull thud as he did every morning, and then he barked, 'Assembly.' Chairs were scraped back and desk lids were opened and slammed shut as we formed a noisy procession and filed out towards the school hall. I assume that on that first morning Ali stood up and joined us, but I really have no idea. He was the new boy and so he was effectively ignored.

During the next few weeks, Ali's palpable sense of isolation did not attenuate. As far as I could tell he had no friends, and nobody went out of their way to rescue him from his segregation. As a matter of daily routine, somebody in the classroom would throw a pencil, or a piece of chalk, and it would strike an unsuspecting boy on the back of the head. The boy who had been struck would turn angrily and try to discern who the assailant was. Fingers would quickly point towards Ali, and raucous cries of 'Hey, Pack it in, Ali' would fill the room. How witty we all were. All the while, an increasingly shy and tormented Ali sat quietly at the back of the classroom visibly shrinking before our eyes. Boys can be merciless, and we certainly were. And because nobody told us to cease, this daily harassment of the newcomer in our midst continued unabated.

It almost doesn't need stating, but Ali was predictably bad at games. You can imagine the scene. On Tuesday afternoons we were bussed to the outskirts of west Leeds, where the school playing fields were located. The cross-country run was a brutal affair, featuring a near-vertical ascent – the so-called 'steep hill' – and untold laps of the football pitches. We were divided into four houses – named after famous scientists. Faraday, Priestley, Newton and Matthew Murray. Competition for house points was fierce, and we were all focused. Most of us had showered and changed back into school uniform by the time Ali rounded the final corner of the football pitch. He could be seen, through the late afternoon gloom, making his painfully slow way towards the school pavilion, his baggy white shirt blowing in the breeze with barely a torso to give it any shape or substance. His spindly legs always appeared to be on the point of buckling, but his arms still pumped like little pistons, and his chin was angled upwards for Ali was determined to cross the line. We all stood and laughed at him. 'Come on, Pack it in, Ali.'

After the games period was over there was no school bus to take us back to town, so we were expected to leave en masse and take public transport to wherever we lived. A few boys lived in west Leeds, but the majority of us took a bus back into the city, and then transferred to whatever bus would take us home. One late Tuesday afternoon, I remember sitting upstairs on the top deck of a bus as it ferried the noisy schoolboys towards the city centre. Ali was sitting by himself some few seats behind me, and then I heard the commotion and turned around. A group of boys had grabbed Ali's haversack and were rifling through it, pulling out his textbooks, his exercise books, his pencil case, everything. I saw terror on Ali's face and immediately understood that he could not afford to lose these things. I knew how hard my own mother was working to make sure that her sons had uniforms and books and sports kit, and I assumed that Ali's family were in the same predicament. One simply could not afford to be frivolous when it came to the practical aspects of getting on in England as a non-white child. And then I saw the bullies open the small top window, and I watched as they threw all of Ali's books, one by one, out of the window of the speeding bus and into the middle of Headingley Road. They then handed him the empty haversack, their stupid faces flushed with success. I turned back around in my seat and faced the front, knowing that something inside me had changed.

When the bus stopped outside Leeds Central High School, I got up and spoke to Ali for the first time. 'Come with me,' I said. Ali followed me down the stairs of the bus and on to the pavement. 'We're going to report this, okay?' He nodded and then traipsed after me, as I walked up the flight of stone steps and into the school. Once there, I made my way to the main office where I was all too familiar with the sour-faced woman whose head poked out of the little hatch. She was the gatekeeper to the headmaster's office, and I had been summoned before him on numerous occasions for various disciplinary reasons. In fact, only the previous week he had bestowed six strokes of the cane upon me for some alleged form of insubordination. As far as his secretary was concerned, I was not just a troublemaker, I was *the* troublemaker. 'Yes,' she said, eyeing the two thirteen-year-old immigrant boys standing before her. I explained what had happened to Ali's books, and I named names. She listened, and then with a triumphant smirk simply said, 'So what do you want me to do about it?' Was she serious? These hooligans had thrown Ali's books out of the window of a public bus. 'Well?' she said. I stared at her and then decided that it was probably politic for me to say nothing further. I walked away in disgust, and Ali shuffled after me. Once outside the school, I turned to face him. 'You can try and report it again tomorrow.' Ali looked at his champion, and he slowly nodded. 'Okay,' he said. I've seldom felt more naïve than I did at that moment. Poor Ali could neither run nor fight, but there was no need for me to feel too sorry for him for this newcomer already understood how things were in England. When tomorrow came he would not be reporting anything to anybody in the school office.

I don't remember having another conversation with Ali. The classroom teasing continued, but I made a conscious effort not to take part. However, I *am* somewhat ashamed that I never again spoke up in Ali's defence. He was the first Muslim that I ever knew, and the first Southeast Asian, but although I felt some immigrant kinship with him, and had instinctively tried to help him, things between us went only so far, and no further. Although we might be enduring some of the same difficulties because of our pigmentation, there was a clear cultural difference which meant that while I was able to find a way to anxiously participate in British life, albeit in a manner that was hardly fulfilling, Ali was enduring the type of hostility that renders any thoughts of participation a distant, and decidedly unlikely, dream. My nominal acceptability to my classmates was in part related to the fact that I was bigger, stronger, and a good deal more outgoing than Ali, but it was also related to my being, at least ostensibly, an Anglican churchgoer who had the good manners not to be able to flaunt another language. Take race out of the equation and I had no place to hide from the English. Culturally, I was very much like them except, as a helpful teacher once told me, 'You've just been left in the oven a bit longer, that's all, love.' I was exposed and the English could see me and keep an eye on me, and even get to know me if they chose to. I could be useful, on the football team or on sports day, but I knew that at any moment the privilege of participation could be withdrawn and, depending on the mood of the person, or people, that I was with, I might suddenly have to fight or run. Ali, on the other hand, had the worlds of religion and language into which he might retreat and hide from the English which, of course, made him deeply untrustworthy.

For a large part of my life I grew up feeling that the real divisive factor in British, and by extension European, life was race; that it was race that was keeping us separate from each other, and that racism had made the greatest contribution to the inequity of opportunity in modern Britain. However, on 7 July 2005 I was reminded that something else is going on which contributes powerfully to divisiveness in British and European life. The cultural 'othering' of another people so that their national affiliation is attacked by pointing to their cultural practices is hardly a new European experience. However, the forceful response of those who feel that their cultural practices are being disrespected *is* something new. The four young men who met just outside London at Luton train station on the morning of 7 July 2005 were as British as I am, and one might have believed that, aside from both the casual and institutional racism which they no doubt frequently endured, they were functioning reasonably well in British society. However, the fact that on that morning they chose to strap backpacks full of explosives to themselves and enter buses and underground trains, where they detonated the bombs to murderous effect, killing themselves and scores of innocent people, speaks to a sense of disaffection with Europe and a culturally informed determination that is truly shocking.

Both before, and certainly since, the events of 7 July 2005, the British media has been replete with articles hostile to Islam, portraying it as a backward faith whose fundamental principles are incompatible with the British way of life. The media would have us believe that this is a religion without any nuances of belief or practice, and they defend their belligerence on the grounds that they are taking a principled stance on behalf of women's rights, or they claim that theirs is a civilised response to a religion that sanctions a barbaric code of punishment, or they insist that they are adopting a necessary position in order that they might maintain our freedom and national security. Of course, most of the discourse is just plain, simple, old-fashioned malevolence towards the outsider, the person who not only looks different, but who dresses differently, or who worships in a place other than a church. It is an old European game and we have all seen and heard it before. But, of late, it is not just the media who have stepped up pressure on 'these people.'

The former British Foreign Secretary, Jack Straw, urged Muslim women to remove full facial veils when talking to him, claiming that the veil was 'such a visible statement of separation and difference that it jeopardised British social harmony'. Tony Blair, of course, echoed him, calling the veil 'a mark of separation'. Other European countries have already passed judgement on this and similar issues. In several German states, Muslim teachers are banned from wearing the hijab (or headscarf) in public schools. In France, nobody – Muslim teachers or students – can wear the headscarf in schools, for Jacques Chirac claimed that schools should be a 'republican sanctuary'. (Somewhat confusingly, Sikh boys are still allowed to wear their turbans.) The former Italian Prime Minister, Romano Prodi, agreed with his European colleagues. 'You can't cover your face,' he said, 'you must be seen . . . It is important for our security.' And in Holland Rita Verdonk, who was the Liberal Party immigration minister, planned to introduce legislation to ban Muslim women from wearing burqas in public places. There are one million Dutch Muslims, who make up 6 per cent of the Dutch population. Best estimates suggest that somewhere between thirty to fifty women in the whole country wear burqas, which makes this a non-issue; one Muslim leader called it 'a big law for a small problem'. Indeed it *is* a big law, for to pass this law would be to violate Dutch constitutional guarantees of religious freedom. However, Ms Verdonk proposed circumventing this irritating fact by embracing the absurd and also making it illegal to wear full-size motorbike helmets or ski masks. In other words, she intended to try and convince the Dutch population that this culturally biased piece of legislation was actually crucial for national security.

These days, on both sides of the Atlantic, many civil rights are being stripped away in the name of 'national security'. The fact is, the wearing of the burqa is becoming increasingly rare in the liberal Muslim world, including Pakistan, and it seems inevitable that European Muslim women will, as the generations turn over, also set it aside. In countries where more fundamental notions of Islam prevail, such as Uzbekistan, the question of women's attire remains a problem, for women *are* beaten and raped over this issue. And it is true that in Europe there *are* Muslim women who are sick and tired of being called whores by their fathers and brothers, and freaks by other men, simply because of how they dress. But instead of condemning Muslims as separate and antisocial, we need to find ways to help those who want help. There is something unpleasant about the judgement of Western men being imposed upon Muslim women. In this sense, Jack Straw, Jacques Chirac, Romano Prodi and others are in a long tradition of male patronage which found its most eloquent expression in the nineteenth century when the British occupation of Egypt was justified on the grounds that the British would 'liberate women from their oppressive veils'. And today, in Afghanistan and Iraq, both Britain and the US have claimed that because of their intervention Muslim women will achieve greater freedom.

Clearly there are a significant number of Europeans who passionately dislike Muslims, and they point to Islamic cultural practices for evidence as to why 'these people' cannot fully participate in European national life. Websites are increasingly filled with the righteous indignation of those who are thrilled that their governments are now legislating against 'these Muslims'. In liberal Holland, the November 2004 murder of the film-maker, Theo van Gogh by a twenty-six-year-old Muslim initiated a backlash of anti-Muslim feeling, but the national tone had already been established by the late right-wing politician, Pim Fortuyn. One recent posting on a Dutch website puts the anti-Muslim, anti-immigrant case very succinctly, claiming that immigrants 'have forgotten that the responsibility and obligation of any immigrant is to conform to the society to which they have moved. They should move if that society is not appropriate for them . . . obviously they don't want to be French, Dutch, Canadian, American or a member of any Western culture because, despising Western culture, they invariably break the traditional immigrant's pact with their host country. Instead of going as an immigrant, they are in fact going as an invader, the vanguard, the first wave.'

To some extent it is indeed the responsibility and obligation of any immigrant to conform to the society to which they have moved. They must, of course, be cognisant of the laws, and aware of the national traditions. Female circumcision is not tolerated in Holland, or in any part of Europe, nor should it be, and one should not expect to be able to practise it, any more than one should be able to attend public beheadings, or see only male drivers on the streets. But European Muslims are not stupid; they know this. The vast majority of Muslims in Europe have never subscribed to a rigid interpretation of sharia, and therefore have no problem at all marrying the practice of their faith to basic human rights as they are understood in the West. There are in the world those who do adhere to a strict interpretation of sharia, and without reform this type of Islam can probably not be reconciled to European cultural practice. But Islam is, like Christianity and Judaism, a flexible faith, which accommodates a multiplicity of differing orthodoxies, and is not a reactionary, monolithic creed as some would have us believe.

And what is this 'traditional pact with their host country' that immigrants are supposed to have? Presumably arrive, do nothing apart from the jobs that none of the locals want to do, make no criticism of the society, keep their heads down and out of sight, keep their hands off the women, and either die or leave in silence. This notion of migration, which I fear remains the model of how most Europeans think, of course removes any obligation for change from the host nation. Not only is it an ignorant misunderstanding of one's own history and how nations are formed, it is a potential recipe for disaster in the present climate. Integrating Muslims into European life is not just about color; it is, as the current debates suggest, about a notion of identity that runs much deeper.

As a boy growing up in England, I knew that the main factor preventing my full participation in British life was the color of my skin. If only they could somehow color me English – in other words, white – then nobody would know the difference. The truth is, I did not want to be white, I just wanted to fit in, and I believed that color was the issue. And then slowly things began to change. In November 1978, Viv Anderson, the Nottingham Forest fullback, became the first black footballer to play for England. Within a few years there were black players on most of the first-division football teams, and then there were other black faces in the English national team; soon after there were many black athletes on the Olympic track and field team, and black people on television reading the news. We were coloring England, and although problems remained one sensed gates being unlocked, rusty bolts being drawn back, and barriers being frequently crossed. However, the shock that most people felt on the morning of 7 July 2005, when it became clear that four non-white Britons had killed themselves and others, was a timely reminder that it is foolhardy to think that race by itself is a barometer of either human disaffection or social progress. It is a factor, but equity of opportunity, especially in housing, education and employment, is determined by race *and* class *and* gender; and then there is something else.

This is what my young Muslim 'friend' Ali knew when we stood outside the school office. I had escorted him there in some kind of gesture of racial − outsider − solidarity, but he was culturally an outsider in a way that I never could be. Back then, I thought that Britain was narrating a harsh tale to me about who I was; however, I had no idea how caustic the narrative was that Ali was being forced to listen to. I was constantly being told, 'Go back to where you come from', but in reality I had nowhere to go back to. Some among my generation did grow dreadlocks and try to retreat into a strangely essential black identity, and they began to speak of Africa as 'home', but I knew that we were not going anywhere and that we would have to wrestle with Britain to make *their* story fit our lives. That's what all migrants do, as their plural selves develop and concessions are made to the new nation while they decide, as time moves on, which of their cultural traditions to hold on to and which they can discard without brutalising who they are. In other words, immigrants decide how, and at what pace, they will adapt.

As England was coloring itself, Ali and his family were obviously hearing the same instructions that I was subjected to regarding England's desire that we should all go back to where we came from, but Ali *did* have some essential place of identity to which he could, should he wish to, turn as an alternative to the perceived hostility of British life. On that July morning in 2005, four young British men felt it necessary to reach out and embrace an alternative place by seizing upon an extreme form of Islamic political identity and demonstrating its potency with tragic consequences. In order to prevent this happening again it is absolutely crucial that we think long and hard about what is happening in Europe. The coloring of Britain, and Europe, suggests a radical and permanent change in the appearance of the European continent that is as dramatic as the changes that came with the post-Columbian settlement of the Americas, or the European settlement of Australasia. To imagine that one can successfully legislate the pace of this change is to fundamentally misunderstand the human desire to belong, and to dangerously misjudge the human capacity to feel slighted. There are those who are willing to pay the highest price imaginable to resist people who would police their identities. And there are those who will pay the highest price imaginable to secure an identity. The European response needs to be significantly more sophisticated than merely telling people that their traditions are barbaric and that they must dress differently.

European borders are porous. European nations have been built, have grown, and have been developed by countless waves of people entering countries and slowly learning the language, adapting to the customs, and enriching the national life by eventually beginning to consider themselves English, or Dutch, or French, or Belgian. In recent years, this process has been complicated and made more difficult by issues of race. How does one have a black face and be European? This has been one of the great essay questions of my life, and it continues to be a vexing issue at the heart of Europe, but I am an optimist. Despite the statement by Georges Frêche – a French socialist politician who recently claimed that he is ashamed because, according to him, the French football team does not represent France because there are too many black faces – I remain convinced that this coloring of Europe, so that one can be both black and European, is not something that might happen; it has *already* happened. However, what if your blackness or brownness comes with a different set of cultural traditions? This is where we now seem to be, and on both sides of the fence the stand-off is filled with violence and distrust. Does it make sense to single out one group and berate them with scant regard for any nuances of difference among them, and then panic into legislating against them? Is this going to help smooth the transition in Europe? I think the so-called *radicalising* of the man who killed Theo van Gogh, and the *radicalising* of the suicide bombers on 7 July in London gives us some part of the answer. Of course, vigorously rooting out those who seek to commit random acts of violence against innocent people going about their daily business is part of our social contract. In Britain, we learned just how deadly and destructive this violence can be during the IRA bombing campaign in the 1970s and '80s. But we also learned that being dogmatic, and passing restrictive legislation, and not understanding our own history, only slows down the movement towards peace and our ability to both tolerate, and cherish, diversity in all its manifestations.

On the morning of 7 July 2005 when I realised that three of the four suicide bombers were from Leeds my heart sank. They were people with Yorkshire accents, exactly like the people I had grown up with. Just what had gone wrong with these young British lives? And, of course, I thought of Ali. I thought of his face as his colleagues threw his books out of the bus window; I thought of his silent, dignified hurt. I felt guilty that, over the years, I had made little effort to try to imagine how it felt to be both British and a Muslim, and I had never stopped to consider how it felt to be called a 'Paki' every day. I was safe in my world where I could wait for colored footballers, and musicians, and newscasters to emerge and ease my passage into the outer circle of belonging in a still defensive and racist Britain. However, at least for me, the journey was beginning. I was being colored English, as opposed to my thirteen-year-old classmate, Ali.

The truth is, Ali's journey had begun from a far more peripheral place than mine, and clearly the pace of his journey would be glacial compared with my own meanderings. In the years that have passed, both of us have witnessed significant changes in English life; for instance, legislation has been put into place which outlaws the use of racist language in public discourse, but those on the right have simply replaced their 'Paki-bashing' discourse with an anti-Muslim rhetoric delivered with a wink and a nudge for they know full well that they are still targeting non-white people. Nominally, at least, I am not affected by such anti-Muslim rhetoric, but Ali and his family remain in the front line of attack, and this being the case I am not sure how much real progress has been made. I often wonder what happened to Ali, and if he ever did complete the journey or if, like the three young Muslims from Leeds, the effort of trying to belong, and the pain of moving slowly into England, caused him to suffer from some sort of assimilation fatigue that eventually led him to simply abandon the whole enterprise. Did Ali get fed up with being called 'Paki', and with being told that he and his family must dress like English people, not speak their own language, knock it off with that mosque prayer stuff, and stop cooking their smelly food? Back then, as a thirteen-year-old, I instinctively knew that some part of me was Ali; I knew that in a time of crisis there is no 'us' and 'them', there is only 'we', and all of us must obey the moral directive to communicate with each other.

I hope that Ali, unlike the three Leeds Muslims who died on 7 July, has not given up on Britain. I hope that over the years he has learned to cultivate a temporary deafness to the knee-jerk proclamations of various politicians and the bitter hostility of thugs who understand neither what is, nor what is inevitable. Successful integration does mean that immigrants adapt to the new country, but it also means that the new country adapts to them. It demands that the residents cultivate the capacity – and courage – to change their ideas about who *they* are. For this to work it is not just those who go to the mosque and wear headscarves who have to look at themselves. Those who eat fish and chips and drink beer or wear clogs or berets have to look at themselves too, they have to look into a mirror and realise that they live in a continent that is in the midst of radical change, and no amount of violence from right-wing racists, or fundamentalists of any stripe, or rhetoric from politicians, or canting from the media is going to halt this change. This transition is as inevitable as the sun rising in the morning and setting in the evening; the only question is, what kind of day are we going to have?

Europe is no longer white and never will be again. And Europe is no longer Judaeo-Christian and never will be again. There are already fifteen million Muslims in the European Union, and the figures will grow. All of us are faced with a stark choice: we can rail against European evolution, or we can help to smooth its process. And, if we choose the latter, the first thing we must remind ourselves of is the lesson that great fiction teaches us as we sink into character and plot and suspend our disbelief: for a moment, 'they' are 'us'. I believe passionately in the moral capacity of fiction to wrench us out of our ideological burrows and force us to engage with a world that is clumsily transforming itself, a world that is peopled with individuals we might otherwise never meet in our daily lives. As long as we have literature as a bulwark against intolerance, and as a force for change, then we have a chance. Europe needs writers to explicate this transition, for literature *is* plurality in action; it embraces and celebrates a place of no truths, it relishes ambiguity, and it deeply respects the place where everybody has the right to be understood, both the thirteen-year-old boy whose books are thrown out of a bus window, and the boys who are throwing the books, and it judges neither party in the hope that by some often painfully slow process of imaginative osmosis one might finally recognise what passed before one's eyes today, what occurred yesterday, and what will happen tomorrow, and it implores us to act with a compassion born of familiarity towards our fellow human beings, be they Christian, Jew, Muslim, black, brown or white. This truly is my hope for Europe, and I *know* that the writer has a crucial part to play in this. I believe this. And this only.

Homeland Security

Ground Zero (2001)

At 8.46 on Tuesday morning I stepped out of my building on Hudson Street and noticed people standing in the street staring south. The Twin Towers of the World Trade Center are less than a mile from where I live, and I knew this was what the small crowd was looking at. I too looked up and saw a huge explosion as a plane crashed into the North Tower. A ball of flames erupted, followed by smoke. Nobody on the street moved – there was total silence. And then we strangers began to look at each other. Everybody was muttering the same phrase: 'Oh my God.'

I walked back into my building and looked at the doorman. 'Mike, come out here. You've got to see this.' I could feel myself shaking. 'Mike, you've got to see this.' He got up from behind his desk and reluctantly came out into the street. Traffic had stopped. Flames were shooting out of the North Tower, which now looked like a Roman candle on bonfire night.

On Tuesday mornings I teach a class at Columbia University, uptown from where I live. In a daze, I walked to the subway station, the only person moving – everybody else was rooted to the spot. I kept thinking of the incident in 1945 when a plane hit the Empire State Building. I convinced myself that everything would be fine. It was bizarre, but clearly some pilot had forgotten to put in his contact lenses. Given that the towers are so large, and there is a lot of air traffic around Lower Manhattan, this was bound to happen sooner or later, wasn't it?

On the subway platform an older black man came up to me. We had been waiting fifteen minutes for an uptown train.

Normally, a train would arrive in three minutes. 'Brother, there's some shit going down,' he said. Up above, on street level, sirens blared. I knew what was going down, so I told him. 'I saw it. A plane hit the North Tower. They'll sort it out.' He shook his head and gave me a piteous stare. A woman further up the platform walked over. 'What's going on?' she asked. We all began to huddle together and talk: 'A plane flew into the World Trade Center.' People looked at their watches. They were going to be late for work.

When the uptown train arrived we rushed on and sat down and pretended we didn't know each other (subway etiquette). The train had come from the southern tip of Manhattan, from the World Trade Center. I looked around and saw a few passengers who appeared to be bruised and dishevelled. Sitting opposite me was a well-dressed man in his late fifties who carried a newspaper. Suddenly, he began to sob loudly. His shoulders shook, his head dropped, and he began to mutter: 'Thirty, forty floors. They're all dead. I know they're all dead.' People began to look at each other, embarrassed and confused.

Twenty minutes later I got out of the subway at 116th Street. From Upper Manhattan one cannot see the World Trade Center. I walked into my office and tried to log on to CNN, MSNBC, and the BBC, but all news websites were jammed. I tried my office phone, but it was dead. A colleague walked into my office, her face wet with tears. 'My husband works in the World Trade Center. Can you tell me if he's all right?' 'I don't know,' I said. I called my mother in St Kitts on my cellphone. She was watching CNN, and she told me that the South Tower had been hit, as had the Pentagon. I covered the receiver and told my co-worker that she should find a television. Then I lost the cellphone connection.

The internet connection, however, was still alive. I logged on to New York City's website, www.nyc.gov. Finally, some information: all subway trains south of 42nd Street were not running; Lower Manhattan would soon be sealed off from the world. I walked to a bar on Broadway that has television sets and watched in disbelief as the Twin Towers collapsed. People were crying and mumbling to themselves. There was a circus of activity as people frantically tried to get their cellphones to work, but to no avail. Somebody said that the payphones were still working, and so there was a rush out on to the street to find them.

I left the bar and flagged down an off-duty taxi and tried to persuade the driver to take me as far south as possible. 'I have to go home,' I said. I told him I lived downtown and he continued to shake his head. He was adamant. 'No sir, you cannot go there.' I pulled some money out of my wallet. 'Take me as far south as you can go,' I said. I climbed in the back of the cab and we joined the screaming rush of ambulances, fire engines and police cars heading south. At Times Square the driver pulled over. 'Sir, no more. No more.' I gave him a twenty and got out of the cab. Times Square was chaotic. Crowds were watching the news live on large screens and holding on to each other. Images of the collapsing towers were repeated over and over again, and the panic on people's faces was unbearable to watch.

I cut west along 42nd Street and then saw the throngs of people crowded outside the Port Authority bus station. It looked like a refugee centre: the streets were blocked and commuters were slumped down, exhausted from trying to get to New Jersey, or Brooklyn, or the Bronx, or Queens. A burly, Hispanic policeman kept braying, 'Is no chance! Is no chance!' They were stranded, frightened, and unable to comprehend what they had witnessed.

I continued to walk south, even though everybody else was streaming north. Below Madison Square Garden at 34th, the streets began to empty. I looked south at the skyline, where the towers should have been. There was nothing but a large, black cloud that was obscuring the whole of southern Manhattan.

Once I reached Hudson Street I walked into my building and up to my apartment. I closed the door and stared out of the window. It was now late afternoon and a beautiful day, with clear blue skies to the north, to the east and to the west. But to the south, the sky was black, and it looked like the darkest moment before dawn. I tried to make some phone calls, but the landline was down and my cellphone was still not working. Anxious, I went outside again. I had to find out what was happening.

I walked the few blocks north to Christopher Street, then west to the Hudson River. Almost every day I run up and down the Hudson River Park, where the view of the towers is not only spectacular, it *is* New York. When I reached the West Side Highway I felt my knees go weak, and tears began to well up in my eyes. The towers were gone, they were not there. I was talking to myself; I was now one of *those* people. 'Oh my God, where are the towers?' I caught the eye of a woman who was also standing with her mouth agape. I heard a sound that began in the pit of her stomach. 'No,' she cried, in one long note: 'No.' I now know what it is to hear somebody wail, and I never want to hear the sound again.

I don't know how long I stood on the West Side Highway, but I know that I heard the almighty crash of World Trade Center Tower 7 as it collapsed. I stood with dozens of others as we saw the enormous mushroom cloud and heard the nerve-shattering noise of the forty-seven-storey tower coming down. A seemingly endless cavalcade of ambulances and fire engines flowed south with lights and sirens blaring. How is it possible for there to be so many fire engines and police cars on one island? Hundreds of them, with grim-faced drivers racing south, and there we stood, a macabre audience witnessing this catastrophe.

I began to walk back home. As I reached the corner of Hudson Street and Morton Street, I saw an elderly man sitting on the sidewalk, covered in dust. He had a smoke mask around his neck. I walked past him and then stopped and walked back. I leaned down and tapped him on the shoulder and asked if I could get him some water or coffee. He looked up at me. His eyes were brimming with tears. He was wrecked with the fatigue of searching through the rubble to the south. He began to shake, and then he broke, simply falling to pieces before my eyes. I looked on helplessly. I thought, 'This used to be a whole man. This morning this was a happy, confident man. And now?'

That night I couldn't sleep. All night long I listened to a continuous screech of sirens beneath my windows, the sounds of a city screaming in pain. Occasionally, the phone rang. 'I'm all right, are you all right? Who is missing? Who works down there? Who do you know?' And then I remembered David, my former student who I'd run into in midtown three weeks earlier. We went to a bar for a drink and he told me that he'd just got a job working for Rudy Giuliani in the Office of Emergency Management. I found his card. His office was in Tower 7. I called his cellphone number. Nothing. His office number. Nothing. Eventually, at 5 a.m. I found him at home asleep. 'David, it's Caz.' He began to cry. 'I'm fine, I'm fine, but . . .' He stopped. Very gently, I put down the phone and I think I too began to fall apart a little.

As dawn broke on Wednesday, I knew that the world of New York City had changed, possibly for ever. Out of my window I could see the National Guard patrolling. My area, Lower Manhattan between 14th Street and Canal, was now effectively sealed off. Businesses were closed. I went out to find a *New York Times*. The streets were deserted. There were no newspapers, no milk, no bagels, nothing. I looked to the south. The skyline was empty. New York City was defeated. The blow to this city's sense of pride is impossible to define. I wandered back to my building but the usual convivial morning banter had gone. Mike shook his head. He had nothing to say.

Later in the day I walked over to the West Side Highway at Christopher Street. The sidewalks were lined with the satellite dishes of television crews from all over the world. I could see the huge plumes of smoke that continued to rise into the air from the carnage. I stood on the central median with hundreds of others who were wielding American flags and signs: 'My heroes', 'New York's finest', 'USA'. They waved their banners at the trucks and ambulances and police cars and fire engines which continued to stream south. The drivers honked their horns and some gave the thumbs-up but the look on their faces was grim. These people had not slept for thirty-six hours and they had colleagues who had already lost their lives. They had to go back but they couldn't tell us what they were seeing down there. They looked straight ahead.

To the north of the West Side Highway it was a different story. Coming up from the carnage were trucks with rubble: bent barriers, bits of wall, chunks of windows, crushed vehicles. And then the refrigerated trucks that would normally transport frozen meat and other food. These were for the bodies. People waved and cheered and showed their signs to these drivers too, but they were often too tired to respond. They looked as though they truly were emerging from the heart of darkness. And then somebody in the crowd with a radio jammed to his ear said that Rudy had ordered more than 6,000 body bags. The rumour swept through the crowd like a bushfire. For a few minutes rescue vehicles flashed by, going north and south, without encouragement. And then we remembered to applaud and cheer.

As night fell on Wednesday I stood in Hudson Street and again looked up at the huge gap in the sky. By now I was used to people around me crying. There was no need to stop or offer help. A fleet of National Guard vehicles crept by with machine-gun-toting soldiers eerily looking all about themselves. I walked a little way east. At St Vincent's hospital there were hundreds of people wandering around with pictures of their loved ones, hoping that somebody would recognise them as having been saved. Inside themselves they knew the truth, but they clung desperately to hope. It was an unbearable sight. For those of us below 14th Street without newspapers, without supplies, without our beloved skyline, the sense of communal trauma is difficult to convey.

I did sleep on Wednesday night, but I had nightmares. I kept waking up but there were no longer any sirens blaring. Just total and utter silence. This morning, the city above 14th Street is trying to function normally. Businesses are open again, subways are running, classes are being taught at schools and colleges. Down here, beneath 14th Street, nothing has changed. We are sealed in. To move north we have to show ID to police. We can't go south of Canal. There are still no newspapers and no supplies. Some shops and restaurants are opening but most remain locked and barred. Over at the West Side Highway the people are still on the median. They have been there all night. The traffic continues to move south and north, sending in the equipment and personnel, bringing out rubble and the dead. It is another beautiful day in Manhattan. Clear blue skies to the north, to the east, to the west. I am learning not to look south any more.

American Tribalism (2003)

I arrived in Amherst, Massachusetts in the fall of 1990 with the understanding that I would be spending a year teaching in a liberal arts college. I had not thought about exactly who I would be teaching, beyond the fact that they would be Americans. When I walked into my classroom on that first morning, I was greeted by a rainbow coalition of faces: black, white, brown, yellow. Even at an institution as famously conservative as Amherst College, diversity seemed to be a wonderfully natural part of the campus culture's make-up. I have to confess that had the classroom been in London, or Paris, or Amsterdam, I might well have wondered – perhaps even asked – how many of them were foreign students. A European education encourages one to employ such clumsy and reductive thinking about notions of identity. However, I was not in Europe. I was fully aware of the long history of racial conflict in the United States, but I arrived in the country believing that for most citizens a sense of pride in claiming the more inclusive American identity would far outweigh any professions of loyalty to a particular racial or ethnic group.

Twelve years later I am now an American resident and I know differently. I have lived through the Crown Heights riots, the Gulf War, the Rodney King beating, the LA riots, the O. J. trial, the Abner Louima case, the crisis of September 11, 2001, and many other events that have further furrowed the nation's creased brow. These have been troubling times. I have also listened to my students, my colleagues and my friends, and I now under-stand that behind the façade of a racially and ethnically mixed society all is not well. I know that the students who sat silently before me in 1990 all harboured different degrees of attachment to the notion of being United States citizens; I know that the imagined harmony of this classroom was a figment of my own romantic imagination, and no matter how much the United States may wish to claim that it is a society in which everybody has a chance to succeed, irrespective of race or ethnicity, this is simply not true.

Back then I think that I desired the United States to be everything that Britain was not. Having grown up in the Britain of the 1960s and '70s, I had been exposed to a society in which diversity of any kind was not encouraged. But this is an old British tale. Minorities, be they religious or racial, have always encountered difficulties as they struggle to adjust to the vagaries of British life. As a young black boy, and a northerner at that, the double yoke of race and class was slipped firmly round my neck. I spent a great deal of my time as an adolescent being the only 'different' face in the room, and this did not change on going to university, particularly as that university happened to be Oxford. After graduation I made frequent business trips to the United States, and from my cursory observations of that society I began to convince myself that there was a world in which one was not going to be judged solely by one's appearance; as far as I could see, being 'different' in the United States did not *necessarily* mean that one would encounter insurmountable obstacles on the journey through life. It was with this mindset that I arrived in leafy Massachusetts in 1990, and arrayed before me in my classroom was the evidence of a healthier, and more palatable, society.

After eight years in Amherst, I left and moved to Columbia University's Barnard College. Only a few days after the collapse of the Twin Towers, I sat in my New York classroom facing my undergraduates. Everybody was understandably still shocked at what had transpired, and my seminar felt more like a memorial service than a forum for lively discussion. The books under scrutiny seemed irrelevant, and no matter how much I wished to make them relevant, they resisted. Eventually I gave up and turned to a Chinese American girl. I asked her why she was wearing a Stars and Stripes bandana on her head. I knew she was a first-generation migrant from Shanghai, and I also knew that on encountering this country she had changed her name and appearance. Hardly unusual behaviour in a migrant, but I was curious about her relationship to the flag that she was displaying.

She took a deep breath and announced to the class that this was her way of expressing solidarity with the victims of the disaster that had occurred. However, she admitted that she did feel somewhat uncomfortable with the symbolism of the United States flag. 'Why?' I asked. And then I became a teacher again. I gestured to the whole room. 'Who in here feels one hundred per cent comfortable with describing themselves as a citizen of the United States of America?' The face of diverse America cracked. Not a single non-white student raised a hand. I felt disturbed, not so much at their response, but at my own stupidity, for I knew that had I asked the same question in 1990 the class-room response would, in all likelihood, have been the same.

I had been duped by the country. Like all great imperial powers, the United States has the capacity to mythologise herself with a conviction that will sweep up all but the sternest doubters. And one of the greatest tenets of United States lore is that irrespective of race, religion or ethnicity, everybody has equality of opportunity. We believe these words because we want them to be true. We believe them because in all likelihood wherever it is we are arriving from, such equality of opportunity has been denied to us. Like all immigrants, we arrive and metaphorically kiss the ground, and then we stand up and look around and slowly we realise — and this process often takes many years — that the place we thought we were travelling to is, in fact, imaginary. In 1990 I had arrived in an imaginary United States of America.

The pattern of one group of immigrants to the United States displacing another at the bottom of the pile is an old game.

Jews, Irish, Italians, Puerto Ricans, and many others, have all served their time in the basement of American scorn. Of course, for Native Americans as original inhabitants, and African Americans as involuntary migrants, the painful process of assimilation has been fraught with very special difficulties. As one century closes and another one opens before us, the truth is that there is not one America, and in all likelihood there never was. There is white America, black America, brown America and yellow America, and they are all to some degree separate and undeniably unequal. This is not the face of the United States that is exported to the rest of the world. American sports teams are integrated. American music and popular culture is similarly 'mixed'. The American armed forces are not only integrated, they are perhaps the most fully functional multiracial institutions in the country. This is what most people outside the United States see, and this is precisely what the self-mythologising American power structure would wish them to see. However, as the facts reveal, and as my students know, up close and personal, things are very different.

What are the facts? The top 1 per cent of Americans have more wealth than the bottom 90 per cent, who are disproportionately African American and Hispanic. The unemployment rate for young men in inner cities is over 30 per cent, while the national rate is under 5 per cent. The leading cause of death among young black men is gunshot wounds. The United States population is 8 per cent African American, but this community accounts for 49 per cent of the inmates in state and federal prisons. The development of what the singer George Clinton has termed 'Chocolate Cities and Vanilla Suburbs' has become a reality across the length and breadth of the country. Gated communities, in which homogeneous groups with siege mentalities cluster behind guarded and patrolled walls, are the norm from the Atlantic to the Pacific. People are not only physically retreating to be with their 'own kind', they are, more worryingly, doing so mentally.

In the United States of the twenty-first century, race and

ethnicity have become essentialist boxes in which people have begun to locate themselves, thus limiting their capacity to function as fully active American citizens. Some are retreating into this space in the belief that they are being pushed there; others believe that a racially or ethnically 'pure' space provides them with the only place in which they feel free and at ease to think and live as they please. However, to submit to the view that race or ethnicity encapsulates the greater part of one's identity or, even worse, determines one's fate, is to surrender to a certain despair. For many non-white people, the feeling of being shut out from American opportunity understandably leads to separation in thought and action. For white people, many of whom regard whiteness as an unexamined norm against which to measure difference, there is a palpable sense of fear of what they perceive to be a growth in culturally centric 'attitudes', as well as a lament for the disappearance of the kind of world they used to see in Spencer Tracy movies.

Americans have always had to learn to become new people and synthesise their old history with their new life in a manner that has ultimately transformed them into larger and more complex individuals. The nation is made up of people whose stories have involved challenging the fragile nature of identity; changing their names, religion, manners, language, in order to begin anew. Sadly, these personal transformations have never led to the kind of open, fluid 'melting pot' of a society that one hears so much about. And today, personal transformations seem to do little more than reinforce separate identities. President Clinton's 'Dialogue on Race' was an attempt to say, 'Can't we at least acknowledge that in this United States of ours there *is* a major problem around these issues of race and ethnicity? Is it not clear to everybody that discrimination against those who are perceived to be different is causing huge sections of our population to accept the label of American citizen, but with increasingly well-flagged modifying clauses?'

The type of society that the United States should be attempting to engender is a plural, non-tribal society in which citizens feel confident enough to communicate with each other, rather than coexist as self-isolated islands. However, before the citizens can begin to reach out to each other they have to recognise the magnitude of the divisions and prejudice that exist, and understand these divisions to be what they are: huge, yawning chasms, not thin fissures that can be papered over with titillating discussions, such as those that grew up in the wake of Clinton's 'dialogue' as to whether the president should offer an official apology for slavery. Really, the situation is more urgent than this. As long as non-white men and women in the United States cannot buy or sell a house, raise and educate their children or get a job without having to factor in race, then there will always be 'aggressive' loyalty to racial and ethnic identity that no amount of talking can ever hope to redress.

Perhaps the two most pressing questions are, is it too late to do anything about this corrosive process, and if not what should we do? First, it is not too late. It cannot be. The United States needs artists, politicians, educators, and those in the media, to undermine fixed and ethnocentric notions of identity, including — some might say *especially* — 'white' notions of identity. Second, there is a clear need for legislation, for this has been shown to be an effective way of combating people's prejudices. Take interracial marriage as an example. Since 1967, when the United States Supreme Court struck out the last anti-miscegenation laws, interracial marriage has risen by 800 per cent. A decade before this decision, *Brown v. Board of Education* had already categorically stated that 'separate' is always 'inherently' unequal. And this decision radically improved educational opportunities for *all* American citizens, not just African Americans.

The United States was founded on legal principles, one of which offers every individual equal protection under the law. Many millions came to the United States because of the ideas that were writ large in the constitution. Strong legislation to address continuing forms of discrimination in American life might go some way towards convincing sceptical citizens that the ideal of human contact, and a concomitant transcendence of self, is a more desirable form of lifestyle choice than a retreat to the essentialisms of race. But legislation by itself will fail. Despite the Supreme Court decision in 1967 that anti-miscegenation laws were unconstitutional, South Carolina, until recently, still had a constitutional clause which afforded the state theoretical provision to ban the 'marriage of a white person with a Negro or mulatto or a person who shall have one-eighth or more of Negro blood'. Although legally impossible to enforce, on 3 November 1998 the provision was finally repealed, but a shocking 38 per cent of South Carolina voters cast their ballot in favour of maintaining the 'irrelevant' ban on interracial marriage. Sadly, we cannot legislate what is in people's hearts, and this fact places increased responsibility on the shoulders of teachers and writers. I remain optimistic that the United States will not allow herself to fracture along racially defined lines. In fact, it is an import-ant part of my job to try and make sure that this does not happen. However, in the twelve years that I have spent in the country, it has not always been easy to live through this difficult period and remain an optimist.

'Give me your tired, your poor, your huddled masses' (2003)

Some years ago I decided that I wanted to live in the United States, albeit for a short while, in part because of the idealised optimism of the country's national motto: '*E pluribus unum.*' One out of Many. Thirteen years later I still live in the United States, in recklessly hybrid New York City, where 40 per cent of the population is foreign-born, where 120 languages are daily spoken, where every major religion is practised. This is a city with an astonishing degree of diversity and an inability to resist dynamic cultural fusion. However, over the years, I have been given reason to pause for thought on a few occasions and wonder about the *true* character of the city. The new, and disturbing, evidence in the case of the Central Park Jogger, and the frequency with which unarmed black men appear to be gunned down by the police, have made me painfully aware that all is not rosy in the city that never sleeps. Yet, over the years I have, in the main, remained pleasantly seduced by the notion of a plurality that is enshrined in the national motto. Rich and poor, black and white, Hispanic and Asian, Jew and Christian, citizen and refugee are, in this teeming metropolis, thrown together and compelled to interact with each other. The tension and energy of the city is positive, if not quite annealing. And then came September 11, 2001, and a different United States began to emerge. After thirteen years as first a permanent resident, and now a citizen, I am beginning to feel increasingly uneasy, for changes in national mood are having an impact upon the great immigrant city of New York. Poets, carpenters, boxers, physicists, movie stars, engineers, lawyers, they have come from all corners of the world and sailed past the Statue of Liberty and on into the heart of the city. It should surprise nobody that on that mournful September morning, people from over ninety countries lost their lives in the Twin Towers. Immigrant city. But after September 11, immigrant city betrayed. In truth, the national motto should now be 'One out of *some*'. This is not the programme that I signed up for. A few days ago I rode out into New York Harbor on the Staten Island Ferry in order to achieve a close-up glimpse of the Statue of Liberty. As I suspected, this different United States of America is also proving difficult for Lady Liberty to bear. I swear that she now has her eyes closed.

Nations are generally built around the notion of closure, most commonly racial or religious closure, but the United States has always promoted itself as an open nation, a place that is happy to accept the stranger without passing judgement, and a country that is willing to offer a home and an opportunity to those of different races, cultures and religions. Immigrants are presented with 'freedom' in the broadest sense, and the opportunity to marry the micronarratives of their often traumatised lives to the macronarrative of their new nation. They might also reasonably expect to be presented with the opportunity to achieve economic prosperity.

Most immigrants are well aware that the United States is a greedy country with a large appetite. Rampant consumerism of all kinds is fed by the likes of McDonald's, CNN, Nike and countless other multinational corporations that conduct their business hand in glove with local, state and federal politicians. But the migrant who arrives hoping to make money and prosper could not care less. Lacking the resources to play the stock market, he can always line up and play Lotto or Powerball or Fantasy 5 or whichever government-sponsored scheme to promote instant wealth is currently in vogue. Of course, he is not supposed to notice that corruption in American corporate life proceeds almost unchecked, and that the bleeding of the social security

system, and the increasing privatisation of health and education, are widening the gap between rich and poor to such an
extent that the disparity is in danger of becoming entrenched.
The migrant came to make money, and the chances are that he
will get on with that and not complain.

And he must not complain if people do not like his weird religion. Because of continual waves of migration, the United States
is by far the most religiously diverse nation in the world and this
has meant that the country has been forced to accommodate many
different moral traditions and value systems. However, without
any doubt, the master narrative of the American tradition is
white, it is Protestant, and it comes from Europe. The power
of the values rooted in this one socioreligious strand has shaped
and defined the nation, and its influence is undoubtedly growing.
In fact, for a society in which state and religion are supposed
to be separate entities there is, these days, a lot of Christian
'God' talk emanating from the White House. There are daily
prayer meetings and Bible study groups in all areas of government, and after September 11 the Attorney General, John
Ashcroft, a man who attends a church where people talk in
tongues, held voluntary Christian prayer services every morning
before work. The Bush administration has consistently funded
religious groups so that they might take over education and
welfare programmes; one might even be forgiven for thinking
that a cabal of right-wing Judaeo-Christian white men, with
the aid of one or two Christian blacks, have set out on a mission
to do God's work.

But the truth is, there has always been a lot of Christian
'God' talk behind the arras in the daily life of the United States.
On the coins it reads 'In God We Trust', and at ball games they
sing 'God Bless America'. However, of late, this Christian 'God'
talk seems to be coming out from behind the arras. The seventy
million Christian fundamentalists in the United States have
found leadership in a White House that carefully positions its
religious zeal in opposition to what they call 'Islamic fundamentalism'. But they are keen not to be too open with their

agenda. On Sunday 23 September 2001 an inter-faith memorial service was held at Yankee Stadium in New York City, which was presided over not only by representatives of the Christian and Jewish faiths, but also by Sikh, Greek Orthodox, Hindu, Muslim and Buddhist clerics. One might well have imagined that this display of diversity was in some way representative of the spirit of religious tolerance in the country. Sadly, this event begins to look, like so many of the public events in the wake of that tragic day, as though it was little more than a by-product of public relations spin. It was undeniably a memorial service held in good faith, but one that most certainly did *not* reflect the mood of the post-September 11 United States, a country in which the citizen was continually being challenged to prove his patriotism, especially if he happened to worship at a mosque or belong to the 'wrong' ethnic grouping.

The present-day United States is a fearful society. Its people are encouraged to tape up their windows, stock up on basic household goods, hoard bottled water, be cognisant of what color alert the nation is on, and be on the lookout for 'terrorists'. The government has established a climate of patriotic fear in which it is good to be afraid *and* vigilant *and* strong, and the stinging events of September 11 have provided the cover for the establishment of a climate which is legitimising the vulgar rush to nationalism and ubiquitous sporting of the flag. However, one cannot help but suspect that the climate is, in part, designed to deflect our attention from the imperialistic tendency of a pernicious foreign policy, and from a domestic policy that is openly hostile to those immigrants the White House now wishes to castigate as the 'other'. The government cannot force through its agenda unless it convinces the people that these are *extraordinary* times in which their very survival is being threatened, hence the demand for expressions of fearful patriotism, and the suggestion that anything less than this is tantamount to capitulation to that most sinful of crimes: being 'un-American'.

✳   ✳   ✳

There are over thirty-three million foreign-born immigrants, both legal and illegal, living in the United States. More than 10 per cent of the country's population is made up of such people, roughly the same percentage as in the period of greatest immigration, which took place in the years immediately preceding the First World War. Americans have always understood that immigrants are necessary to the health of the country's economy, be they fruit pickers, pizza deliverers, landscapers, nannies, baggers at the supermarket, or computer-literate Indians in Silicon Valley already armed with green cards. Yet Americans have always been very uneasy about being 'invaded' and having their cherished 'American way of life' spoiled. What they seldom pause to think about is the fact that many of these foreign-born immigrants are filling low-paid positions in restaurants, factories and textile mills, despite their having professional or management expertise in their countries of origin. If Americans want fresh sheets on their hotel beds, clean offices to work in, and their restaurant tables bussed, then they should be happy to have immigrants, both legal and illegal, among them. If they want a society with ambition and creativity, then they should be begging immigrants from around the world to continue to migrate in their direction and reinvent both themselves and the nation at large. But, even before September 11, the vast majority, although recognising their necessity, were not happy about foreign-born immigrants. Of course, these complainants were themselves, at some point in their history, foreign-born immigrants.

Back in the late nineteenth century, when immigrants were pouring off the boats from Europe, the anti-immigrant sentiment was much the same. A great number of the large influx of immigrants from Ireland, Russia, Germany and other European countries were Roman Catholic or Jewish, which encouraged Americans of the time to publicly voice anti-immigrant, and specifically, anti-Catholic and anti-Semitic, sentiments. They reasoned that not only was there not enough room, but these people with different accents and customs might cost them their employment. They imagined the economy as a zero-sum game with only so many jobs to go round, and they failed to understand that immigrants yearning for freedom and opportunity actively stimulate an economy. The hostility to these outsiders was, of course, most directly related to their perceived exoticism and 'difference'. After all, before 1865, the identity of the United States had been crudely constructed along lines of race. However, after the emancipation of the slaves, and with continual waves of exotic migration from Europe, ethnicity began to play a larger role in national identity as strangers from many lands sought to gain admission into the American family.

On arrival, these Irish and Russians and Germans were regarded as 'not-quite-white', but most were in the transitional stages of becoming white. This mobility would, of course, eventually open doors for them to union membership, social benefits and housing. Inevitably, as they moved up they locked non-whites, particularly African Americans, into the lowest-paying jobs or, worse, kept them from jobs altogether. In today's United States, immigrants from the Hispanic world, or those from the Far East, are in the transitional stage of becoming white and, a century on, their upward mobility merely confirms the existence of a racially discriminatory system which effectively keeps blacks pegged to the bottom rung of the socio-economic ladder. After September 11, however, immigrants from the Arab and Muslim worlds, many of whom might, in normal circumstances, have been considered transitional in today's United States, now find themselves trapped at the bottom of the pile, and *below* blacks.

This situation has come to pass because, in the wake of the attacks on New York City and Washington, DC on September 11, 2001, the founding principles of the American legal system have been severely undermined. On 25 October 2001, Attorney General John Ashcroft presented the USA Patriot Act for ratification. Astonishingly enough, ninety-eight out of ninety-nine voting senators passed the 342-page document without public debate and before most of them had even read it. This act ushered into being the Terrorist Information Awareness programme, which actively encouraged individuals to spy on their neighbours, and it allowed the FBI to collect data on the ordinary activity of citizens, including their credit card charges, library book withdrawals and enrolment in university courses. Anti-war demonstrators, pacifists and members of certain groups were to be systematically listed in computer databanks of potential 'traitors', and the programme gave the government the right to indefinitely seize and hold US citizens deemed to be 'enemy combatants'. The secret detention and deportation of immigrants without charge was now permitted, and the administration had the right to refuse to release the names of any detainees, and to hold their court proceedings behind closed doors.

One of the first consequences of this act was that 10,000 immigrant workers at airports lost their jobs as the new legislation barred foreign nationals from employment in aviation. These were cleaners, or people who prepared in-flight meals, or baggage handlers, all of whom had work visas or green cards. Of course, there is no legislation that prevents non-citizens from fighting or dying for the United States, and 38,000 foreign nationals are currently enrolled in the military. Shortly after the dismissal of the airport workers, 762 illegal immigrants were detained – mainly Arab, Southeast Asian and Muslim men – who were suspected of having links to terrorism. Of these men only one, Zacarias Moussaoui, was ever charged with any crime related to terrorism. Nevertheless 500 of them – who had been held on minor immigration violations such as overstaying a visa, or entering the country as a tourist and staying on – were summarily deported, having been subjected to everything from petty bureaucratic humiliation to gross violations of their human rights.

In June 2003, following a litany of complaints from organisations and individuals about the detention of the 762 suspected terrorists, the Justice Department's Inspector General released a highly critical report. Allegations of physical and verbal abuse against the detainees were confirmed, and individual cases cited. One man was arrested when an acquaintance wrote to officials that he had overheard the man making 'anti-American statements'.

The statements, according to the report, 'were very general and did not involve any threats of violence or suggest any direct connection to terrorism'. Yet the man was brought in for questioning, found 'guilty' of the misdemeanour of overstaying his visa, and held for months in detention, and away from his family. The report asserted that the administration made no distinction between those accused of breaking immigration laws, and those suspected of being terrorists, thus neatly linking immigration to terrorism, and stoking the public's already hostile feelings towards immigrants, legal or otherwise. The result, of course, was that a so-called 'war on terror' very quickly became a war against immigrants. It took Edward Kennedy, Democratic Senator of Massachusetts, and a senior member of the Judiciary Committee, to state the obvious. He pointed out that he was deeply troubled by the Inspector General's findings on the USA Patriot Act, and went on to compare the treatment of post-September 11 detainees to Japanese Americans interned during the Second World War 'when the government ran roughshod over basic rights in the name of national security'.

In the wake of September 11 the people who were most affected by these developments were not immigrants who were white, or well on the way to becoming white; they were immigrants who because of their religion or ethnicity *looked* as though they might be terrorists. This post-September 11 government crackdown on targeted immigrants was extended in November 2002 when the Immigration and Naturalization Service issued a Special Registration directive that announced that men over sixteen years of age from twenty-five 'suspect' Arab, Southeast Asian and Muslim countries were to register with the Department of Justice. Those with green cards or citizenship were exempted, but those teaching, or studying, or those on extended business trips, on tourist visas, or visiting family or friends, were to report. This included individuals whose visas or papers had expired, or those with pending applications for either a green card or naturalisation.

Eighty-two thousand people came forward and registered and

approximately 13,000, or 16 per cent, of them suddenly found themselves facing deportation for immigration violations. Many were arrested for simply not having 'sufficient' documentation with them when registering. Such 'violations' committed by a Mexican or Albanian immigrant would not be pursued, enforced or punished in the same way. A number of those who have now been deported were entirely innocent people who had been waiting for months or years for their official and legal applications to be processed, and then suddenly found themselves caught up in a bureaucratic nightmare. They were profiled because of their Arab-sounding names, their countries of origin or their religion. The situation would be farcical, were it not so tragic. Take, for instance, the case of a New Jersey man who one afternoon received a package from a delivery service at his home. He was subsequently arrested and detained for nearly six months because a vigilant and patriotic neighbour saw Arabic writing on the box. Sadly, this man's case is not untypical.

Take the case of Mohammed Junaid who went to 26 Federal Plaza in downtown Manhattan to comply with the Special Registration programme. Mr Junaid never returned home, and his pregnant wife, his daughter and his father-in-law suddenly found themselves facing eviction, having lost their breadwinner. Mr Junaid's crime? It transpires that, after ten years living and working in the United States, there was an order of deportation for him that neither he nor his family knew about. But, in a sense, Mr Junaid is one of the lucky ones. Many men have been subjected to 'the knock' on the door and been arrested by federal officers in the middle of the night, and in front of their terrified families; their workplaces and homes have been raided, or they have simply disappeared into the 'system' leaving their families distraught with anxiety, often unable to track them down for weeks. Deporting the parents of children who are US citizens, usually for minor violations which would ordinarily not be regarded as deportable offences, has become commonplace. This profiling of an entire ethnic and religious group has had serious repercussions for the police, who now have the power to arrest anyone they suspect of immigration irregularities, something that used to be restricted to the INS. Understandably, the relationship of the police to the Arab and Muslim communities has become fraught with tension.

Sadly, a sharp increase in violence against these communities has been a natural corollary of the events of September 11 *and* the government's subsequent behaviour. In January 2003, Zakir H, a young Muslim, was assaulted and stabbed by five men as he walked home in Midwood, Brooklyn, but he never filed a crime report for he was afraid that the police would inform immigration authorities that his visa had expired. Such hate crimes are a daily occurrence, and New York City taxi drivers, 60 per cent of whom are from the Indian subcontinent, are particularly prone to attack, which accounts for the plethora of flags and patriotic stickers that now decorate the city's taxicabs. Delivery men, grocery store owners and restaurateurs are also habitually attacked by people who think it acceptable to call their victims 'Bin Laden' or 'Osama' before punching or stabbing or shooting them simply because they *look* like the 'enemy'. Shortly after September 11 a man murdered a Sikh in Arizona, then shot at a Lebanese clerk at a nearby Mobil station before firing into the home of an Afghan family. 'I'm a patriot,' said Frank S. Roque, as he was arrested. 'I'm a damn American all the way.' And then earlier this year, there was the tragic case of Larme Price, a somewhat deranged African American man from Brooklyn who, blinded by ethnic hatred, went on a six-week spree and killed four immigrant merchants in Queens and Brooklyn claiming that he was targeting people of 'Arabic descent'. He told the police that he considered himself to be a 'patriot killer'.

Perhaps the most insidious and shameful element of all the discriminatory legislation enacted in the wake of September 11 has been Operation Liberty Shield, which became effective in March 2003. Part of this national programme proposed the compulsory detention of asylum seekers from thirty-three countries. If people from these countries attempted to claim asylum in the United States of America they would, quite simply, be locked up for an indefinite period until their cases could be heard. The usual course of action is that anyone seeking asylum in the United States has to go through a hearing to show that they have 'credible fear', and the burden is on them to prove to the immigration authorities that they are not a threat to the United States. While their cases are being heard, most are given help to orientate themselves in society. However, under this new legislation asylum seekers from thirty-three specific countries – in other words Arab, Southeast Asian or Muslim countries – were to be incarcerated on the basis that their mere arrival in the United States constituted a threat to national security. Tom Ridge, Homeland Security Secretary, claimed that the policy was to prevent terrorists – especially those from the so-called 'axis of evil' – from trying to enter the United States, thus once again equating terrorism with immigration in general, and with specific ethnic or religious groups in particular.

The good news is that only a month after initiating this part of the national programme the Department of Homeland Security quietly terminated it, having been subjected to a barrage of criticism from legal, advocacy and faith-based organisations. Thousands of individuals also wrote to Tom Ridge expressing their opposition, including the UN High Commissioner for Refugees, who stated that the 'Detention of asylum seekers should be the exception, not the rule, and should be based on an individualised assessment of the security risk the person poses.' Similar pressure also led to the government quietly dropping the Justice Department draft bill entitled the Domestic Security Enhancement Act of 2003, commonly known as Patriot Act II, which sought to further browbeat the nation with the ludicrous, almost Faustian choice of liberty or security. Incredibly enough, this bill would have granted the executive the ability to strip citizenship from an American who supported a group that the Federal government decided was sympathetic to terrorism. As if that were not enough, the act also proposed the establishment of a DNA database for people whom the government suspected of having links to terrorism. Of course, the criteria for being hauled in and probed for inclusion in the government's DNA database was entirely within their discretion. Mercifully the pressure of individual voices and many agencies around the world has led to the administration dropping this act, although an attempt is being made to slip many of the same proposals through in other bills. In the past two years much damage has been done, not only to civil liberty and people's rights, but to the moral fibre of the country. A religious and ethnic group is regularly being profiled by the government; meanwhile, immigrants have become the fastest-growing section of the US prison population, and the whole question of belonging and national identity has become a decidedly more complex issue than it was before September 11, 2001.

The United States Defense Secretary Donald Rumsfeld was recently asked if he was worried that 'the United States is becoming an imperial, colonial power'. He responded with some indignation. 'That's just not what the United States does. We never have, and we never will. That's not how democracies behave.' When speaking to the graduating cadets at West Point in June 2002, President Bush insisted, 'America has no empire to extend or utopia to establish.' A few months later he announced to veterans gathered at the White House that America 'has no territorial ambitions. We don't seek an empire. Our nation is committed to freedom for ourselves and for others.' The facts don't seem to support these denials. The United States possesses 31 per cent of the world's wealth; it has 750 military bases in three-quarters of the countries in the world; it has more than a million men and women permanently armed and deployed around a globe that it has neatly divided into five military commands; and in 137 countries it has soldiers who are on active duty. Furthermore, the country *guarantees* the safety of Israel and South Korea and, perhaps most bizarrely, its leader, George Bush, a man who avoided military service in Vietnam by enlisting in the Air Force of the National Guard, has become the first president in living memory to don a military uniform. Not even Dwight D. Eisenhower, who *was* a general and war hero before he became president, ever pulled on a uniform while in the White House. And then there is the problem of swagger and attitude. In July this year, while referring to the Iraqis who have had the temerity to attack US forces in Iraq, President Bush drawled 'bring 'em on', suggesting that he had been killing those long hours on Air Force One by watching too many John Wayne films.

The truth is, most Americans don't believe they have an empire for two reasons. First, they have little sense of history, and they therefore don't understand that the United States's overseas imperial phase began long ago, in the wake of the Spanish–American War of 1898, when the country annexed the Philippines, Puerto Rico, Guam and Hawaii. Since 1898 the country has become over-fond of 'short-term interventions' in a wide range of countries including Panama, Grenada, Haiti, Lebanon, Vietnam, Korea . . . the list is endless. After the Second World War, the United States settled into Germany and Japan, where they remain to this day, and they began to exercise an increased influence in Africa, the Far East, and in huge sections of Latin America. Since 1945 the United States has been less than shy about utilising treaty-breaking, non-defensive, pre-emptive strikes against other nations, and they have succeeded in extending the global influence of the country to a level not seen since the heyday of the British Empire.

The second reason that the accusation of 'empire-building' is vigorously denied is that Americans equate the imperial agenda with residence which, of course, is expensive. From the moment they make an incursion into somebody else's territory the United States government begins to talk in terms of 'liberation' and 'withdrawal'. However, the ever-spiralling military budget would suggest that the American people – particularly the poorer members of society – have, for some time now, been obliged to find a way to fund this 'empire', or global sphere of influence. They are being asked to pay dearly for this state of perpetual, media-scripted war against often mythical, and certainly difficult to locate, enemies. The bill for the latest escapade in Iraq has been, so far, in excess of $70 billion. Estimates for the 'rebuilding' phase put the figure at ten times this amount, which is patently immoral in a country in which over forty million people, including eleven million children, have no health care whatsoever.

The overseas antics of the United States of America have always threatened to damage the country from within. This was powerfully demonstrated during the anti-war protests of the sixties, when opposition to the Vietnam War generated a huge backlash of violence and unease within the country. The protestors knew that 'freedom' was no longer the guiding principle of the republic, and a rapacious foreign policy began to affect the nation's domestic health. The nation survived this crisis, and for a while it was careful to be more oblique about its interventions into other people's countries. The destabilising of the Pinochet regime in Chile occurred hard on the heels of Vietnam, but this was a covert operation, as were the ones in Nicaragua, in Panama, and elsewhere. However, the events of September 11, 2001 dispelled any such caution, and while the leaders still protested that the country was not an empire-builder, and that 'liberation' and 'withdrawal' remained its guiding principles, some among them were now openly 'hawkish' about describing what they were *actually* doing. Shortly after September 11, Deputy Secretary of Defense Paul Wolfowitz said that the Bush administration would be '*ending* states who sponsor terrorism'. Not much caution there, nor was there any coyness about the imaginatively named 'Operation Infinite Justice', although it is interesting to note that only days after its announcement the name was changed to the less hawkish, but equally absurd, 'Operation Enduring Freedom'.

But why should Paul Wolfowitz worry? As long as the administration can persuade the nation that all policies are being introduced in the name of those two 'buzzwords', 'freedom' and 'security', then surely nobody can question the 'integrity' of pursuing a policy of 'regime change' in either Afghanistan or Iraq, nor should anybody be too sentimental about a few minor sidesteps around the Bill of Rights at home. 'Supervision', or 'indirect rule', is the stated aim of this present administration's foreign policy, and 'containment' is the euphemism used to describe its actions. Given the United States's extraordinary military might, and its economic and cultural power, it all begins to smell suspiciously like Empire to me. However, the folly of Empire is that eventually the imperialists begin to believe that 'containment' is not enough; they decide that nothing short of control and domination will suffice.

It was John Quincy Adams who pointed out in 1821 that if the United States were tempted to 'become dictatress of the world, she would no longer be the ruler of her own spirit'. For much of the twentieth century this great nation of immigration, reinvention, new beginnings and, yes, freedom for so many people, has managed to maintain its vigour and enthusiasm. But it has done so, in part, by averting its eyes from the stain of genocide and slavery at the inception of the republic, and the bullying and posturing that have characterised its adventuring in other people's countries throughout the entire past century. This present administration has brazenly used the events of September 11 to justify its expansionist foreign policy, quickly fusing the name of Osama Bin Laden with that of Saddam Hussein, and suggesting that a 'war on terror' is somehow the same thing as a military assault on Iraq. This is lamentable, but perhaps the most heinous of all deeds carried out by this present administration has been its assault, in the name of 'security', upon immigrants. The United States has, to use a phrase ascribed to the Russian poet Vladimir Mayakovsky, stepped on the throat of its own song. John Quincy Adams was right: this administration's policy of targeting immigrants – the very lifeblood of the nation – because of their ethnicity or religion, means that the country has betrayed herself. She is no longer the ruler of her own spirit.

* * *

It is difficult to explain just how dreadful it was to be in Lower Manhattan on the morning of September 11, 2001. There is, however, one image from the many hundreds that affected count-less millions around the globe, that I simply cannot get out of my head. It is a photograph of the Statue of Liberty as viewed from the water on that morning. Beyond the statue we can see the burning towers of the World Trade Center dominating the skyline. Some time later a journal of remembrances was opened at Liberty Island and visitors from all over the world were invited to share their thoughts. The sentiments ranged from the insightful and thought-provoking to the truly banal, but the word most commonly used was 'freedom'. An entry from Georgia is typical: 'They may have taken the Trade Centers, but they can never take our freedom or pride. This gorgeous statue repre-sents so much!'

Located in New York City Harbor, the Statue of Liberty was a gift of international friendship from the people of France to the people of the United States, and it was intended to recognise the close relationship that had been forged during the American Revolution. Dedicated on 28 October 1886, it is one of the most universal symbols of political freedom and democ-racy, and it became an emblem for the twelve million anxious immigrants in steerage and third class who, between 1892 and 1954, entered the United States through the port of New York. For them the sight of Lady Liberty with her upraised torch meant that their journey to the New World was almost complete. They knew that they had finally reached a place of refuge that would shelter them from poverty, religious persecution, hostile oppressive governments and tyrannical dictators, and they knew that in this new land they would be free to embrace opportu-nity. Although this sighting of the Statue of Liberty stirred such feelings in the hearts and souls of the immigrants who clambered on deck, not until 1903 was there any official recog-nition of the relationship between the statue and immigration. In that year a bronze plaque was affixed to the pedestal of the statue, and inscribed on the plaque was a short poem entitled

'The New Colossus' by a poet who had died some sixteen years earlier, aged only thirty-eight.

Emma Lazarus was born in 1849 into a prominent Jewish family in New York City, and she devoted her short life to literature. She published a novel, a play and two collections of poetry, and she regarded Ralph Waldo Emerson as her model. Her concern with nature, her undefined faith and her transcendentalist ideas gave her writing an ethereal quality, although 'The New Colossus' was, for her, an entirely different type of poem. Moved by the lamentable conditions of the hordes of immigrants arriving in New York City, in 1881 Emma Lazarus visited a temporary immigrant shelter on Ward's Island in the East River and she soon became an advocate of refugee interests. Her poem honours the Statue of Liberty, and its enduring genius is that it gives the statue a *raison d'être* that it previously lacked. In the poem she calls Lady Liberty 'the mother of exiles' and imagines her standing at the 'golden door', the threshold of this new American land, and speaking with her silent lips, crying out to the old, pompous lands across the seas,

> 'Give me your tired, your poor,
> Your huddled masses yearning to breathe free,
> The wretched refuse of your teeming shore.
> Send these, the homeless, tempest-tost to me.
> I lift my lamp beside the golden door!'

The entry from Georgia read: 'They may have taken the Trade Centers, but they can never take our freedom or pride. This gorgeous statue represents so much.' Indeed it does. But in a way 'they' – the catch-all word for terrorists – have, in fact, succeeded in taking away so many, many freedoms along with the Twin Towers. But let us be clear: the people who *organised* the removal of these freedoms were, of course, the United States government. Not only are Lady Liberty's eyes closed tight, but she is squirming in shame.

*   *   *

The great, and enduring, strength of the United States is that it *is* an immigrant society that is subject to continual waves of replenishment from outside. Such is the desire to participate that one person every day is killed trying to enter the country. These 'new' people bring with them new narratives which grow and flourish in the very heart and bosom of the society, narratives that find expression in music, theatre, dance, film and literature. These 'new' people are not only vital to the economic health of the country, they are also the keepers of the cultural and artistic flame. However, since September 11, it is precisely these people who have been hounded and persecuted by the government, and their fealty to the country is being questioned. Their desire to construct narratives has not been stilled, but their new tales are *counter-narratives* which seek to explain their situation. The impulse to tell a story is the oldest of human impulses for it clarifies and orders the relationship between the private and the public, our inner and outer worlds, and it records the dissonance between these two spheres of existence. This being the case, storytelling has always been a logical form for the migrant to utilise in order that he might try to capture the conundrum of his own, often precarious, situation in the world. While I remain dismayed by the domestic and foreign chaos that the United States continues to unleash upon her own people, and upon millions of foreign citizens, I am comforted by the knowledge that her folly will be recorded and exposed by the narratives of those whose private and public lives have been thrown into turmoil by the iniquities of the policies emanating from the White House.

This new work will be written or performed in English, and it will tell us what happened when the FBI came to lock up daddy. Or why grandad ended up in a jail cell in New Jersey for two years, having committed no crime. This work will tell us what happened when one morning, after ten years of tax-paying, law-abiding residence, the police threw us out of our home. What happened when a neighbourhood gang burned down our mosque. Beat up Uncle Mohammed. Tore the headscarf off Cousin Fatima. What happened when the immigration officer took away our passports. Narratives of belonging and betrayal. Earlier this year in New York City, *In What Language?*, a piece of musical theatre by Vijay Iyer, the son of Indian immigrants, opened Off-Off Broadway. The work explored how ill-formed suspicions of Arabs, Southeast Asians and Muslims in American airports is making life in transit impossible for this section of the population. (The phrase 'Flying While Brown' can now be added to that equally pithy description of American discrimination, 'Driving While Black)'. At another theatre in the city, a play entitled *Come Undone* recently premiered; a series of moving monologues, from a young girl's bewilderment at her father's disappearance, to an INS agent's rant, to a Sikh woman's humorous conversation with an arsonist. *In My Own Skin* is a filmed documentary meditation with five young Arab American women talking about their lives in the unforgiving climate which most have had to endure during the past two years. Films, plays, poetry, dance pieces, art installations, short stories and monologues already exist, but more work will follow. I believe we are witnessing the birth of a new kind of American artistic and literary expression: work which brings us the voices of people who feel stunned and bruised by the abuses of American power at home and abroad.

The present-day United States of America is faced with a familiar situation, in some ways the eternal stand-off. On the one side we find the poet and on the other side the emperor. Whose version of history do we trust? Whose version of history will prevail? My ear is to the ground and I already hear an insistent whispering from the poet. I believe that ultimately it is the poet who will revive the spirit of the nation, and it is the poet who will lend dignity to the people. During the past century we have heard, in Latin America, in Eastern Europe, in Africa, in China, the moral authority of the individual voice raised against tyranny, the voice of a person who refuses to look the other way, who is determined to explain himself, who is un-afraid to challenge the might of the emperor, who is determined

to tell his truth. It is the poet who will finally enable Lady
Liberty to once more open her eyes, and when she does so she
might glance down to her feet and there she will find the words
of a poet. 'Give me your tired, your poor, your huddled masses.'
Such dignity. Such dark times.

American Stories, American Silence (2006)

I live in a country in which I am constantly being told by the president that the world is becoming an increasingly dangerous place. Red alert. Orange alert. 'We'll have that suspicious-looking tube of toothpaste, thank you very much.' There is a website (www.nationalterroralert.com) sponsored by the Department of Homeland Security that is so melodramatic in appearance and content that, having logged on to it, I thought for one moment that this must be a joke. Of course it is not. I have lost all track of when anxiety is supposed to harden into dread, or dread give way to fear; I just know that I am supposed to be scared – pretty much all of the time – because there are bad people out there who menacingly congregate around a place called 'the axis of evil'. Apparently, they are all fundamentalists of one type or another. The irony is that the man who is telling me this seems to exhibit all the characteristics of the men he is supposedly warning me against. He is a dogmatic man, and he appears to tolerate little dissent; he is wedded to violence as a means of achieving his ends, and he believes that a higher being is guiding him towards his ultimately religiously inspired destiny. Unless I have missed something, this man is as much a fundamentalist as the bad men who supposedly threaten what the leader likes to speak of as 'our way of life' in the American homeland.

The suggestion that there is a cohesive 'way of life' in the disunited and fractured United States of America is in itself a deeply questionable conceit, but in the early twenty-first century, platitudes about 'national security', often sponsored and promoted by the right-wing media, easily triumph over truth, or just plain common sense. After all, this is a nation which bought into the idea that the possible existence of so-called 'weapons of mass destruction' justified ploughing billions of dollars into a war against a nation whose regime they helped to establish in the first place. Successive US administrations both armed and fully promoted Iraq during the 1980–88 Iran–Iraq war, continuing a policy of support, which dated back to the early 1970s, of bolstering Saddam Hussein as a 'friendly' counterweight to revolutionary Iran. And then suddenly this staunch ally became the uncontrollable enemy. The White House has assured us that the present war against Iraq is not motivated by vengeance; this 'moral crusade' has nothing to do with oil or punishing an ungrateful upstart. Walt Disney could not have made up a more fantastical narrative than that which has emerged from Washington, DC. And today, on almost every American television news channel, the foreign policy catastrophe that is Iraq is still being reported as a righteous war against so-called terror. This obvious fiction is made all the more offensive by the debasement of the English language that accompanies the bulletins. 'Bring 'em on,' says George W. Bush. The whole misadventure would be laughable were it not for the gross misappropriation of tax dollars in a country where basic health care remains a privilege. It would be laughable were it not for the open, and now state-sanctioned, use of torture, the hundreds of thousands of deaths – both civilian and military – and the apparent inability of the Bush administration to learn from previous mistakes and negotiate a semi-dignified withdrawal before any more innocent blood is shed. But it is not laughable. Meanwhile this leader keeps telling me, with a straight face, that the world, through no fault of his own, is becoming an increasingly dangerous place.

To be an artist one has to be able to see. There are, of course, other attributes that are necessary if one is to pursue this vocation: talent, discipline and some good fortune all help. But first one must be able to *see* into the heart of society and understand what is going on in one's world. The artist may well comment very clearly and directly about what he sees, as is the case with Marvin Gaye's 'What's Going On', or Picasso's *Guernica*, or Solzhenitsyn's *One Day in the Life of Ivan Denisovich*. Or the commentary may be more consciously indirect – J.M.W. Turner's 1840 masterpiece, *Slavers Throwing Overboard the Dead and Dying, Typhoon Coming On*, or Beethoven's 'Eroica' symphony are works of art forged in the crucible of political change and turmoil – but these seemingly more oblique political artists were *also* acutely aware of their responsibility to 'see'. Whether overt or cunningly covert, all artists see, and writers see with at least the same degree of acuity as any other artists.

There is a directness about storytelling, involving as it does human beings as the central players, which means that we often look first to our writers for news of who and what we are. Words cohering into language form the bedrock of our identity, and to explain our human condition, our first port of call is generally words. The storyteller who first sees and then tells his story often places himself in an extremely exposed situation. But exposed to what? More often than not, to the wrath of those who do not approve of what the writer is seeing and reflecting upon. The writer's frowning opponent has usually invested in promulgating a different type of story, and the authority of this disapproving man, whom the Nigerian writer Chinua Achebe once called 'the emperor', is traditionally fuelled by power that emanates from the ballot box or from the barrel of a gun, or both. However tangential the relationship of the emperor's story to factual evidence, the emperor very much desires that *his* story should be received as an evident communal truth.

But what are we to make of the story of the exposed writer? Are those listening able to detect the moral authority of a story unsupported by the flying buttresses of political power? The writer hopes that *his* story will offer up an alternative, and certainly more palatable, narrative about the contemporary world, and he hopes that there might be an audience out there who are receptive to his words. The squabble between the emperor and the writer is an old one, but in our present unpredictable world, with self-aggrandising fundamentalism to the right and to the left, it is a struggle in which it might be increasingly problematic for the writer even to consider presenting his counter-narratives. 'Tell your potent stories, but with caution,' might be the mantra for the modern writer. While nobody would wish any harm, and certainly not death, on a writer who is pursuing his art, writers, perhaps more than other artists, should understand that if, as is often the case, the emperor has invested in a different story, then it is they, the writers, who will be most vigorously attacked, not their stories.

Ovid was sent by Emperor Augustus from Rome into exile on the Black Sea, and he eventually died there. Solzhenitsyn, a man born into troubled times, was exiled from the Soviet Union, but in the end he returned to a place that he had to learn to comprehend anew. Other writers have attempted to cosy up to power, like the Georgian poet Vladimir Mayakovsky who eventually shot himself, while others like Czeslaw Milosz fled Poland and wrote about how perilously close he came to allowing his mind to be captured by the emperor, while lamenting the fate of former colleagues who had succumbed to this seduction. Recently, two writer friends of mine died, both Cuban, both exiled. Antonio Benítez-Rojo and Guillermo Cabrera Infante. My abiding memory of these two extraordinary writers is their dignified melancholy for a land lost to them because of their inability to sing choral words they knew to be false.

There is another type of exile that is not the political exile of somebody being ejected by, or having to escape, the emperor and his stories. Sometimes the writer simply has to travel to another country in order to see himself and his own society clearly. This is what Ibsen was doing in Italy when he wrote his great plays, or what James Baldwin was doing in France in the 1950s, or what Henry James and T.S. Eliot were doing in London. A writer goes to where he can see, he engages in a conversation with himself, what Eudora Welty calls 'daring to do with one's bag of fears', and then he makes his story available to the tribe. To know how to see, and where to go to see, is difficult. To sit in judgement on oneself is difficult. But to then take the next step, and speak to the tribe, is when the job of the writer becomes potentially treacherous.

It is night. A group of people sit cross-legged around a bonfire. The storyteller stands up and begins to tell his story. If the story is good it will hold the attention of the people. If it is not good the members of the tribe may well nod off to sleep. But good or bad the tribe will never punish the story-teller. It is the so-called leader of the tribe, the emperor, who will punish the storyteller, even though the emperor himself may not be seated by the bonfire. Somebody will tell him about the story. Somebody will tell him that it was a dangerous tale. He himself has no time for such tales, but he knows that he should be wary of the storyteller and his stories. He now knows that there is a problem and he wants to make sure that there are no further tales. He cannot attack the tale, for it already exists. Instead, he attacks the storyteller to prevent further tales, and if the storyteller does not flee in time he may well be punished or even put to death. Such worries have descended on the shoulders of a great many writers in the world today, and many writers have sought asylum, often in the United States of America, a country that is sometimes directly or indirectly responsible for the writers' plight in the first place. What is it about the air of this country that encourages storytellers, American or non-American, to believe that they can construct their narratives without a real fear that they might suffer reprisals from the American emperor? After all, the United States is not above passing legislation which blatantly undermines the civil liberties of citizens and non-citizens alike.

Have writers spoken out against the widespread attack on human rights since September 11, 2001? Of course they have. New Muslim American writers have begun to write work which speaks back to the centre, and established American writers are also speaking out and challenging the legitimacy of President

Bush's policies, but we hear precious little of these writers' statements; so much so that Derek Walcott recently stated that he was appalled by the apathy he sees among American writers regarding torture and social injustice. 'I'm not disappointed,' he said. 'It's not my country, but I *am* embarrassed about the silence of the American intellectual.' The truth is that, in these dark times, American writers have *not* been silent, but on closer inspection it is possible to detect something that may well be even more disturbing than perceived silence.

In the land of the free and the home of the brave, a writer's voice which rises up against state orthodoxy would appear to be comfortably accommodated. It is nearly forty years now since the late Mary Lee Settle, a remarkably courageous southern writer, vowed that if 'that asshole' Richard Nixon was elected president she would leave the country. She was, of course, true to her word and in 1969 she went to live first in England, and then in Turkey, and only after Nixon resigned in 1974 did she return to the United States. I sometimes wonder who noticed, or, if they did, who cared. She was an outstanding writer, who later gave money to establish the PEN/Faulkner Award, one of America's most prestigious literary prizes, but when she died last year her anti-Nixon stance was largely overlooked by most of the obituary notices. And then more recently, the award-winning poet Sharon Olds wrote an open letter explaining why she would not be participating in one of Laura Bush's Literary Symposiums at the White House. Many well-known American writers and critics such as Tom Wolfe, Arnold Rampersad, Colson Whitehead, David Levering Lewis and others have attended, but not Ms Olds. In a letter published last year in *The Nation*, Sharon Olds could not have been clearer about her feelings.

'. . . I could not face the idea of breaking bread with you. I knew that if I sat down to eat with you, it would feel to me as if I were condoning what I see to be the wild, highhanded actions of the Bush Administration.

What kept coming to the fore of my mind was that I would be taking food from the hand of the First Lady who represents the Administration that unleashed this war and that wills its continuation, even to the extent of permitting 'extraordinary rendition': flying people to other countries where they will be tortured for us.

So many Americans who had felt pride in our country now feel anguish and shame, for the current regime of blood, wounds and fire. I thought of the clean linens at your table, the shining knives and the flames of the candles, and I could not stomach it.'

The Nation printed a few letters to the editor, which divided along predictable pro-Olds/anti-Olds lines, but the gesture did not stimulate a larger debate, and Laura Bush's Literary Symposiums continue to attract a wide range of writers who are happy to participate. This public statement by a nationally acclaimed poet elicited the same indifference that disappointed Mary Lee Settle some years earlier.

Perhaps the seriousness of the times demands that writers should raise their voices and be a little less delicate, and a little more shrill, in their outrage. Kurt Vonnegut is certainly no shy retiring flower when it comes to polemical statements, but his online anti-Bush rant in 2004 stimulated little press coverage and barely a raised eyebrow. 'But I know now,' he said, 'that there is not a chance in hell of America's becoming humane and reasonable. Because power corrupts us, and absolute power corrupts absolutely. Human beings are chimpanzees who get crazy drunk on power. By saying that our leaders are power-drunk chimpanzees, am I in danger of wrecking the morale of our soldiers fighting and dying in the Middle East? Their morale, like so many bodies, is already shot to pieces. They are being treated as I never was, like toys a rich kid got for Christmas.' One can imagine Kurt Vonnegut's narrative seizing the emperor's attention and causing him some offence, but this American emperor was not only unmoved by Vonnegut's vitriol, he seems to be indifferent to the many alternative stories that are being narrated by the writers in his tribe. Neither the storytellers, nor their stories, seem able to provoke a response in him.

Some have claimed that it is not indifference but censorship that is at the root of this perceived lack of opposition in the United States. In other words, the emperor hears the stories but he quickly finds ways and means to control their dissemination. It is undoubtedly the case that the American news media has censored itself, and shamefully so. CNN's top war correspondent, Christiane Amanpour, admitted as much when she said, in 2003, 'I think the press was muzzled, and I think the press self-muzzled. I'm sorry to say, but certainly television and, perhaps, to a certain extent, my station, was intimidated by the administration and its foot soldiers at Fox News. And it did, in fact, put a climate of fear and self-censorship, in my view, in terms of the broadcast work we did.'

But censorship in literature and the arts? American libraries and school boards have continued to ban books, most frequently *The Catcher in the Rye, Of Mice and Men, The Adventures of Huckleberry Finn, To Kill a Mockingbird,* and *One Flew Over the Cuckoo's Nest*. The familiar list. However, this form of literary censorship is hardly new in American life, and its existence generally has more to do with perceived morality than contemporary politics. There were some adjustments to cultural product after September 11; an episode of *The Simpsons* that takes place in New York (called 'The City of New York versus Homer Simpson') which features many scenes of an animated World Trade Center, was deemed not suitable for transmission, and when it was finally broadcast it was heavily edited. However, this 'censorship', as some saw it, seemed to owe more to sensitivity about the images of the towers than to any attempt to silence the satirical, dangerous voice of Homer Simpson. In fact, films such as *Men in Black II, Zoolander* and *Serendipity* were also re-edited to cut out images of the towers, but this is not censorship. I see no real examples in the United States of censorship in publishing or the arts comparable to the repression that exists in many other parts of the world. John Updike's latest novel, *Terrorist*, concerns a thoughtful teenager in New Jersey who is a devout Muslim and who finds himself recruited to the cause of violence; and Jonathan Safran Foer's *Extremely Loud and Incredibly Close* explores loss and love through the eyes of a nine-year-old boy wandering New York City after his father's death on September 11. These authors, and many others, are dealing directly, and not uncritically, with the current state of modern America and the nation's subsequent descent into a questionable domestic, and a chaotic foreign, policy, and they appear to be doing so without any real fear of retribution or punishment.

In many parts of the world, past and present, the writer is the person to whom one looks, in times of trouble, in the hope that he or she might provide an alternative to the dominant narrative. The writer as the moral voice of the tribe; the writer as the keeper of a people's conscience. We are back to my initial image. It is night. We are seated around a fire. The storyteller stands up and begins to tell his tale. And if it is a tale that the emperor does not like, then the emperor may attempt to punish him. As was the case with Arthur Miller who, as one among many other writers, stood before the House Un-American Activities Committee in 1956 and refused to name names. He displayed both courage and moral leadership – such as we might expect from the man who had written *The Crucible* three years earlier – but he was still fined $500, sentenced to thirty days in prison, blacklisted, and disallowed a US passport. In 1958 his conviction was overturned by the court of appeals, but not every writer who was punished by McCarthy's committee was this fortunate.

In the present-day United States of America, there is no Senator Joe McCarthy, no perception of the writer as a dangerous person that one must call to heel. Most people consider themselves too busy to sit around a fire and listen to a whole story. The truth is, the writer in the early twenty-first-century United States of America is *not* perceived as a purveyor of moral leadership. In this new American world, the culture of celebrity has legitimised a dumbing down of intelligence so that people now believe that *anybody* can be famous, and that fame is the goal; a fame, of course, that bears no relationship to achievement. In this brave new world, the writer's voice is no more important than that of a model or an actor, and many writers are now beginning to panic and desire celebrity status, perhaps out of a fear that without this kind of profile they will be perceived as 'losers' and not real societal 'players'. Ironically, it's possible that from the moment, fifty years ago, when Arthur Miller married Marilyn Monroe, things began slowly to go downhill as far as the American writer being taken seriously as a voice of reason was concerned.

Both at home and abroad, the United States is struggling and in desperate need of somebody other than the White House or Fox News to interpret what is going on. We do get different versions of events, most often in the form of satire, from comics such as Bill Maher or Jon Stewart. But we also get them – loudly and clearly – from writers such as Sharon Olds and Kurt Vonnegut, who *do* take a stance and speak out; but who, in the United States at least, cares what an American writer thinks? When William Styron died recently, one obituary pointed out that he was part of the last generation of American writers who could assume that literary quality might be married to a large audience. In other words, he was one of the last American authors of literary fiction who could imagine that he had an audience. Am I lamenting the changing role of the writer in the United States? Absolutely.

The serious storyteller in the United States can no longer assume that he has an audience who are interested in his make-believe. Nor, given the results of the recent midterm elections, can one assume that the American public is necessarily interested in hearing what the emperor is saying. The truth is, the average American may well be indifferent to *any* narrative, and interested only in pursuing their own non-scripted roles as studio guests in the reality show called 'The United States of America'. The most powerful country on earth may well have already dispensed with the role of the author as social commentator or moral guide and replaced him with the author as B-list celebrity beneath the A-list of sportsmen, actors, comedians and politicians. This being the case, we know that the emperor is entirely content with this development. If nobody is listening to anybody, then the emperor can simply get on with what he does best, which is translating power into material gain, until somebody presses a buzzer and his time is up.

There is dignity and responsibility to being a storyteller, but when a tribe descends into decadence and no longer appears to be interested in stories which tell them who they are, and what they have done, and what they are doing, then the storyteller can either stubbornly keep talking, or decide to bellow a simpler story in an attempt to make his voice rise up above the relentless celebrity babble, or he can just sit down and retreat into dignified silence. I worry that American writers will eventually fall silent, the very act that Derek Walcott claims has already happened. But I have a greater fear: I fear that a new generation of writers is emerging whose notion of storytelling is that they should submit to being packaged for the American consumer, good alongside bad, so that any moral weight is evenly distributed and therefore diluted, so that any possibility of real vision or originality rising out of this democratic morass will become increasingly difficult with the passing of each new year. Of course, these days one doesn't need to formally publish to call oneself a writer. Anybody can keep a blog and share their 'writing', no matter how bad, or inept, or mindless it is. The United States of America has fully entered the age of celebrity babble and it is effectively killing the art of storytelling at precisely the time that the country needs to hear something other than its own mindless whining on chat shows, reality shows and television news. In the inaugural issue of the *Paris Review*, in the spring of 1953, William Styron commented that 'The times get precisely the literature that they deserve . . .' President Bush is right; these *are* dangerous times.

American Dispatches

Colored People (1995)

Henry Louis Gates is well known in American academic circles as a phenomenon. Having moved quickly through the Ivy League ranks as a student, with degrees from both Yale and Cambridge, he has since taught at Yale, Cornell, Duke and Harvard, each 'transfer' being accompanied by promotion and more administrative power. He is presently W.E.B. Du Bois Professor of Humanities, Professor of English and Chair of the Afro-American Department at Harvard.

His new book, *Colored People* (1994), marks a significant departure in the writing of Gates, who has hitherto been best known for his critical essays, particularly the American Book Award winner, *Loose Canons* (1992), and the ground-breaking *The Signifying Monkey* (1988). His rewriting of African American literary history, and his reshaping of the critical vocabulary that one employs to define it, have been work of the highest importance. With this new book Gates temporarily leaves the academy and writes about himself and his upbringing in the small town of Piedmont, West Virginia (Population: 2,565. Colored Population: 351).

The book traces the first eighteen years of Gates's life, from 1950 to his departure for Yale in 1968. Gates came of age in a period when the adjective changed from the quaint 'colored' of the 1950s, to the rather more dynamic 'negro' of the Civil Rights Movement, to the out-and-out angry affirmation of 'black' that came in the wake of the death of Martin Luther King Jnr and the emergence of the black power movement. Gates is clear about where his preference lies: 'I don't mind any of the names myself. But I have to confess that I like 'colored' best, maybe because when I hear the word, I hear it in my mother's voice and in the sepia tones of my childhood.'

The dominant tone of the book is nostalgic recollection, a tone which is not to be found in the recent spate of black autobiographical writing such as Brent Staples's *Parallel Time*, or Nathan McCall's *Makes Me Wanna Holler*. There is precious little in the way of humour in modern African American writing, much of which seeks to capture the essence of how the author 'got over'. *Colored People* is a valuable corrective to this, but at times one does wonder about the accuracy of the author's memory. Early in the book Gates talks about 'the day in 1951 when Bobby Thompson hits a home run in the bottom of the ninth to beat the Dodgers and win the pennant for the Giants'. His elated father began to jump all over the furniture to the extent that it scared young Gates. In fact, 'It scared me so much that I started to cry.' It is a delightful anecdote, but only when one examines it more closely does it become evident that Gates could, at best, have been a year old at that time. Did he really 'remember'?

Gates's narrative may be slightly romanticised, the memories of a man who has 'made it' and can therefore afford to imbue what must have been a difficult childhood with a gloss that stops well short of real hurt and anger. For long stretches of the book one is left with an uncomfortable feeling that much of what happened might have occurred solely in the hip, fertile imagination of a very intelligent young boy, whose upbringing was only tangentially connected to what was going on in the rest of the world. Politics beyond Piedmont are alluded to, for instance when Gates describes the 'colored' town's first encounter with the Civil Rights Movement. But can it all have been this simple?

The simple truth is that the civil rights era came late to Piedmont, even though it came early to our television sets. We could watch what was going on Elsewhere on television, but the marches and sit-ins were as remote to us as, in other ways, was the all-colored world of *Amos and Andy* — a world full of black lawyers, black judges, black nurses, black doctors.

At moments such as this, one longs for Gates to put aside sentiment and tackle the issues of his own development, of the racial politics of Piedmont, and of the Civil Rights Movement, in a more vigorous manner.

Colored People attempts to chart the territory where a 'colored man' might dwell without having to choose between Bach and James Brown. To define a place where a man can be a man and still be culturally black. Where achievement does not mean that one has to straighten one's hair and stop acknowledging other black people in the street. In this respect *Colored People* is an attempt by a man who has journeyed far beyond Piedmont to say, 'What's up? I still speak your tongue!' But in order to understand the nature of the journey one has to be fully aware of where its author has now arrived. In other words, to achieve its fullest resonance the book needs to be viewed through the prism of Harvard. Gates is uncomfortable with such a reading. *Colored People* is an attempt to subvert the notion of a book about the loss that accompanies progress. Instead, the author seeks to introduce Professor Gates the academic to 'Skippy' Gates the homeboy. A synthesis of these two persons into one offers the black intellectual a way to reclaim the romance of his past without giving up the perks of his present. Precisely the task which this author hopes to achieve in his public and professional life.

Men at Sea: African American Sailors (1997)

During the years immediately preceding the Civil War, by far the greater part of the American merchant marine was registered in the northern states. The maritime blockade established by Abraham Lincoln's administration sealed the ports of the southern states, effectively causing a severe decline in coastal trade. The Confederacy was quick to send out raiding parties to attack any of the Union's merchant ships which dared to venture south, and during the course of the war 258 Union vessels were captured or destroyed. This devastation undermined confidence in the shipping industry, and by the end of the Civil War the merchant marine was in a lamentable condition.

For African Americans, the decline of American-owned and American-operated shipping marked the end of a remarkable period in their history, in which the vast shipping lanes of the Atlantic and the eastern seaboard not only provided a means of employment but offered them a chance to escape the harsh realities of slavery. Life at sea also had given African Americans the opportunity to educate themselves, for the maritime world was truly multiracial and often multi-lingual, and black sailors were able to frequent foreign ports and exchange information and ideas far removed from the crushing restrictions of the United States.

Crispus Attucks, Denmark Vesey, Robert Smalls, Paul Cuffee, and many more African American leaders of the eighteenth and nineteenth centuries were schooled on board ships, and their maritime 'education' bred within them a deep resistance to an onshore system which denied them even the most fundamental of rights. Although the vast majority of African Americans served as ordinary seamen, many rose through the ranks and became officers, and some even rose to become captain. And these positions were earned by dint of ability and experience.

W. Jeffrey Bolster's study of these men and their world, *Black Jacks: African American Seamen in the Age of Sail* (1997), begins in 1740 and finishes in 1865 with the end of the Civil War. Bolster is a cautious scholar, and he concludes the first paragraph of his preface with the disclaimer that: 'It may be germane that I am not black; again, possibly germane that I am a seaman of sailing ships.' The former fact would appear to be of little significance, but Bolster's experience of sailing ships has clearly affected his narrative. And not always for the better: he sometimes assumes that his readers are also seamen and that they can therefore find their way through the technical jargon of the sea unaided by either footnotes or a glossary. What are we poor landlubbers expected to make of a sentence such as, 'Refinements in rigging were modest, such as the substitution of a gaff-rigged spanker for a lateen mizzen'?

But the extraordinary story that Bolster tells makes such complaints moot. With the onset of the transatlantic slave trade, many Africans soon had their first experience of life beyond the horizon of sea and sky. Olaudah Equiano, whose memoir (1789) is the most important slave narrative of the eighteenth century, remembers that the crew on his slave ship was careful to make sure 'that we could not see how they managed the vessel'. This meant that the relationship between the cloth and the masts remained, at least for the time being, a mystery to Equiano and his fellow African captives. Yet a great number of captains did release slaves from their chains, and put them to work during the voyage. Malaria, dysentery and yellow fever often carried off crew members during the coastal loading process, and this careful utilisation of 'cargo' was a common practice. Accordingly, some captives arrived in the Americas with their own traditional maritime skills enhanced by experience in the white man's ways of sailing.

In the years immediately preceding the Revolutionary War, the only way in which a slave could realistically escape the plantation system was by going to sea. This often happened with the approval of the slave's owner, to whom the slave might remit an agreed amount each month. In 1747 Briton Hammon, a Massachusetts slave, came to an agreement with his owner that he might go to sea in exchange for paying his master $15 a month. Hammon's *Narrative of the Uncommon Sufferings, and Surprizing Deliverance of Briton Hammon, a Negro Man* (1760) contains the first account of a sea voyage published by an African American.

Most black sailors in this pre-Revolutionary period hired themselves out to whomever would pay. It was a precarious business in which they risked capture by pirates, being sold back into slavery in the South, imprisoned, or worse. Many planters and slave-owners resented blacks being allowed to go to sea: they claimed that it bred an unacceptable independence in them. But blacks at sea became an increasingly common sight during the eighteenth century. For a white man to go to sea suggested a certain marginalisation within his own society. Black seamen, on the other hand, were the aristocrats of African American society. Seamen wrote the first six autobiographies of blacks published in English before 1800, and nearly all those works are characterised by the author's ability to place his own life vividly in the context of more than one world. The autobiographies of Equiano and Ukawsaw Gronniosaw in particular make connections between the worlds of Africa, Europe and the Americas with a diasporan ease that we do not see again until the twentieth-century writings of Claude McKay, C.L.R. James and Richard Wright in our own time.

Bolster is keen to stress the broader Atlantic significance of the African American world of sail, but his enthusiasm often finds him tearing down the wrong path and arriving at implausible conclusions. Thus he cites the case of Joseph Johnson, an early nineteenth-century merchant sailor who, with a model of a ship balanced neatly on his head, begged in the streets of London. He claims that Johnson's existence and practice are not only evidence of the exchange of human traffic across the Atlantic in the time of slavery, but signify something larger:

> In a classic case of cultural cross-over, Johnson appropriated a European artefact, one that had become meaningful to him through his own years of sea service, and reinvested it with African meanings to create a characteristically black cultural expression. Most white contemporaries looked at Joe Johnson through the distorting glass of race and saw an old black sailor cleverly manipulating a full-rigged ship on his head. London blacks, on the other hand, saw an aged mummer bobbing through the streets, connecting them with his coded ship to West Indian and Carolinian slaves, and to people on the Gold Coast and the Niger Delta. Forced to represent himself with fawning propriety to white almsgivers, Johnson undoubtedly took psychological refuge in their inability to comprehend him fully, even as he shook his creolized African past in their faces.

It is entirely possible, of course, that Johnson appeared to most London blacks as nothing more than 'an old black sailor cleverly manipulating a full-rigged ship on his head'. London blacks of the late eighteenth and early nineteenth century constituted a very sophisticated and diverse section of society. Still, it is highly unlikely that they would have interpreted the paraphernalia on this beggar's head as a 'coded ship' connecting them to 'West Indian and Carolinian slaves', any more than Johnson would have felt that he was shaking his 'creolized African past' in anyone's face. The man was begging: he knew it, and those he met on the streets of London knew it.

Bolster's book too often attempts to draw meaning from a dry academic well, and shake its doctoral credentials in our face. He seems determined to extend his study beyond the domestic confines of the nascent United States, and out into the more amorphous zone of 'the black Atlantic'. At almost every juncture where he attempts an 'Atlantic' reading, however, his examples are unconvincing, and his claims for them often unacceptably speculative. But there is a towering exception to this rule, and it is his wonderfully vivid examination of the events at Dartmoor prison in southern England during the War of 1812.

By 1814, nearly one thousand African American seamen, and 5,000 of their white shipmates, found themselves imprisoned in the notoriously bleak and harsh conditions of Dartmoor prison. The first African Americans had arrived in April 1813, but as the war gathered momentum, and captured Americans of all colors refused to be pressed into the service of the Royal Navy, Dartmoor quickly filled up. Eventually whites petitioned to be separated from the 'thieving' blacks, who in turn began to organise themselves and establish their own codes of discipline and government. A charismatic native of Massachusetts, Richard Crafus, was elected 'King' and he set about organising his men in an autocratic manner. He made daily rounds, checking each berth for mess, punishing those who were dirty and drunken, and arranging recreation and gambling.

The imprisoned African Americans had their own theatre group, which performed Shakespeare among its many productions, and they organised dances and church services to which whites were welcome. They offered instruction in boxing, dancing and music; but, as Bolster points out, although 'black and white sailors gambled, prayed, talked, and formed mobs together, racial expectations in Dartmoor exercised more influence than did shared experiences'. As was true of life on board ship, shifting allegiances between groups of white sailors and black sailors sometimes cemented temporary alliances, but the reality of racial prejudice was always lurking just beneath the surface.

The American Revolution significantly changed the nature of black maritime activity. Before the American Revolution, practically every person of color in the Americas was a slave; but by the war's end almost 60,000 African Americans were free. The majority of these men were sailors who during the war had served aboard privateers or in the Continental navy.

Massachusetts and Connecticut in particular enlisted all the black sailors they could find, and at the conclusion of the war the abolition of slavery in the northern states allowed black men to freely enter the labour market.

Those seamen who remained enslaved could look to the free northern ports as places of refuge; and after the Haitian Revolution any black sailor arriving in Haiti was able to manipulate the political situation to his own advantage and claim freedom. But Haiti was little more than one-third of a Caribbean island in which the Catholics spoke French and had cultural and spiritual practices that were entirely foreign to sailors from New York or Chesapeake Bay. The assumption of Haitian citizenship was, for most sailors, simply a way of circumventing the authority of the United States. According to Bolster, most African American sailors had no desire to give up their citizenship in the United States, but neither did they wish to risk being sold to southern plantations.

The African American sailor who existed in the precarious twilight zone of transience and freedom became a model for those of his own race left behind in the harsh world of the plantation. Frederick Douglass, who himself escaped to freedom dressed in the garb of a sailor, remembered the general respect for sailors on the Maryland plantation of his youth in the 1830s: 'My cousin Tom . . . was sometimes a cabin boy on board the sloop Sally Lloyd (which Capt. Thomas Auld commanded), and when he came home from Baltimore he was always a sort of hero amongst us . . .'

Bolster's writing is intelligent and strong, as he stresses his central point that the life of a black sailor in the age of sail was essentially a dignified one. Life on the plantation involved endless menial labour, with few opportunities to develop meaningful skills of any kind, or to come to terms with responsibility and self-discipline. Yet life at sea meant working alone and without white supervision, and provided the black man with the ability to earn an income from labour and petty trading while roaming freely and observing the world. Bolster argues convincingly that for any ambitious African American trapped in the plantation world of the Americas, the life of a sailor represented a huge leap forward in circumstances and possibilities.

By the early nineteenth century the most influential 'middle class' black families in the North habitually sent their children to sea. The maritime 'finishing school' inculcated values of equality and worth into their children for they were working side by side with white men on an equal footing. Paul Cuffee and James Forten, a Philadelphia sailmaker who patented a device for handling sails, were men whose families 'shipped out'. The principal danger was the immorality which was inevitably associated with life at sea, but the 'best' northern families were prepared to run this risk if it meant that future generations might secure for themselves an independent financial life.

No matter how successful a black mariner might be, however, his wealth or his status could be wiped out by legislation or prejudice, or a combination of both. As southern attitudes hardened in the antebellum South, making it increasingly difficult for black sailors to step ashore without fear of being seized, the sea became a less attractive option. Physical abuse on board ships, and a dramatic fall in the wages being paid to both black and white, led to the advantages of black maritime life being slowly eroded, and to the collapse of the status enjoyed by maritime families. Paul Cuffee's son spent his life at sea as little more than a common sailor, and by 1864 Cuffee's granddaughter Joanna was reduced to seeking public assistance in New Bedford.

'The contagion of liberty emanating from northern ships', as Bolster nicely describes it, received official legislative attention in the wake of Denmark Vesey's attempted insurrection in Charleston in 1822. Vesey, a former mariner himself, used the 'network' of black mariners to spread his 'revolutionary' doctrine. An 'Act for the better Regulation and Government of Free Negroes and Persons of Color' was passed in December 1822 in South Carolina, and in three months in 1823 some 154 black seamen found themselves in prison. Their captains, or the shipowners, were required to pay their costs while the seamen languished in jail, and this naturally made white captains more wary of taking on black crew.

In the years leading up to the Civil War, the period of relative freedom for black men on the sea came to an end. Changes in hiring practices, which now included the utilisation of a middleman rather than the captain directly choosing his own crew, meant that the middleman (or the 'crimp') tended to favour his own white mariners. On board ship blacks, now an ever shrinking minority, found themselves marginalised as little more than cooks or stewards, and by the time of abolition no truly ambitious African American would think of risking life and limb, to say nothing of dignity, on the sea.

That black sailors had been crucial mediators in the assertion of a dignified notion of black people is ably illustrated by Bolster's book. Yet he insistently makes claims for the achievement of African American sailors to be viewed in a broader context. He asserts, for example, that black seamen 'clearly worked in an international world as members of the Atlantic community of color' but it is highly debatable whether such a community ever existed. That there were black communities in the Caribbean, in England and in the United States is beyond any doubt. And that African American seamen travelled the waters between these communities is also beyond any doubt. But the idea of 'the black Atlantic' world is a relatively new concept, as fostered by pioneering historians such as James Walvin, the late Paul Edwards (who edited Equiano's memoir), and more recent scholars such as Stuart Hall and Paul Gilroy, whose book *The Black Atlantic* has become an important and influential text.

Of course, the notion of 'the black Atlantic' world is a useful one for contemporary scholars and for writers of fiction. The final sentence of Bolster's text acknowledges this: 'And for those concerned with the creation of America, Black Jacks' story splices together African American and Atlantic maritime histories, fusing them in ways that storytellers worth their salt can no longer ignore.'

But 'the black Atlantic' world is one that neither the individual seamen nor their respective communities would have recognised. It is only by looking back through the long telescope of history that we are able to impose order and coherence on a universe that would have appeared irreconcilably fractured to the black individuals who were trying to ride its powerful and adverse currents.

The real achievement of *Black Jacks* is to remind us that black seafaring in the age of sail was not limited to the Middle Passage, and that black sailors were the eyes, the ears and the mouth-pieces of the African American community at a time when America was attempting to stifle the community's collective cry of outrage. In the nineteenth century the pulpit would eventu-ally replace the forecastle as the wellspring of liberty, but Bolster shows us that for over a century, while seafaring remained a contemptible occupation for the white man, it was not only a noble occupation for the black man, but it played a central role in the creation of an African American identity.

Literature: The New Jazz? (1997)

Ten years in the compiling, the *Norton Anthology of African American Literature* (1996), is an exhaustive and comprehensive cataloguing of 250 years of literary creativity. Under the editorial guidance of two distinguished academics (Henry Louis Gates Jnr and Nellie Y. McKay), and backed by a further nine editors all of whom are leading scholars in their fields, including Arnold Rampersad, Houston Baker and Barbara Christian, the present volume not only establishes itself as the definitive collection of African American literature, it is likely to remain so until well into the next century.

There is nothing surprising about the chronological periods into which the editors have chosen to divide the volume. They begin with 'The Literature of Slavery and Freedom: 1746–1865', which in turn gives way to 'Literature of the Reconstruction to the New Negro Renaissance: 1865–1919', 'Harlem Renaissance: 1919–1940', 'Realism, Naturalism, Modernism: 1940–1960', 'The Black Arts Movement: 1960–1970', and finally the longest section in the book, 'Literature since 1970'. However, within these groupings some curious choices have been made regarding which writers to anthologise.

In their introduction the general editors point to the number of women that have been included, noting that 52 out of the 120 writers are female. Laudable as this may be, on closer inspection one is left wondering if the shadowy hand of political correctness might not have been lurking behind some of this decision-making. Sojourner Truth and Maria W. Stewart would seem to belong more to the realm of speech-making and religio-political agitation than literature. Two writers from the Harlem Renaissance, Angelina Weld Grimké and Helene Johnson, are allotted only two pages each, which serves to confirm one's suspicion that their work is not particularly distinguished. Among contemporary writers, neither Wanda Coleman nor Octavia Butler (both of whom were new to this reader) seemed to merit inclusion in such a canon-shaping venture, and the inclusion of Terry McMillan is quite frankly baffling.

The question of nationality also appears to be problematic in a number of cases. To claim Olaudah Equiano as an African American seems a trifle bold. He was born in West Africa and as a young man spent only the years between the ages of seventeen and twenty-one in America. The greater part of his life, and all his writing, was done in England. Similarly the Caribbean-born writer Eric Walrond lived in England for most of his life. Jamaica Kincaid (born and raised in Antigua), and Michelle Cliff (born in Jamaica and largely educated there and in England) surely lie outside the scope of this volume. The inclusion of the Jamaican Marcus Garvey highlights this same problem, but also points to a larger issue with which the anthology wrestles.

The editors have chosen to introduce, as a curtain-raiser to the written literature, a chapter entitled 'The Vernacular Tradition'. They argue that the written tradition has grown out of, and may indeed be partly dependent upon, the oral. In their attempt to justify this oral 'tradition' the editors have included a compact disc with the anthology so that one can actually 'hear' the vernacular tradition. Although they make a vociferous case for this oral material, the practical evidence of the weak 'writing' undermines the theoretical framework upon which they have constructed their case.

'The Vernacular Tradition' is divided into 'Spirituals', 'Gospel', 'The Blues', 'Secular Rhymes and Songs, Ballads, and Work Songs', 'Jazz', 'Rap', 'Sermons' and 'Folktales'. At a mere 125 pages it is by far the shortest section in this weighty anthology, and while one acknowledges the importance of the oral, especially the musical, influence on the literature, one is still left with the feeling that the majority of the material is somewhat redundant. Perhaps the two most notable exceptions are Martin Luther King's 'I Have a Dream' speech, which is a magnificent testament to the power and grace of the English language, and Grandmaster Flash and the Furious Five's 1982 rap classic, 'The Message', which is a brilliant analysis of the despair of inner-city life, and far more expressive than much of the so-called urban 'poetry' collected in the section entitled 'The Black Arts Movement: 1960–1970'.

With very few exceptions, such as Amiri Baraka's play *Dutchman*, the 'angry' political literature of the 1960s is chiefly characterised by its lack of subtlety or sophistication. Coming hard on the heels of much elegant writing in the 1940s and '50s by writers like Margaret Walker, Robert Hayden and Lorraine Hansberry, it is difficult to read Eldridge Cleaver, Jayne Cortez and Haki R. Madhubuti and detect much in the way of a literary sensibility. Their writing seems to do little more than cry out in protest against the troubled social and political times they were living through, but there is precious little art to the wailing.

Time both makes and breaks reputations. One of the virtues of such an anthologising enterprise is that it affords the reader the opportunity to reassess the merits of 'important' writers, and to situate them in the great sweep of the tradition. For instance, it is surprising that only five pieces of James Baldwin's *oeuvre* are included: four essays and one short story. However, when one reads (or rereads) the anthologised fiction and non-fiction of Ralph Ellison, one immediately recognises not only the most outstanding writer and intellectual that the tradition has so far produced, but undoubtedly one of the truly great American writers of the century.

The writers included in the final section, 'Literature since 1970', continue to deal with themes which relate to slavery, or Africa, or poverty and deprivation, but the variety of forms they are currently employing is truly remarkable. There are the traditionalists such as Toni Morrison or Rita Dove, both of whom beautify the language with poetry and prose that is at once ornate and clear. There are the self-conscious stylists such as John Edgar Wideman, a devotee of Joyce and Faulkner, and Charles Johnson, a follower of Western and Eastern philosophies whose ideologies have been incorporated into his work, particularly so in the case of his novel *Middle Passage* which won the 1990 National Book Award. There are those who are disrupting both form and language in an unapologetically postmodern manner; Ntozake Shange and Ishmael Reed would appear to be at the head of this movement. Finally, Walter Mosley's hard-boiled detective fiction and Samuel Delaney's science fiction writing extend African American literature into genres that are still relatively new to the tradition.

If one can detect any major development in African American literature during the second half of this century, it would be a growing love for and dependency upon music in general, and jazz in particular. A quite astonishing number of the very best writers, including Ralph Ellison, Michael Harper, Albert Murray, Langston Hughes, Robert Hayden, Gwendolyn Brooks and James Baldwin, have tipped their hats in the direction of musicians such as John Coltrane, Duke Ellington, Count Basie, Louis Armstrong, Bessie Smith and Billie Holiday. The formal structures of music, its profound effect on the masses, and the individual talent of the performers, have obviously inspired the writers. It is no accident that African America's first Nobel Laureate in Literature, Toni Morrison has written a novel called *Jazz*.

Music is the art form which has benefited most from African American creative genius in the twentieth century. However, what this anthology demonstrates is that in the twenty-first century, African American literary endeavours are likely to take centre stage. Countless young men and women are now studying the tradition that stretches back to the eighteenth century, and they want to write. The plethora of stories that have to be told and retold will challenge both form and language; after all, this is what both jazz and rap have done. This anthology of African

American literature is as much a reminder of what has gone before as a signifier of the work to come. A storm is about to break in American literature and, in the words of the American singer-songwriter Curtis Mayfield, the harbingers of rain may well be 'darker than blue'.

Warren Beatty's *Bulworth* (1998)

A few weeks before the 1996 California primaries, a distressed Senator Jay Bulworth (Warren Beatty) sits alone in his office listening to one of his insincere campaign ads. Some time later, before a predominantly African American congregation in South Central Los Angeles, Bulworth finds himself unable to read a well-rehearsed speech. Instead he decides to tell the 'truth'. Politicians, he says, do not really care about you people. Furthermore, unless you 'put down that malt liquor and chicken wings and get behind somebody other than a running back who stabs his wife', they never will.

Predictably enough, Bulworth's politically suicidal speech wins him a cult following. Suddenly he is free to rant about race, class, the power of money, and the corrupt nature of politics. This is a clever and interesting conceit, and one which is a good deal more engaging than anything in *Wag the Dog* or *Primary Colors*. But after about forty minutes *Bulworth* begins to go off the rails.

A ghetto girl named Nina (Halle Berry) catches Bulworth's eye, and she accompanies him to an all-night party in the 'hood where a newly 'liberated' Bulworth starts to rap. Soon we see the senator dressed in the garb of black youth – baggy shorts, athletic shoes, a wool cap and a warm-up jacket. He testifies with the rest of the brothers. 'There's a time when every homey got to risk his neck and fight / For the thing that he believe in, and he got to preach it right.' If that's not clear enough for their bad selves, he offers the brothers and sisters this insight into the modern world: 'Now over here we got our

86

friends from oil / They don't give a darn how much wilderness they spoil.'

Nina educates Bulworth about racism and inner-city poverty, and he spouts these 'lessons' back to the black people he encounters in the grand tradition of the nineteenth-century missionary, urging these lost inner-city souls to clean up their act. His appropriation of their dress, their mannerisms, and the culture of rap in no way disguises the patronage that is being dispensed. But things get worse. The film makes verbal and visual references which equate Senator Bulworth with Malcolm X, Martin Luther King and Huey Newton. Absurd? Hold on.

This is a Warren Beatty film, and sixty-one-year-old Beatty must get the girl, even though she's a twenty-nine-year-old designer fly girl who wouldn't have to step ten yards down her block to stumble over something 'finer' than our senator hero. The senator's most profound thought on race relations is the following. 'We should just keep fucking each other until we're all the same color.' At the end of the film when Nina says, 'Bulworth, you know you my nigga', this is intended to be the highest form of 'black' compliment that can be paid to a white man. It is, of course, nothing of the sort. It is simply embarrassing.

Beatty is suggesting that a politician who would dare to tell the truth might begin as a hyped celebrity, but will ultimately end up marginalised – like black people. This may be the case, but the ludicrous ease with which Bulworth appropriates black culture, and is thereafter taken seriously as a 'leader' by the very people he's patronising, suggests a profound misunderstanding of contemporary American society, not to mention a profound misunderstanding of black people. The black community in America has, over the 130 years or so since the end of the Civil War, had to deal with a variety of white politicians who have presented themselves as saviours. None, however, have been so 'short-sighted' as to risk their political career for black people, none have had the temerity to grow an Afro, or jeri-curl their hair, or don baggy shorts and gold jewellery in order that they might get down with the people, and none have been crowned honorary 'nigga'.

Beatty has a fine track record of political commitment, having worked with Robert Kennedy and countless other Democrats over the years. One might have imagined that insights gleaned from the real world of politics might have sharpened his artistic vision. But apparently not. Mr Beatty appears to be unaware of the fact that his country is full of black men and women at the city, state and federal level who are providing firm and clear-headed political leadership to both the black and the white community. Which makes this pernicious fairy tale little more than a film about a powerful limousine liberal claiming victim status. An absurd Robin Hood in the 'hood. Ageing white liberal gets fly girl. Warren Beatty should know better.

'O': All alone in Charleston (2001)

Tim Blake Nelson's film 'O' (2001) attempts to update Shakespeare's *Othello* to the contemporary world of Charleston, South Carolina. Othello is reborn as Odin James, high school basketball star recruited to the all-white Palmetto Grove Academy. Desdemona is Desi, his girlfriend; Michael Cassio is Mike, his best friend; Iago is Hugo, his jealous teammate, and so on. We have to imagine the world that Odin has come from, for we never see where, or how, African Americans in Charleston live. We also never meet any of Odin's family. Blake Nelson's African American hero is spectacularly disenfranchised from any personal or social history.

There is an African American drug dealer who supplies Hugo (Iago) with steroids, and eventually Odin with cocaine. We have a brief glimpse of a black basketball team, all shaven heads and attitude, although none of them speak with Odin; and there is a foul-mouthed young black boy who confronts Odin when he is seized with jealous rage, but Odin simply pushes the boy to the ground. We must therefore assume that Odin has little connection with the African American world of Charleston, although we are never told why this might be. The film suggests a rootlessness to the African American condition, which means that individuals such as Odin are likely to be dependent upon, and therefore liable to be duped by, whites.

Our modern-day African American Othello is initially a grinning wonder-child of the backboard whose coach is proud to declare, 'I love him like my own son.' However, the slightest provocation from one of the white boys soon kindles an anger that returns Odin to his 'natural' condition. His best friend Mike puts it pithily: 'the nigger's out of control'. For the avoidance of doubt he continues, 'the ghetto just popped out of him.' Midway through the film Odin climbs into bed with Desi who, referring to his performance on the basketball court, describes him as 'a little cocky'. 'Hey, don't be saying little and cocky in the same sentence with me,' says our hero. The next time we find them in bed together, Desi invites him to 'do anything he likes' to her. Odin, still smarting from his suspicion that his girlfriend might be cheating on him, promptly 'rapes' her. Desi screams and begs him to stop, but ghetto homeboy has to do what he has to do.

By stripping Odin bare of history, or family (although he does make reference to a mother who we assume to be dead), Nelson denies us the possibility of understanding Odin's irrational and violent actions. What apocalypse has blighted this boy's life so that his coach is able to claim that 'we' are his family now? Why does he not call his father, or another relative? Why does he not go for a walk in his old 'hood, or talk to his friends from his previous school, or call an old girlfriend? Charleston is an American city with a profound connection to African American history and a sizeable contemporary African American population. Odin James in Charleston is not Othello in Venice. If he is feeling temporarily unmoored in the 'civilised' world of Palmetto Grove Academy, then he has a large community to turn to for help and guidance.

When Shakespeare's Othello commits suicide, we understand that he is a vulnerable man who is a long way from home. He is lonely and isolated. However, when, at the end of 'O', Odin turns the gun on himself, he is an African American in America. Are we really supposed to believe that this eighteen-year-old has no idea of how to comprehend the American world around him? Are we supposed to believe that Odin James is little more than a helpless boy from the Charleston 'ghetto' who, when given the opportunity of making something of himself in the white world, simply could not rein in the urban beast within him? If this is what we are supposed to believe, then the less one shows of the African American world, beyond drug dealers, arrogant ballplayers and foul-mouthed kids, the better. A church, a family or a home would disrupt the somewhat simplistic thesis of the film, which reads as follows: 'Poor O.J., we gave him a chance but the ghetto just popped out of him.'

Luther Vandross (1951–2005) (2005)

In the early 1980s the word on the street was that there was 'a new guy' on the music scene. There was no reckless talk of his replacing the ruling triumvirate of Marvin Gaye, Teddy Pendergrass and Barry White, but he was being spoken of as somebody who perhaps belonged in their company. His first recordings were not easy to find, but bootlegged tapes of his music were being freely passed from hand to hand. A friend dubbed a tape for me and I was hooked, but I had to wait until 1983 when he made his long-awaited debut in Britain to see him live. His sold-out concert was electrifying, and one critic declared that Luther Vandross 'represents something very special indeed'. He had no idea just how special – none of us did – but twenty-two years later, Vandross has died at the age of fifty-four, and we can now look back at an extraordinary body of work by a man who is undoubtedly the most influential American male vocalist of the past quarter-century.

A few weeks ago, I lined up for two hours in the driving rain outside Riverside Church in Upper Manhattan in order that I might pay my respects at Vandross's funeral service. It quickly became clear that this was no ordinary service. Jesse Jackson and Al Sharpton were present, as were the women who had been so significant in Vandross's career: Dionne Warwick read the obituary, while Patti LaBelle, Cissy Houston and Aretha Franklin all took their turns at the microphone and sang. Stevie Wonder paid his own tribute in words and then sang a heart-rending version of the gospel 'I Won't Complain', while the younger generation was represented by, among others, Usher and Alicia Keys. Eighteen years ago I witnessed a similar demonstration of love and sorrow, some few blocks away at the Cathedral of St John the Divine, when I attended the funeral of the writer, James Baldwin, a man who, like Luther Vandross, was utterly convinced of the refining power of love.

The theme of thwarted love, familial and romantic, forms a strong line in the African American narrative tradition. After all, the participation of Africans in the American world was preceded by the tearing asunder of lovers and families, first on African soil and then during the Middle Passage. Any possibility of reconstructing a new narrative of loving responsibility was further disrupted by the grim realities of American plantation slavery. In this system a man's bond with his 'wife' was always liable to be undermined and broken, because his master could choose to sell the man and woman to different owners in far-flung parts of the country or, even worse, force himself upon the woman. In such circumstances, it was difficult for black men or women to know just how to love each other.

Female singers from Bessie Smith to Billie Holiday, and through to Aretha Franklin, have taken up the challenge of singing about difficulties with men who have simply let them down. However, it is only relatively recently that African American men have begun to introduce such painful narratives of loss in love into their own music. Nat King Cole and Billy Eckstine illuminated the middle years of the twentieth century; they were succeeded by a posse of mellow-voiced balladeers, including Sam Cooke, Otis Redding, Donny Hathaway and Al Green. These men were unafraid to expose their bewilderment and despair, and they soulfully laid bare their helplessness in matters of love. When Vandross appeared on the scene at the start of the 1980s it was immediately apparent that not only did he fit squarely into this tradition of vulnerability, he also possessed both a God-given voice and technical brilliance as a producer/arranger.

Luther Vandross was born in New York City in 1951, and he grew up on the Lower East Side and then in the Bronx. His father died of diabetes-related problems when Luther was seven, and his mother, who worked as a nurse, raised her two boys and two girls with a stern fist. Throughout his teen years Vandross was obsessed with music, particularly Diana Ross and the Supremes, and he spent all his spare time writing and arranging and forming bands among his friends. He left school and spent a year at Western Michigan University, where he studied engineering, before returning to New York City and a career in music.

His first break came in 1972 when he wrote 'Everybody Rejoice', a song that was included in the Broadway musical, *The Wiz*. In 1975 he was invited by a friend to a studio where David Bowie was recording his Philly-soul inspired album, *Young Americans*. Bowie overheard Vandross idly singing along and he asked him not only to sing background, but to arrange all the vocals on the album. Vandross subsequently toured with Bowie before finding work arranging vocals and singing background for a wide range of artists from Chic to Carly Simon. His knowledge of the studio was further enhanced as he began to record advertising jingles for Pepsi-Cola, Kentucky Fried Chicken, the US Army and many others. Although he became extremely wealthy as the voice of these various companies, he was frustrated by the fact that he was finding it difficult to start his own career as a solo recording artist.

In 1980, Vandross scored his first 'underground' hits as the lead singer for the studio band, Change. On both 'The Glow of Love' and 'Searching' there is a transcendent quality to his lead vocal. Vandross seems reluctant to dominate the music in the manner of a Teddy Pendergrass or a David Ruffin, both of whom were schooled fronting Harold Melvin and the Blue Notes and the Temptations respectively. Lead singers for live acts have a tendency to interject, proclaim and make demands on their audience, whereas Vandross, who was studio-trained, was far more subtle and carefully distributed his voice within the overall structure of the songs. On both hits he effortlessly rides the driving bass line, complements the complex rhythm guitar, and paints a thrilling, seductively haunting pattern with a voice that seems to hover and float through these two early gems.

In 1981 Epic Records allowed Vandross to record and produce his own album, and *Never Too Much* went platinum. It was this album, and the 1982 follow-up, *Forever, For Always, For Love* that were being passed from hand to hand in the London of the early 1980s. They contained a series of bold, soulful tracks that eschewed the politics and social observation of Stevie Wonder, Curtis Mayfield or Marvin Gaye, and focused tightly, and some-times ironically, on love lost and found. The complex vocal arrangements had none of the aggressive punchiness that one had come to expect from such luminaries as Quincy Jones. As a producer, Luther teased musically, he left silences, built bridges with deft rhetorical flourishes, made heart-stopping and unex-pected transitions and, having drawn emotion out of a song until he'd exhausted all possible meaning, he would finish with a sigh as opposed to an exclamation point.

Vandross's signature work was his recording of standard ballads, but he performed these in such a manner that they were not so much remade as reinvented and heard for the first time. Hal David and Burt Bacharach's 1964 classic 'A House Is Not a Home' was originally, and lovingly, interpreted by Dionne Warwick. When Luther Vandross got hold of it in 1981 he made a masterpiece of the song, convincing us for the first time that the house really was empty by the way in which he would pause and allow the song to appear to momentarily lose its way in the cavernous 'house' before pulling everything together, and then faltering again and 'climbing the stairs' of the song with a vocal crescendo that is not only technically exquisite but perfectly illustrates the emotional turbulence at the heart of the piece. And later, in 1994, when he recorded the almost irre-deemably saccharine 'Evergreen' he rephrased the song so that for the first time we understand, and believe, that true love does last for ever. As the final note fades it is clear that, as I once heard a woman at a Luther concert exclaim, 'the song ain't Barbra Streisand's no more'.

The 1980s releases that followed were uniformly outstanding and, in 1989, Vandross won his first Grammy, albeit for the somewhat bland 'Here and Now', a song which became the anthem for countless weddings. In the 1990s he began to record material that was sometimes unworthy of his prodigious gifts, and on such occasions he did little more than decorate these songs with his sweet voice. He claimed that Epic were steering him towards middle-of-the-road material against his wishes, and his return to form with the eponymous *Luther Vandross* (2001), which he recorded for Clive Davis's new J label, suggested that there may have been some truth to his claims.

I saw Luther's last concert at New York's Radio City Music Hall in February 2003, an event that is preserved on a live CD. Who knew then that two months later a massive stroke was going to lead to over two years of attempted rehabilitation before Vandross finally succumbed to the same diabetes-related condition that took his father and all three of his siblings before him? That night at Radio City Music Hall the audience was largely comprised of women – there was a particular bond between Luther and the ladies. Quite simply, he respected them; they were never bitches or hos, or honeys or shorties; he didn't growl at them, or try to seduce them, or beg them for anything; he simply wanted to give them a flower. He promised to be true, and, of course, they believed him.

In the United States, black men who feel deeply are an endangered species, for the country loves and embraces its black males if they are tough like Tyson or crude like 50 Cent. Classically poised, sensitive and smart is not an image that is always rewarded, but Luther persevered and embraced contradiction. He was a major iconic figure for gay black men, and although he never disclosed his sexuality it was generally assumed that he was gay. For legions of gay black men, he was singing their song on tracks such as 'Your Secret Love' and 'My Sensitivity (Gets in the Way)'. There was undoubtedly great loneliness in his personal life but, to the end, he remained an extremely private man. He lived alone in a twenty-five-room mansion in exclusive

Greenwich, Connecticut, his nearest neighbour being the somewhat reclusive former tennis star, Ivan Lendl, and he battled
occasional bouts of depression, and a serious weight problem
that saw him frequently soar from 190 to 340 pounds. However,
Luther always suggested that music was his only real partner,
and he poured the truth of his own story into his art so that
his best work spoke directly to fear, isolation, and the anguish
and ache of unrequited or hidden love.

Luther Vandross will be remembered as a great producer/
arranger whose original harmonies and production skills will
be studied and spoken of in the same breath as those of Brian
Wilson or Phil Spector. He produced music for many artists,
including Dionne Warwick, Diana Ross, and of course Aretha
Franklin's magnificent *Jump To It* album. He was a superlative
technician who possessed a rare understanding of what was
possible in a recording studio, and the young pretenders,
including Babyface and R. Kelly, have learned much from him.
But Luther Vandross will also be remembered as a vocal artist
who sang with the nuanced phrasing of a master craftsman.
Working within a tradition that had been thoroughly explored
by some of the greatest voices in history, he discovered a new
and beautiful sound which he delivered in a superbly modulated tenor that had a range and flexibility that invariably took
one's breath away. When Luther held a note he often deviated
from the line, not in a self-conscious display of technical bravura,
but in order that he might squeeze every last drop of truth
from the moment. Like all great artists, Luther understood that
the gift of his astonishing voice was displayed to fullest advantage when it enhanced rather than obscured the subject matter,
and at such moments he could transform even the direst schmaltz
into pure gold.

His closest female equivalent might well be Aretha Franklin.
When she rose to her feet at his funeral service and began to
sing 'Amazing Grace' the women on either side of me stopped
dabbing their eyes with damp handkerchiefs and began to rock
with grief. Franklin soared with dignity and complete authority

as she fearlessly revealed to us the source of her passion and her pain. Luther would have been proud. As his gold coffin was raised on to the shoulders of the bearers, the tearful congregation rose to its feet and began a thunderous storm of applause. People screamed 'Luther!' the way they would at concerts, but there was nothing blasphemous about this moment as the secular came face to face with the sacred. God's heavenly choir had been waiting for quite some time, but now they were ready to welcome their lead vocalist.

Strange Fruit (2007)

In late 1979, I finished writing my first stage play, but long before I put the final full stop in place I had decided that I was going to call the play *Strange Fruit*. The drama concerns the relationship between a single mother and her two rebellious sons, both of whom are in danger of 'going off the rails'. The mother is understandably worried, and she begins to question the nature of the relationship that she enjoys with her children. I took the title of the play from the Billie Holiday song of the same name, but at the time I knew very little about the full history of 'Strange Fruit'. I understood that the name of the song made reference to racially motivated violence in the American South, but 'Strange Fruit' also seemed to me to be evocative of the puzzling situation that many parents unwittingly find themselves in with their children and, this being the case, I felt it was an apt title.

The play premiered at the Sheffield Crucible Studio Theatre in October 1980, and a year or so later it was produced in London. I don't remember doing any press interviews, so no journalist ever asked me what I intended by naming the play *Strange Fruit*. Perhaps more surprisingly, neither the director nor any of the actors ever questioned me about the significance of the title. Accordingly, I just assumed everybody understood that the play's title made reference to the dilemma of intergenerational communication and so I was perfectly content.

In early 1983 I found myself in Alabama, being driven the 130 miles from Birmingham to Tuskegee by the father of one of the four girls who had been killed in the Sixteenth Street

Baptist Church bombing of 1963. Chris McNair is a gregarious and charismatic man who, at the time, was running for political office and he was scheduled to make a speech at the famous all-black college, Tuskegee Institute. This morning, as he was driving through the Alabama countryside, he took the opportunity to quiz his British guest about his life and his nascent career as a writer. He asked me if I had published any books yet, and I said no. But I quickly added sheepishly that my first play had just been published. When I told him the title he turned and stared at me, then he looked back to the road. 'So what do you know about lynching?' I swallowed deeply and looked through the car windshield as the southern trees flashed by. I knew full well that 'Strange Fruit' meant something very different in the United States; in fact, something disturbingly specific in the South, especially to African Americans. A pleasant, free-flowing conversation with my host now appeared to be shipwrecked on the rocks of cultural appropriation.

I had always assumed that Billie Holiday had composed the music and lyrics to 'Strange Fruit'. She did not. The song began life as a poem that was written by Abel Meeropol, a schoolteacher who was living in the Bronx and teaching English at DeWitt Clinton High School, where his students would have included the Academy Award-winning screenwriter Paddy Chayefsky, the playwright Neil Simon, and the novelist and essayist James Baldwin. Meeropol was a trade union activist, and a closet member of the Communist Party, and his poem was first published in January 1937 as 'Bitter Fruit' in a union magazine, the *New York School Teacher*. In common with many Jewish people in the United States during this period, Meeropol was rightly worried about anti-Semitism and he therefore chose to publish his poem under the pseudonym of 'Lewis Allan,' the first names of his two stillborn children.

Abel Meeropol was motivated to write the poem having seen a photograph of two black teenagers, Thomas Shipp and Abram Smith, who had been lynched in Marion, Indiana on 7 August 1930. Their bodies were hanging limply from a tree. The image greatly disturbed him, and his poem opens with the following lines:

> Southern trees bear a strange fruit
> Blood on the leaves and blood at the root
> Black bodies swinging in the Southern breeze
> Strange fruit hanging from the poplar trees.

Hoping to reach a wider audience, Meeropol set his poem to music, and the song 'Strange Fruit' was first performed at a New York City Teachers' Union meeting, where it created an immediate stir. Meeropol sang it himself, but as 'Strange Fruit' grew in popularity his wife began to perform the song.

According to figures kept by Alabama's Tuskegee Institute, between 1889 and 1940, 3,833 people were lynched in the United States, over 90 per cent of them in the southern states and approximately four-fifths of the victims were black. The brutality of this mob 'justice' invariably went unpunished, and when asked, in 1971, why he wrote the song, Meeropol replied, 'because I hate lynching and I hate injustice and I hate the people who perpetuate it'. Those who heard 'Strange Fruit' in the late 1930s were shocked, for the true barbarity of southern violence was generally only discussed in black newspapers. To be introduced to such realities by a song was unprecedented and considered by many, including left-wing supporters of Meeropol, to be in poor taste.

At this time, twenty-four-year-old Billie Holiday was head-lining at a recently opened Greenwich Village nightclub called Café Society, the only integrated nightclub in New York City, and a place which advertised itself as 'the Wrong place for the Right people'. The manager of the club, Barney Josephson, introduced Billie Holiday to Abel Meeropol and his new song, and she immediately loved 'Strange Fruit'. She decided to sing it at Café Society, where it was received with perfect, haunting silence. Soon she was closing her shows with the song, and it was understood that before she sang 'Strange Fruit' the waiters had to stop serving, the lights had to be dimmed to a single spotlight, and only then would she begin, with her eyes closed. Once she had finished the song she walked offstage and never returned to take a bow.

The song was revolutionary, not only because of the explicit nature of the lyrics, but because it effectively reversed the black singer's relationship with a white audience. Traditionally, singers such as Billie Holiday were expected to entertain and to 'serve' their audiences. However, with this song, Billie Holiday found a means by which she could demand that the audience stop and listen to her, and she was able to force them to take on board something they were not comfortable with. She often used the song as a hammer with which to beat what she perceived to be ignorant audiences, and her insistence on singing it with such gravitas meant that she was not always safe while performing 'Strange Fruit'. Occasionally members of her audience were not fully appreciative of her treating them to this song when they had stepped out for the evening to hear 'Fine and Mellow' and other cocktail lounge ditties.

Billie Holiday was keen to record 'Strange Fruit' on her label, Columbia Records, but her producer, and the man credited with discovering her, John Hammond, was concerned that the song was too political and he refused to allow her to go into the studio with it. However, the singer would not back down. In April 1939 she recorded 'Strange Fruit' for a speciality label, Commodore Records, and the song became a bestseller and was thereafter forever associated with her. When Barney Josephson introduced her to Abel Meeropol and his song, Billie Holiday knew that she could sing this song like nobody else could, or *would*, ever sing it. She glimpsed truth in the song and that was enough. She, perhaps more than most artists, understood that if you live the truth then you will pay a price, but without the truth there is no art. Whenever she performed the song she could *see* the two teenagers, Thomas Shipp and Abram Smith hanging from the tree, which is, of course, why she closed her eyes whenever she sang the song.

Five years later, a southern writer published a novel called *Strange Fruit*. Lillian Smith was born in 1897 in Florida, the eighth of ten children. Hers was a relatively comfortable white middle-class background, and her childhood was divided between Florida and a summer house in the mountains of Georgia, where her father ran a camp for girls, called Laurel Falls. As a young woman, Smith travelled to Baltimore to study music, and she then spent a few years teaching in China. In 1925 she returned to the United States and became principal of the Laurel Falls Camp, placing a great emphasis on the arts in the curriculum, and on music and drama in particular. Aware of southern injustice and oppression, in 1936 Lillian Smith founded a literary magazine, *Pseudopodia*, which the following year changed its name to the *North Georgia Review* and in 1942 became *South Today*. Smith published writing by blacks and whites which agitated for social change in the South, and her politically progressive magazine quickly gained notoriety.

Strange Fruit told the story of an interracial relationship in the pre-First World War South. The narrative charts the mounting violence which eventually overtakes the relationship, and it thematically examines the same issues that inform Meeropol's lyrics. Despite being banned by many bookstores, the novel was the nation's best-selling title in 1944 and sold over one million copies. It was adapted for the Broadway stage, and by the time of Smith's death in 1966 the novel had sold three million copies. In the year of her death, while being honoured by the all-black Fisk University in Tennessee, Smith succinctly identified the enemy against which she had worked as both a teacher and a southern writer. 'Segregation is evil,' she declared. 'There is no pattern of life which can dehumanise men as can the way of segregation.' And segregation's natural corollary is, of course, violence.

On that hot southern morning, as Chris McNair drove us through the Alabama countryside, I knew little about the background to the Billie Holiday song, and I had never heard of Lillian Smith. After a few minutes of silence, Chris McNair began to talk to me about the history of violence against African American people in the southern states, particularly during the era of segregation. This was, of course, a painful conversation for a man who had lost his daughter to a Ku Klux Klan bomb. I had, by then, confessed to him that my play had nothing to do with the United States, with African Americans, with racial violence, or even with Billie Holiday. And, being a generous man, he had nodded patiently, and then addressed himself to my education on these matters. I did have some knowledge of the realities of the South, and not only from my reading. A week earlier, while staying at a hotel in Atlanta, a young room service waiter had warned me against venturing out after dark because the Klan would be rallying on Stone Mountain that evening, and after their gathering they often came downtown for some 'fun'. However, as the Alabama countryside continued to flash by, I understood that this was not the time to do anything other than listen to Mr McNair.

That afternoon, in a packed hall in Tuskegee Institute, Chris McNair began what sounded to me like a typical campaign speech. He was preaching to the converted, and a light shower of applause began to punctuate his words as he hit his oratorical stride. But then he stopped abruptly, and he announced that today, for the first time, he was going to talk about his daughter. 'I don't know why, because I've never done this before. But Denise is on my mind.' He studiously avoided making eye contact with me, but seated in the front row I felt uneasily guilty. A hush fell over the audience. 'You all know who my daughter is. Denise McNair. Today she would have been thirty-one years old.' Indeed, strange fruit.

Growing Pains

A Life in Ten Chapters (2005)

There are ten chapters to this story.

Chapter One

He lives in Leeds, in the North of England. His is a strange school for there is a broad white line in the middle of the play-ground. The boys and girls from the local housing estate have to play on one side of the line. His immigrant parents own their small house and so he is instructed to play on the other side of the line. He is the only black boy in the school. When the bell signals the end of playtime the two groups, one neatly dressed, the other group more discernibly scruffy, retreat into their separate buildings. The five-year-old boy is beginning to understand difference – in the form of *class*. The final lesson of the day is story time. The neatly dressed children sit cross-legged on the floor at the feet of their teacher, Miss Teale. She begins to read them a tale about 'Little Black Sambo'. He can feel eyes upon him. He now wishes that he was on the other side of the line with the scruffy children. Either that, or would the teacher please read them a different story?

Chapter Two

He is a seven-year-old boy, and he has changed schools. At this new school there are no girls. His teacher asks him to stay behind after the lesson has finished. He is told that he must take his story and show it to the teacher in the next classroom.

He isn't sure if he is being punished, but slowly he walks the short way up the corridor and shows the story to the other teacher, Miss Holmes. She sits on the edge of her desk and reads it. Then Miss Holmes looks down at him, but at first no words are exchanged. And then she speaks. 'Well done. I'll hold on to this.'

Chapter Three

The eight-year-old boy seems to spend his whole day with his head stuck in books. His mother encourages him to get into the habit of going to the local library every Saturday, but he can only take out four books at a time and by Monday he has read them all. Two brothers up the street sometimes let him borrow their Enid Blyton paperbacks. The Famous Five adventure stories. Julian, Dick, Anne, George and Timmy the dog are the first literary lives that he intimately engages with. However, he tells his mother that he does not understand why the boys' mother warms the Enid Blyton paperbacks in the oven when he returns them. The two brothers have mentioned something to him about germs. His mother is furious. She forbids him to borrow any more books from these two boys. He begins to lose touch with Julian, Dick, Anne, George and Timmy the dog.

Chapter Four

His parents have recently divorced. He is nine and he is spending the weekend with his father, who seems to have little real interest in his son. He senses that his father is merely fulfilling a duty, but the son needs his father's attention and so he writes a story. The story includes the words 'glistening' and 'glittering' which have a glamour that the son finds alluring. When the son eventually hands the story to his father, the father seems somewhat baffled by this offering. His father is an immigrant, this much he already understands. But it is only later that he realises that imaginative writing played no part in his father's colonial education as a subject of the British Empire. His father's rudimentary schooling never embraced poetic conceits such as those his son seems determined to indulge in. As the father hands back the story to his son, a gap begins to open up between the two of them.

Chapter Five

He is only ten years old when his father decides that it is fine to leave him all alone in his spartan flat while he goes to work the night shift at the local factory. There is no television. No radio. Nothing to seize his attention beyond the few comic books and soccer magazines that the son has brought with him from his mother's house. Then, late at night, alone in the huge double bed, he leans over and discovers a paperback in the drawer of the bedside table and he begins to read the book. It is a true story about a white American man who has made himself black in order that he might experience what it is like to be a colored man. The ten-year-old boy reads John Howard Griffin's *Black Like Me* and, alone in his father's double bed, he tries hard not to be afraid. That night he leaves the lights on, and in the morning he is still awake as his exhausted father slides into bed next to him.

Chapter Six

At sixteen he has no girlfriend. The truth is, his brothers aside, he has few friends of any kind, and he seldom speaks with his father or stepmother. During the long summer holiday he locks himself away in his bedroom and he reads one large nineteenth-century novel after another. He learns how to lose himself in the world and lives of others, and in this way he does not have to think about the woeful state of his own life. At the moment he is reading *Anna Karenina*. Towards the end of one afternoon his heart leaps, and he has to catch his breath. He puts the book down and whispers to himself, 'My God.' His stepmother calls him downstairs for dinner. He sits at the table in silence but he cannot eat. He stares at his brothers, at his father, at his stepmother. Do they not understand? Anna has thrown herself in front of a train.

Chapter Seven

He is eighteen and he has completed his first term at university. He cannot go back to his father's house and so he travels 150 miles north to his mother's place. Mother and son have not, of late, spent much time in each other's company. His mother does not understand that her eighteen-year-old son is now, according to him, a man. They argue, and he gets in the car and drives off in a fit of frustration. He stops the car in the local park and opens his book. However, he cannot get past the sheer audacity of the first sentence of James Baldwin's *Blues for Mister Charlie*. 'And may every nigger like this nigger end like this nigger — face down in the weeds!' This eighteen-year-old 'man' is completely overwhelmed by Baldwin's brutal prose. He reads this one sentence over and over and over again. And then he closes the book and decides that he should go back and make up with his mother.

Chapter Eight

His tutor has asked to see him in his office. Dr Rabbitt informs the student that he has passed the first part of his degree in Psychology, Neurophysiology and Statistics, but he reassures the student that at nineteen there is still time for him to reconsider his choice of a degree. Does he really wish to pursue psychology? The student patiently explains that he wishes to understand people, and that before university he was assiduously reading Jung and Freud for pleasure. His unmoved tutor takes some snuff, and then he rubs his beard. So you want to know about people, do you? He patiently explains to the student that William James was the first professor of psychology at

Harvard, but it was his brother, Henry, who really knew about people. The student looks at Dr Rabbitt, but he is unsure what to say. His tutor helps him to make the decision. 'Literature. If you want to know about people study English literature, not psychology.'

Chapter Nine

He is twenty, and for the first time since arriving in England as a four-month-old baby he has left the country. He has travelled to the United States, and crossed the huge exciting nation by Greyhound bus. After three weeks on the road, he knows that soon he will have to return to England and complete his final year of university. In California he goes into a bookstore. He buys a copy of a book that has on the cover a picture of a young man who looks somewhat like himself. He takes the book to the beach, and sits on a deckchair and begins to read. When he finishes Richard Wright's *Native Son* it is almost dark, and the beach is deserted. But he now knows what he wishes to do with his life. And then, some time later, he is grateful to discover that mere ambition is fading and is being replaced by something infinitely more powerful; purpose.

Chapter Ten

He sits with his great-grandmother in the small village at the far end of St Kitts, the island on which he was born twenty-eight years earlier. He has now published two novels, and on each publication day he has asked his editor to send a copy of the book to his great-grandmother. But she has never mentioned the books and so gingerly he now asks her if she ever received them? *Does* she have them? When she moves it is like watching a statue come to life. She reaches beneath the chair and slowly pulls out two brown cardboard bundles. The books are still in their packaging. She has opened the bundles, looked at the books, and then neatly replaced them. Again she opens the packaging. She fingers the books in the same way that he has seen her finger her bible. Then she looks at her great-grandson and smiles. 'I was the teacher's favourite,' she says. She was born in 1898 and so he realises that she is talking to him about life at the dawn of the twentieth century. 'And,' she continues, 'I missed a lot of school for I had to do all the errands.' Suddenly he understands what she means. She cannot read. He swallows deeply and lowers his eyes. How could he be clumsy enough to cause her this embarrassment? She carefully puts the books back in their cardboard packaging and tucks them back under the chair. She looks at her great-grandson. She doted on this boy for the first four months of his life. The great-grandson who disappeared to England. The great-grandson who all these years later now sends her stories from England.

1978 (1993)

The year is 1978. The place, Oxford. The month, October. There exists a photograph of me with a clenched fist that might have been taken in a photo booth at Gloucester Green bus station. Or somewhere behind Broad Street. Or just off Cornmarket. I simply can't remember. I must have recently had my hair cut, for in 1978 I used to wear it long. Or, more accurately, wide. In those days even Michael Jackson had an Afro. Not that I wanted to be Michael Jackson. Not then. Not now. In 1978 my people were Earth, Wind and Fire. Wide hair, funky clothes, thumping, danceable rhythms. 'Got To Get You Into My Life', 'September'. In 1978 they 'conquered' Britain. As did *Saturday Night Fever*. Both the movie and the album. Oxford was full of over-confident young men in white suits, pumping their pelvises in time to 'Night Fever'. Disco was having a last, desperate throw of the dice. Punk had muscled in on the scene. For those of us who took unashamed pleasure in sporting flares and platform soles, things were heading rapidly downhill. In 1978 a man named Jilted John tortured us with a spectacularly inept single entitled 'Gordon Is A Moron'. Ian Dury and the Blockheads livened things up a little by hitting us with their rhythm sticks, but, all things considered, 1978 marked the end of an era for the generation who had come in with Gary Glitter, Marc Bolan and Ziggy Stardust. In October 1978 I had my photograph taken for my National Union of Students card. I was embarking upon my third and final year as a student. Decisions would have to be made. Freedom lay just around the corner, as of course did the ominous presence of Mrs Thatcher.

At the start of 1978 I still clung to the idea of being a theatre director. In March of that year I directed what turned out to be my last production: Ibsen's *Ghosts*. The redeeming feature of this production was a startling performance by a brilliant actor in the role of Oswald. I haven't seen Adam Thorpe for some years, but he now lives in France with his wife and children, and writes both poetry and prose. We toured the production all over England, to what the critics call 'mixed reviews'. After our last night, in Durham as it turned out, I wheeled Adam around the streets in a hastily borrowed wheelbarrow. He played his saxophone. I whooped and hollered appreciatively. We were both alcoholically challenged. We parked by the moonlit River Wear and Adam played a long Coltrane style solo. Then a fish leapt clear of the water — a salmon? I've no idea. I swear it did a triple toe loop. I gave it a 9 for degree of difficulty, and 9.5 for artistic impression. Adam and I stared blankly at each other. Then I wheeled him back to our lodgings. The following morning I woke up to find a police officer staring down at me. 'Okay, son, where's your Joe Loss friend?' It appeared that one of Adam's more sinewy solos had been delivered beneath the window of the vice-chancellor of Durham University. Adam and I 'beat the rap', but I never directed again. And he never acted.

In the summer of 1978 I made two decisions which subsequently changed the course of my life. I decided to go to the United States, courtesy of Freddie Laker's Skytrain. This would mark the first time that I would leave Britain since arriving as a screaming infant from the Caribbean in the late fifties. It would also be my first time in an aeroplane. In short, I decided to undertake the biggest adventure of my life. For five weeks I travelled aimlessly on Greyhound buses, reading, thinking, watching, dreaming. I travelled from New York to Los Angeles. From Detroit to San Francisco. I went to Canada. To Mexico. I 'discovered' Baldwin, Wright, Ellison, George Jackson, Malcolm X. For the first time in my life I had time to think about Britain objectively, to think about the Caribbean, to think about myself.

And, funnily enough, no longer did it seem appealing that I should spend the rest of my life locked up in rehearsal rooms with Ibsen, Tennessee Williams, Shakespeare et al. The United States removed the blinkers from my eyes, and made me aware that the accident of my birth had perhaps prepared me for something other than directing plays. In the United States I encountered an unapologetic, upwardly mobile black middle class. A group of people who dared to aspire, who – quite rightly – did not regard themselves as immigrants, and who were therefore not subject to the nervous hesitancy which characterises the lives of the newly-arrived, whether black or white. In the United States I discovered, by reading and observing, that I had a common history with black Americans, and I wanted to write about them. And about myself. I wasn't really sure what I wanted to say, but I *knew* – with alarming conviction – that I wanted to write. I now realised that I belonged to a larger tradition than that of black working-class kids from Yorkshire, who spoke like Freddie Trueman. I returned to Oxford in October 1978 a very different person.

What I do remember is feeling that I had only one more year to survive. Yes, survive. Before I embarked upon the adventure of being a writer. I looked into the camera and made a mischievous gesture of defiance. A clenched fist. But beneath the irony, my mind was set. 'Home' from America. One more year to go. I used to take great delight in watching people's faces when I presented my union card. But my mind *was* set. I had changed. I threw away my flares and platform soles. For the first time I could see beyond Oxford. The Irish writer Brian Moore said recently that the door closes on a writer at twenty. This may well be the case. If so then my door closed with this photograph. In 1978. And another door opened.

Northern Soul (2005)

As a child growing up in Leeds in the sixties, I remember occasionally crossing the River Aire. My memories are of a dank and uninspiring stretch of water, with gloomy sheds and ware-houses lining both banks. When I looked past these buildings, I could make out the brooding outline of Leeds Parish Church and, if the soot-blackened sky was clear enough for me to see beyond this grand nineteenth-century church, there, in the distance, was the grim, vertical evidence of countless chimneys that day and night spewed soot into the air, casting a pall of wintry bleakness over the whole city.

In the centre of Leeds the river runs close by the uninspiring Leeds–Liverpool Canal. Occasionally we schoolboys were encouraged to undertake educational walks along the towpath of the unhappy canal, and march, two by two, out into the so-called 'countryside' so that our teachers could introduce us to 'nature'. However, the sight of an odd tree could always be quickly put into perspective by glancing back to the city, which was a place where – aside from the grass which decorated our beloved football pitches – we understood that 'nature' did not really exist. To stand shivering on the towpath in blazer, short trousers, and school cap set at a jaunty angle, and scrutinise the skyline was to immediately understand that this vast forest of tall chimneys and towers constituted the reality of our home city. The trees of the 'countryside' were merely a brief illusion.

My parents arrived in Leeds towards the end of the fifties, carrying me as hand luggage. They had heard that opportun-ities for employment were greater in the North of England,

and somewhere at the back of their minds they hoped that should they find work and make a home then perhaps, one day, it might be possible for their son to achieve an education in this northern city. They found a house on a cobbled street, where people hung their washing out to dry as though their vests and pants and bras were some form of celebratory bunting. But there was precious little to celebrate. I remember being taken down to the end of 'our street' by my teenage babysitter and hoisted up into the wintry air so that I might peer over the wall and stare at the murky canal. But, even as a small child, I already understood that there was something distinctly unsatisfactory about both 'our street' and the canal.

Neither of my parents came from wealth or privilege – far from it – but, on the long journey across the Atlantic Ocean, it never occurred to them that they might find themselves living in such dismal conditions. They soon discovered that their back-to-back house, which stood at the open end of the cobbled cul-de-sac, was no different from thousands of other red-brick houses that dominated the narrow streets and gentle hills of Leeds. The stinking privies were located in the middle of the block, and my whole childhood seems to have been dominated by olfactory assaults, both those in the street, and those that had their origins in the house itself. I distinctly remember the musty smell of the open coal fire, the acrid sting of the paraffin heater on particularly cold nights, and the lingering bouquet of chamber pots that were discreetly tucked under the bed, but which saved my parents the nightmare of having to venture outside in the middle of a freezing night to relieve themselves.

During the day I used to sit on the doorstep and dream of owning a tricycle on which I could explore my city. My English playmates were as thin and gaunt as their parents. I used to watch their mams and dads sloping off to work, the men proudly sporting their flat caps, with lunch and a newspaper tucked under their arms and a fag sticking out of their mouths. From my doorstep I surveyed the bell-shaped towers of the gasworks, and the grey sky spiked with chimneys that never seemed to tire of belching smoke, and the dramatically shaped spires of the many churches which were, in their own way, as darkly ominous as the factories. To my young eyes, Leeds never appeared to be truly glum or depressing. But this was not the case for my parents, who, back in the technicolor Caribbean, had sternly refused to believe that English people were crazy enough to actually light fires *inside* their houses. Strange new world to their immigrant eyes, but their son was clearly seeing something else.

I remember occasional glamorous sightings. Men in bowler hats carrying rolled umbrellas, representatives of Edwardian courtliness, emerged from the pubs and clubs of Leeds and mingled with the Lowry-like figures on the street. A sighting of the crumpled elegance of these 'posh' men, who had no doubt levered a post-work reflective half-pint before deciding now to make their way home, lit up my day. As did a glimpse of the rag-and-bone man, with his horse and cart, bellowing as he came down the street to collect junk. At the end of *his* day he would retire to the neighbourhood dump where he would scour through debris in the hope that he might make one or two scavenged 'discoveries' before taking his horse back to the yard for the night.

Today, I look back on my 'glamorous' Leeds childhood and remember it as being peopled with somewhat stoic individuals, each of whom seemed to move in purposeful isolation. But this was *my* world, and I was not unhappy with it. After all, I knew nothing else. Neither on television, nor at the pictures, did I hear others who spoke like us with broad flat vowels, and I hardly ever saw images of narrow, bumpy streets like ours, or people who looked anything like us, but it didn't matter. Leeds was my city, and I slowly developed a great pride in it, a pride that was enhanced by the existence of Leeds United Football Club with their spotlessly white kit, a team who tormented their opposition with industrial efficiency and bestowed upon me, and tens of thousands of others, a reason to walk tall and declare, 'We are Leeds.' From the late sixties, and on into the seventies, we were the best there was. We knew it, and 'they' knew it. If this decidedly unmodern city lacked charisma, the football team more than made up for it.

I left Leeds in the 1970s, but even before I left there were signs that the city was beginning to change and enter the modern world. Double-decker buses had long since replaced the antiquated trams, and the various local railway stations had closed down and Leeds now possessed just one large, central station. Plans were set in motion for soot-blackened civic buildings to be blasted back to their original sand color, and Leeds City Council announced its intention to construct a number of major new structures and lay out a complex urban motorway system. My city which, long after the Second World War, still seemed to be trapped in an era of Dickensian poverty and faded Edwardian gentility, was now attempting to embrace the new, but it was precisely at this point that I left Leeds and travelled south to start university. I was no longer a child, and the 'glamour' of the city had begun to fade for me. While I could never be ashamed of Leeds, largely because of the football team, I was no longer sure whether I still liked the place. I did, however, know that I had begun to imagine that bright lights and opportunity lay elsewhere.

It was over thirty years later that we found ourselves getting to know each other again. There had, of course, been sporadic visits in between, but I had never lingered long enough to take a deep breath and absorb the full nature of the transformation. However, on my most recent visit I was able to explore, and so here it was, the new twenty-first-century Leeds which civic leaders were now comparing to Barcelona. They had to be kidding me, right? My city of dark, satanic mills was many things, but surely nobody would have the temerity to compare it to Barcelona! As I walked the streets, and retraced the footsteps of my childhood and youth, it soon became apparent why the *boosters* for the city would think of the bustling, colorful Catalonian city, with its sidewalk cafés and humming nightlife, as the yardstick for this new Leeds.

The city centre has been largely rebuilt in an architectural fusion of glass and metal. Everywhere there are strangely angled, honeycombed buildings which form a brightly colored backdrop for the multicultural medley of people who now constitute the population of Leeds. In this new Leeds, the new buildings frame the new people. But the old stone buildings of the city, most of which *have* now been sandblasted clean, sit with a solid, patient, sobriety tolerating the transitory evidence of this overtly self-conscious technological age.

Transitory, yes. Leeds has seen it all before, this history of rushing to embrace the modern, only to eventually turn around and tear it down. In the 1930s Quarry Hill flats were constructed right in the heart of the city centre, a huge, vast sprawling housing estate, a kind of urban Colditz and the biggest estate of its type in Britain. But as I walked about the city I soon discovered that Quarry Hill flats were no more, and in their place I could see the grand structure of the West Yorkshire Playhouse, and the even grander edifice of the national head-quarters of the Department of Health and Social Security, a building so lacking in architectural elegance that it is already something of a local joke.

I walked out of the city centre towards the south and in the direction of Hunslet, where thirty-five years ago I lived briefly in a brand-new purpose-built complex of flats called 'Hunslet Grange'. When I got there I was shocked to discover that the whole mini-metropolis had been razed to the ground. A local man informed me that the flats lasted little over a decade before they were declared unfit for human habitation. 'Fit for bloody rabbits,' was his succinct summary of their merits.

In many parts of this new Leeds, 'modern' buildings have been torn down and replaced with 'modern' buildings, while the evidence of the old and durable sits staring the city in the face. To my middle-aged eyes, the great majority of these older buildings, far from shrinking with the years into old-fashioned obscurity, seem to have doubled in size, including the stunning Town Hall which, when Queen Victoria opened it in 1858, was one of the largest civic buildings in Europe. Leeds Town Hall and the vast majority of the other 'old' buildings seem to me to be representative of the enduring strength of the city; its backbone against decay, its defence against architectural vandalism, its moral core.

In this new Leeds one doesn't have to travel far to see that back-to-back houses still exist, although many of the streets are no longer cobbled. Yet the people in these streets live with the evidence of transition all around them. Their houses may now have indoor plumbing, but the privies are still there in the middle of the block, and at the end of many streets there are rubbish-strewn clearings which suggest that demolition began but has now been abandoned. The truth is, for all their cramped poverty, there is a durable history to these red-brick streets that is simply not present in the ephemeral glitter of a Leeds city centre that is trying so hard to reach out and appropriate modernity as though it is a commodity to be bought on credit at the local supermarket.

Late in the afternoon I walked down to the river and gazed at the new buildings which complement the recently renovated mills and storerooms. These days greenery fringes the water where previously filth and debris triumphed. Here warehouses have been transformed into boutique hotels and apartment blocks for the newly affluent, and right down by the water's edge cafés and restaurants lend a bohemian raffishness to the newly vibrant area. It seemed to me miraculous that the water was no longer polluted and lifeless, and I was actually tempted to linger and marvel at this transformation.

Back in the city centre, I looked closely at the anxious faces of the latest batch of youngsters readying themselves for a night out. Their faces appeared pinched and slightly weary, and I felt sure that behind their impish smiles and sugar-sabotaged teeth these young people knew that soon it would be their turn for unemployment and early parenthood. These 'kids' were old souls dressed in bright new clothes, much like the city itself; 'modern' kids. As I stared at them, I remembered that when I was a boy we used to play football against a secondary school with the somewhat hopeful name of 'Leeds Modern'. The joke, of course, was that there was precious little that was modern about Leeds, including this school. This is definitely not the case now.

Leeds was the city that took us in, back in 1958. My parents and I were assimilated into cobbled streets, introduced to dark gloomy buildings, and situated around the corner from pubs that still operated a color bar. But whatever the difficulties, this was our home. Today's newly constructed city centre, with its young multiracial population, speaks eloquently to a kind of self-belief that the city has probably not known since its mid-nineteenth-century industrial heyday. But, as in many great cities, the true ethos of Leeds is most plainly discernible in the buildings. The rush to modernity in the architecture might suggest confidence to some, but the very flimsiness of the enterprise is clear in the reflected solidity of the buildings that sit all around. I walked through this new Leeds marvelling at change, but I also felt relieved at just how much of the old, including the dark, satanic, soot-blackened fifties, still remained. After all, these are my roots. And those of the city.

Necessary Journeys (2004)

Twenty years ago, in the early autumn of 1984, I was travelling by myself in Morocco and Spain. I had already been on the road for some time, and ahead of me lay many more countries, many more border crossings, and journeys to places, and encounters with people, which I hoped might help me to better understand the world surrounding me. I was, at the time, a young man in my mid-twenties who was based in Britain and who was trying to make his mark as a writer. I felt comfortable with my chosen vocation, for I understood that I was working in the lee of a robust literary history. Britain has a long heritage of producing and valuing writers, and I saw no reason why, with assiduous application, and some good fortune, I might not develop as a writer in Britain. However, I already sensed that in order to progress I would have to remain particularly vigilant about the way in which my identity was being buffeted and twisted by societal forces.

Like any black child in Britain who grew up in the sixties and seventies, it had long been clear to me that the full complexity of who I am – my plural self, if you like – was never going to be nourished in a country which seemed to revel in its ability to reduce identity to clichés. The first time one is called a 'nigger' or told to 'go back to where you come from', one's identity is traduced and a great violence is done to one's sense of self. Thereafter, one fights a rearguard action to keep other elements of oneself in focus, and it's hard to get through the day without the shoulder coming into play. I don't mean the 'chip on the shoulder', I mean the 'glance over the shoulder'.

Once somebody has mounted a stealth attack on a part of who you are, you had better be wary for you know it's coming again.

Twenty years ago, I felt as though I was striving to do two things simultaneously. First, I was trying to become a writer. Second, I was still engaged in a struggle to recognise and protect my own identity, in all its intricacy, for I knew that I had to view it as unique, complicated, open to inspection and re-examination, and binding me not just to a particular tribe, clan, or race, but to the human race. I always understood that acknowledging this would be a prerequisite of writing well, for the more vigorously one resists a narrow view of self, the more one sees. In many ways, the task of trying to recognise and protect my identity was just as exhausting as the task of trying to become a writer. But, as I've already suggested, these enterprises are, of course, not unrelated.

There is a long tradition of writers from Britain who have found it necessary to travel. In many respects this tradition of departure, and sometimes return, was at its most furious during the period of empire and colonisation when countless British writers sought to define themselves, and their country, by travelling and encountering strange others who might, to some extent, affirm their sense of their own place in the global scheme of things. From Sir Walter Raleigh's *The History of the World*, to Robert Louis Stevenson's *The Amateur Emigrant*, to Patrick Leigh Fermor's *A Time of Gifts*, British writers have moved out beyond the horizon and produced books which have grappled with these vexing issues of British identity and belonging.

However, I not only belong to the British tradition, but I am also a writer of African origin, and for African diasporan people, 'home' is a word that is often burdened with a complicated historical and geographical weight. This being the case, travel has been important for it has provided African diasporan people with a means of clarifying their unique position in the world. Whether one is thinking of Langston Hughes in Moscow, or W.E.B. Du Bois in Berlin, or Ida B. Wells or Phillis Wheatley in London, or Claude McKay in Marseilles, or James Baldwin in Paris, the ability to leave and see oneself through another prism – hopefully one that is less racially cloudy – has long been a part of the legacy of being a writer of African origin in the West.

There was also a third tradition that was pressing on me back in 1984: that of being a writer of Caribbean origin. Between 1980, when I first returned to the Caribbean as an adult, and 1984, I had frequently journeyed back and forth between the eastern Caribbean and Britain, trying to explore and understand the impulse to migrate that had informed my own parents' lives, and the lives of many of my family and friends. This journeying had been written about by C.L.R. James, Jean Rhys, George Lamming, V.S. Naipaul, Samuel Selvon, in fact by the greater number of my Caribbean literary antecedents, all of whom understood what a profound contribution travel – often in the form of migration, forced or voluntary – had made to their own sense of themselves in the world.

A triple heritage of journeying: British, African diasporan, Caribbean. Looking back across twenty years, I can now see clearly just how unlikely it was that I would have developed fully as a writer while remaining rooted in Shepherd's Bush. However, back in 1984, I was not thinking in such a clinical manner of travel as fulfilling an obligation to follow in a specific tradition. I was thinking of it as an absolute, and very personal, necessity. I had to leave Britain. Pure and simple. I had to get out of this country which seemed determined to offer me only unpalatable, and racially determined, stereotypes as models for my own identity.

I should say that I was, of course, free to do what so many people in such situations do, which is to decide to see themselves as the embodiment of whatever facet of their identity is being thrown back in their face. In other words, I did have the option of embracing blackness as a form of essential identity. However, to use *any* element of oneself as either a weapon or a shield is restrictive. Given the type of writer that I was trying to become, I knew that such a course of action would not serve me well. The fact is, I was more interested in writing about the human heart than I was in addressing 'issues' – black or otherwise. The contemporary social, political and cultural milieu of Britain would inevitably, and rightly, find its way into my work, but I was keen that at its centre there would be the human heart. And, as we all discovered in the late sixties when the first heart transplant operation took place in South Africa, the human heart has no color.

At the beginning of 1984, the manuscript of my first novel was accepted by the publishing house Faber and Faber. In a meeting in a cramped office in London's Queen Square, my new editor asked me what I now know to be the usual questions about a jacket cover for the book, and then we discussed something called 'publishing strategy'. When he raised the question of what I might write next, I answered without hesitation. 'I want to travel through Europe and write a book about what I see, about who I talk to, and about what I'm thinking.' My editor was visibly unimpressed. He essayed a suggestion. 'What about a new novel?' What he meant was, 'What about another novel about West Indians in Britain?' Perhaps, if I had been in his position, I might have asked the same question. But I dug my heels in. 'I want to travel across Europe.' My editor looked uncomfortable, and then he came up with what he imagined to be a suitable compromise.

'What about travelling around Britain?' Always eager to please, my response was the very helpful, 'Yeah, what about it?' He got the idea, and soon after that we signed a contract for a minuscule amount of money, all of which would be immediately swallowed up by train and plane tickets and hotels. I was seriously out of pocket long before I had left Britain, but at least I was leaving.

Britain in 1984 was not a place I cared to spend much time in. There was considerable racial and cultural confusion in the air, which continued to manifest itself in an upsurge of far right-wing activity, and a concomitant backlash from young black people that was principally directed against the police force.

As British society reluctantly began to make the transition from 'West Indian' to 'Black British' as the acceptable, and more accurate, term with which to describe non-white citizens, things only seemed to get worse. Lines of demarcation were quickly established, so that one was perceived either as a challenge to the established system or as part of it. Of course, one could sometimes be perceived as both, but it was difficult to be seen as neither. Either way, it was a pointless business, and not really conducive to one's maturing as a writer. All too often I found myself being called upon by the media to explain my generation of black people to Britons – meaning white Britons: a predicament that can quickly reduce a writer to little more than a social commentator.

In such a situation, what is in danger of being lost is the narrative of self. My ability to focus on the interior personal journey was being undermined by a media-driven pressure that required little of me beyond my agreeing to report back to British society. I soon understood that in this Britain I would find it difficult to take time out and look inwards and explore a personal identity that is rooted both in *and* beyond Britain. I was to be given an image; or rather, the choice of an image. I could choose to remain on the side of the West Indians and be a rowdy, most likely dreadlocked, youth who threw bottles in the street, abused the police, and generally made a nuisance of himself; or I could enter into the brave new world of Black Britain, and dissociate myself from this dissolute, ganja-smoking element and attempt to gain a white-collar job. In case I was in any doubt as to what this new black Briton looked like, in 1983 the Conservative Party produced an advertisement which featured a photograph of a smartly suited, briefcase-wielding, well-groomed black man under the heading 'Labour says he's black, Tories say he's British.' Unsurprisingly, this black Briton neither looked like me, nor did he look like anybody I knew. The Conservative Party were quickly forced to withdraw the advertisement, having had it pointed out to them that the terms 'black' and 'British' were not, in fact, mutually exclusive. At least we non-white Britons had been afforded a glimpse of one of 'their' images of 'us'.

The truth is, in a country such as Britain, it is difficult to exercise any authority over one's own identity. Britain is a deeply class-bound society, with a codified and hierarchical structure which locates the monarchy at the top, with a roster of increasingly 'marginal' people as one filters down to the bottom. It is a largely inflexible system whose survival is dependent upon the maintenance of the status quo, and any societal change or development, such as immigration, is likely to cause instability. It would be reasonable to suggest that in the seventies Britain endured a fair degree of upheaval. Aside from the turbulence of domestic politics, with the three-day week and the electoral see-sawing between the Conservative Party and the Labour Party, the trauma of the decline of Empire was *still* palpable, and anxiety over decimalisation and the country's membership of the European Economic Community was seriously gnawing away at national pride. If one adds to this mix the overwhelming, and seemingly permanent, evidence of the legacy of Commonwealth migration in the high streets of the country, it is easy to see why British identity became, in the 1970s and '80s, a hugely contested area of debate.

For black people in Britain during this period, conflicting signals about their membership of society were rife. Black footballers would play for England one week, and the following week, while playing for their club sides, they would be racially abused and have bananas thrown at them by the very same fans who had cheered them when they wore an England shirt. Linford Christie, the captain of the British Athletics team, was stopped by a police officer while driving. When the officer noticed what he was wearing he asked, 'What's a nigger like you doing in an England tracksuit?' Although one tried hard to navigate this period it was sometimes difficult not to just throw one's hands up in the air. I remember canvassing for the Labour Party during the 1983 general election in the housing estate between Uxbridge Road and Goldhawk Road in Shepherd's Bush. I pressed one doorbell, and a girl who can hardly have been more than seven years old answered the door. 'Hello,' I said, 'is your mother or father in?' The girl looked at me, and without turning around said, 'Mum, there's a nigger at the door.' But I'm a stubborn type of fellow. A few doors down the same block I tried again. An older man, in vest and carpet slippers and with a cigarette dangling from his mouth, opened the door. 'Will you be voting Labour in the forthcoming election?' He slowly looked me up and down. 'Well,' he said, 'I was till I saw you.' I went back to Labour Headquarters and gently intimated to them that perhaps I wasn't their best canvassing tool.

When my editor suggested that I travel around Britain and write a book, my mind was already made up. To stay in Britain would undoubtedly have enabled me to better understand and analyse the profound 'identity crisis' which seemed to have descended on British society in this period. I could have looked at the regional differences in attitude, examined rural versus urban behaviour, and I would have happily done so for I was genuinely interested in such subjects. But a domestic journey would not, to my mind, have helped me to fully understand the more serious question of the degree to which my own identity was being compromised by the society I was living in. I did feel an acute obligation to examine the issues clouding British society, but I felt an even more important responsibility to grow and develop, and that was not going to happen effectively in a society in which I daily had to grapple with images of myself that were laughably restrictive, generally insulting and obviously false.

The fact that I was born in the Caribbean and journeyed to Britain in the late 1950s as an infant has had an incalculable effect upon who I am. That I grew up in Yorkshire as a working-class boy has also had a deep-seated effect upon me. That I went first to grammar school, then to a comprehensive school, and from there to a prestigious older university, this has all fed who I am. The evidence of these migrations over water and across land, through nations, class and geography had, twenty years ago, already bequeathed to me an exceedingly multifarious sense of self. Add to this the ingredient of race, in an institutionally racist society, and it becomes clear that I was dealing with a personal identity that resisted easy classification.

Identity, as perceived in Britain, is often little more than an outer garment handed to you at birth that you learn to recognise, wear, feel proud of, brag about, and that in the end you are buried in. The difficulty of either discarding it or re-tailoring it has bedevilled countless generations of Britons and this, I believe, has encouraged many people, including writers, to flee the country, however temporarily, in the hope that they might see themselves in a new light. I too was convinced that in order to be free to explore and construct my own independent identity, and therefore write with some degree of freedom and compassion, I would have to leave; and so, in 1984, I left Britain for Europe to look at other places and people and encourage them to gaze upon me. There was no way that I was handing over the responsibility for defining me to a country that was under the leadership of Mrs Thatcher, a woman who had little respect for people such as myself. After all, it was her own daughter, Carol Thatcher, who in her book *Below the Parapet* revealed that her mother and father used to joke that the Commonwealth Heads of Government Meeting (the CHOGM) should be more correctly known as 'Coons Holidaying on Government Money'.

I have in the past been asked — and asked myself — what would have happened to me if my parents had not left St Kitts in 1958? Would I have migrated to the United States or Canada instead of Britain? Or would I have stayed in St Kitts? I used to think about this a lot, most often when sitting in the Caribbean with friends or family, and looking around me at the evidence of their own non-migratory lives. But I have now come to understand that a far more important and difficult question is, what would have happened to me if I had not left Britain in 1984 and begun a process of border crossings that I've continued to this day? Of course, I have no real answer to this question.

What I *do* know is that it is difficult to grow as a writer in any society at any time. The pitfalls are many, and the distractions multiply with each new book. To attempt to grow as a writer while grappling with the pernicious labelling that society wishes to impose upon those whose identities they find disruptive, is doubly difficult.

Some of my contemporaries from 1984 have managed to forge ahead and write with great success, while others seem to have stumbled, and some have even fallen silent. I am not sure what would have happened to me had the autumn of 1984 found me tucked away in Shepherd's Bush, as opposed to moving between Cordoba and Madrid on a journey that would, many months later, conclude in Moscow. The gift of travel has been enabling for me in the same way that it has been enabling for writers in the British tradition, in the African diasporan tradition and in the Caribbean tradition, many of whom have found it necessary to move in order to reaffirm for themselves the fact that dual and multiple affiliations feed our constantly fluid sense of self. Healthy societies are ones which allow such pluralities to exist and do not feel threatened by these hybrid conjoinings. Of course, I soon discovered that in continental Europe many countries suffer from the same myopia as Britain, but that is another topic altogether. As a young writer, travel enabled me to understand that constantly reinterpreting and, if necessary, reinventing oneself is an admirable legacy of living in our modern, culturally and ethnically kinetic world. The most dangerous thing that we can do to ourselves is to carelessly accept a label that is offered to us by a not always generous society that seeks to reduce us to little more than one single component of our rich and complex selves. Somewhere between Morocco and Moscow the truth of this struck home, and by the time I returned to Britain I was ready to begin.

'Rude am I in my speech' (2008)

Perhaps the most arresting moment in the first act of Shakespeare's *Othello* occurs when the soldier is asked by the Duke of Venice to respond to the accusation that he has 'beguiled' Brabantio's daughter, Desdemona, away from the protection and safety of her father's house. The soldier is an outwardly confident man, full of pride and bombast, and hugely aware of his celebrity in Venice. He addresses the Duke. 'Rude am I in my speech,' he says, then spins a masterfully persuasive narrative full of lyrical eloquence which the Duke acknowledges would have ensnared his own daughter too. The poised, silver-tongued soldier is vindicated and the play can proceed. What is firmly established in this first act is that Othello is an outsider both racially and socially. In this thoroughly demarcated Venetian world where Michael Cassio is simply 'a Florentine', the 'old black ram', although he claims to be descended from 'men of royal siege', is regarded as little more than an 'extravagant and wheeling stranger'. For the full length of the first act, what Shakespeare does *not* allow us to see is that for all Othello's public success there is at the centre of his personality a kernel of self-doubt, a tight knot of anxiety, which is eventually exploited by his ancient, Iago. During this first act the soldier appears to be in control. He plays games, protesting that he has a clumsy tongue even as his language betrays no hint of rudeness or foreign taint. If Othello possesses any self-doubt or inner discomfort, its origins are not rooted in language. What if he had begun his mellifluous speech with, 'Rude am I in my visage'? Would this self-assured black migrant to Europe have had the confidence to stand before the Duke of Venice and play fearlessly with notions of identity and belonging that are rooted in race as opposed to language, or would this be to trespass too close to the source of his well-hidden self-doubt?

Almost ten years ago, I arranged to meet my father at lunchtime in a hotel in Manchester. The night before I had given a reading at a local bookshop, and that afternoon I was planning to move on to Liverpool and give another reading at the university. My father lives maybe an hour away from Manchester, and so this seemed an opportune moment to get together. What made the meeting unusual was the fact that we had not seen or spoken with each other for some years. I came down into the hotel lobby a little early, but there he was already sprawled out on a sofa and watching the news on the television. He saw me and stood up. I was glad to see him. He had not changed much, and we hugged and I suggested that we go to another hotel around the corner which had a nicer restaurant. There were very few people in the place and the hostess seated us and gave us our menus. She asked if we would like a drink to start with. My father ordered a Scotch and I asked for a glass of Sauvignon Blanc and, having informed us of the specials, the hostess left us alone. Five minutes later a waitress arrived with our drinks. As she withdrew we raised our glasses and clinked, and then I sipped and grimaced. My father asked me if there was a problem and I said that the wine was not Sauvignon Blanc. It tasted like Chardonnay. I signalled to the waitress and then I saw a flicker of panic pass across my father's face. He asked me if I couldn't drink it. I said, 'Why? It's not what I ordered.' The waitress came over and I explained the situation. She shrugged her shoulders and took up my glass. There was no apology, but there was no surliness either as she disappeared from view. My father remained quiet and I could see that he was uncomfortable. For a few moments I made inane conversation; at last the waitress returned with the new glass of wine and I tasted it. Better, I thought, so I nodded and thanked her and she left us alone. However, this incident caused the atmosphere between father and son to become strained.

First-generation migrants to Europe, from wherever they may originate, have to learn quickly how to read the new society in order to successfully navigate their way forward. Sometimes this involves learning when to remain quiet, and somewhat compliant, and not risk causing offence. When West Indians first arrived in England in the 1950s, countless pamphlets were thrust into their hands which explained to them the ways of the English. They were instructed that they must line up at bus stops in an orderly fashion, and not keep working when their fellow labourers were on a tea break, and it was suggested that they should try to join a trade union, and perhaps they should not bring food that smelt 'foreign' to work. In common with many immigrants, they were being taught how to tread carefully, the unspoken contract being that in time they would learn the rules and become familiar with how the society worked; so much so that one day they might be considered domesticated. Whether they would ever become fully fledged insiders was not discussed, but for many first-generation migrants this was not something that was necessarily desired. The hope on both sides was for some vestige of tolerance and respect.

There are, of course, two places where new immigrants can find some relief from these anxieties of belonging. First, at home with their families, where the rules are of their own making and no local person can prevent them from being kings and queens in their own castles. Behind closed doors they can cook their own food, listen to whatever music takes their fancy, and curse the locals in whatever tongue or dialect they choose. And then of course there is the world of the pub, or the club, or the café, where immigrants gather together socially and over a drink compare notes with others of their own tribe. The home and the social gathering place constitute zones of psychological relief for immigrants. In such spaces one doesn't have to be called 'Sam' or 'Son', or take aggressive orders from ignorant people half one's age. In the kingdom of the home, or in the citadel of the club, first-generation migrants are free to be whoever they imagine, or remember, themselves to be, and there is no expectation that they should perform the shape-shifting dance that immigrants often have to execute in order to safely negotiate a passage from sun-up to sundown. Of course, the more successful the immigrant the more difficult it can be to keep in touch with the 'club'. Upon assuming a white-collar job as a foreman, or an executive role in a company, the rules become more complex for there are now men and women above you and men and women below you, and with the job comes a salary increase and perhaps a move to a new neighbourhood where there are less of you and more of them. To keep contact with fellow migrants one now has to travel further, both physically and psychologically.

During the first, Venetian, act of Shakespeare's play, before the action moves off to Cyprus, it is clear to us that Othello, this 'extravagant and wheeling stranger', is a man who is a long way from home. In Venice he is an exotic celebrity, and as such the Duke is inclined to overlook the social and cultural transgression of not only an interracial marriage but a secret one, therefore allowing Othello to indulge in behaviour that would almost certainly be frowned upon if attempted by a non-celebrity. This being the case, this extravagant stranger appears to be untroubled by the fact that he has recourse to neither home nor club as places to which he might retreat and recuperate from the daily fatigue of living a performative life, and he appears content to veer dramatically between rhetorical swagger and self-deprecating bluster like a kite snapping in the wind. Apparently he feels that his success is such that there is no need for him to be aware of the unwritten Venetian rule book which tells him that he must line up in an orderly fashion for a gondola, and don't even think about cooking chickpeas or couscous, and whatever you do don't mess with the local ladies, especially the titled ones. Our celebrity migrant considers himself above and beyond such restrictive nonsense. By the end of Act One the newly married man truly believes that he has crossed over into full acceptance, but the truth is, without family or peer group, and without societal knowledge born of vigilance and judicious interaction, he is incapable of making sound decisions about something as basic as knowing who to trust. It soon becomes lamentably evident that, far from being in control of the situation and participating as an insider, our black, first-generation migrant to Europe is about as unmoored as any man can be.

My father is no Othello. He may have polished up a few words and phrases here and there, and done a little studying of the dictionary, but to this day he remains admirably rude in speech. But then again he has never been a vital or essential cog in British life and occupied the role of super-migrant. What West Indian immigrant has? In fact, what immigrant has? As a first-generation migrant he has always been aware of the home and the club as zones of sanity in which he can be himself. Like most second-generation children I have, at times, been puzzled and frustrated by his dependence upon one form or another of the 'club', and irritated by the taciturn manner in which he often exercised his authority in the home; not that he was always wrong. When I was fifteen or sixteen, I remember one Saturday night standing upstairs in front of the mirror and preparing myself to go out to the church discotheque. Eventually I ventured downstairs wearing tight blue nylon bell-bottoms, black platform shoes, a pink shirt with a huge collar that was trimmed in brown piping, and a black and white checked jacket. My father was sitting at the kitchen table and he looked up at me over the top of his newspaper. He shook his head and said, 'Somebody tell you that shit matches?' The second generation was stepping out into England with a confidence and brashness that, in retrospect, could have used a little more of his cold water being poured upon it. It was his house and he was trying to tell me something about how to look and comport myself out there on the streets, like the time a year or two later when I passed my driving test and he told me that I must be very careful if I was out driving at night with a white girl in the passenger seat. He warned me that I should be prepared to have the police stop and harass me for no other reason than the fact that I was with a white girl. Again he was passing on knowledge which was meant both to help prepare me for life in England, and to reaffirm who he was when in his own private sphere. I listened, and I assumed that my father knew what he was talking about for, at the time, he had a white wife.

As a reader and a writer, I am interested in loneliness and isolation, and I have found myself returning time and time again to consider those who have suddenly realised themselves to be marooned. Richard Wright's Bigger Thomas in that huge Chicago mansion, scared out of his mind and not knowing whether to stay put or flee; Ibsen's Oswald, recently returned to Norway with his body eaten away by disease and his mind racked with pain at the bleakness of his own country; James Baldwin's David, alone in a house in the South of France at precisely the time his lover Giovanni is about to be guillotined in Paris; Shusaku Endo's medical intern, Suguro, whose conscience begins to torment him as he remembers the past and finds himself increasingly detached from daily reality. However, I know of no character in literature more profoundly alone and isolated than Shakespeare's pioneer migrant Othello, who, once he passes beyond the imaginary security of his life in the great city of water, suddenly finds himself adrift with no son or daughter to measure his situation against, no peer group to bond with at the end of the day, no Venetian home to return to, and loving a local woman whom he eventually decides he cannot trust. No wonder he loses his mind.

Immigrants will continue to enter Europe, and initially they will be unsure of how to be an Italian, or how to be a Dane, or Irish or Greek. It takes many years for a first-generation migrant of any race to become socially confident, and perhaps, in the end, it is only those closest to them, the second generation, who can fully understand the price they pay as they grapple with self-doubt and attempt to hitch their fortune (and talent) to a new country. I am beginning to feel that witnessing and recording the predicament of the first generation is a responsibility, because by the time we reach the commendably brash third generation, a parental comment about one's dress, or how to be circumspect in the street, is likely to be met with a bemused and slightly disdainful, 'what are you on about?' As the grandchildren enter fully and boldly into the country with not only the temerity of an Othello but, crucially, armed with the social knowledge and understanding that the Venetian resident didn't have, or seem to desire, the kernel of self-doubt which speaks to either social standing or race is, in their lives, beginning to disappear. Nervous hesitation will once again be visited upon the next wave of first-generation migrants, wherever they might hail from, and to the list of potential sources of anxiety to be negotiated we might add religious belief. Rude am I in my speech. Rude am I in my visage. Rude am I in my faith. When I left my father in Manchester that lunchtime, and took the train to Liverpool, I began to think about first-generation diffidence, and again I reflected upon the supreme loneliness of the migrant to Venice, who also had a white wife but it never occurred to him that the police were going to pull him over until, of course, it was too late.

Overtures

E.R. Braithwaite (2005)

To Sir With Love (1959) was the first published book of Edward Ricardo Braithwaite, who was born in 1920 in British Guiana (present-day Guyana), the large English-speaking territory on the north-east coast of South America. His was a relatively comfortable upbringing, being the son of two Oxford-educated parents, and as a young man he quickly absorbed the conservative, middle-class manners of the Caribbean intellectual. He attended Queens College, an elite colonial school in British Guiana, and went on to study at City College in New York, before enlisting as a Royal Air Force pilot in England. Braithwaite states in *To Sir With Love* that, like many other Caribbean men, he joined the British armed forces out of a sense of duty and during the war years he was ready to die for *his* country.

Upon being demobilised at the end of the war, Braithwaite fully expected to be absorbed into the upper levels of his chosen profession of engineering. Not only has he studied in New York, but he will soon earn a Master's degree in Physics from Cambridge University. However, at interview after interview he is refused an appointment because of his color. Unfortunately, the camaraderie of the service does not transfer to civilian life, and the realisation of this fact strikes him a hard blow. 'I had just been brought face to face with something I had either forgotten or completely ignored for more than six exciting years – my black skin . . . Disappointment and resentment were a solid bitter rising lump inside me; I hurried into the nearest public lavatory and was violently sick.'

After eighteen months of unemployment and faltering

confidence, Braithwaite decides to try teaching, for the profession is in desperate need of educated men and women. He successfully negotiates an interview, but then finds himself posted to one of the worst schools in the East End of London. He is further dismayed to discover that his charges are an unruly, disruptive group of fifteen-year-olds who stand cockily on the threshold of adulthood.

Braithwaite's somewhat haughty attitude towards his new pupils is entirely predictable. After all, this is a man who, on the very first page of the book, has made it clear how superior he is, both intellectually and physically, to the disappointing English. 'They reminded me somehow of the peasants in a book by Steinbeck: they were of the city, but they dressed like peasants, they looked like peasants, and they talked like peasants.' And, even before he has travelled out to the school, he muses aloud on the East End of London and wonders about its history in a manner that shows the extent of his distinguished education.

> I had read references to it in both classical and contemporary writings and was eager to know the London of Chaucer and Erasmus and the Sorores Minores. I had dreamed of walking along the cobbled Street of the Cable Makers to the echoes of Chancellor and the brothers Willoughby. I wanted to look on the reach of the Thames at Blackwall from which Captain John Smith had sailed aboard the good ship *Susan Lawrence* to found an English colony in Virginia.

Predictably, the fetid air, and the dirty streets of the recently bombed-out East End disappoint, as do the unwashed, uncouth youngsters now ranged before him. We are left in no doubt that Braithwaite's manners are impeccable, and that his dress is always smart and tidy, but also that an unmistakable, almost anthropological, sneer permanently decorates the colored teacher's face.

The girl who rose to comply was fair-haired and slim, with a pair of heavy breasts which swung loosely under a thin jumper, evidently innocent of any support. I wondered at the kind of parent who would allow a girl to go out so sloppily attired.

There is, however, no doubt that Braithwaite would, during this period in the late 1940s and early 1950s, have had to endure a fair amount of anthropological sneering himself. *This* colored man in London would be a double oddity: first for his color, and then for his class. Those few West Indians who did walk the streets of England would, despite the prejudice they endured, have had far more in common with white working-class people than with this Cambridge-educated former officer. In fact, throughout the course of the book there is no sense of 'Ricky' having a community of any sort beyond his white 'mum' and 'dad', and we do feel some sympathy for this rather isolated, patrician man who attempts now to make a community out of the pupils in his charge and his fellow teachers in the staffroom.

Braithwaite displays a great aptitude as a teacher, but we are aware that there are lessons that he too must learn, particularly with reference to humility and patience. Unsurprisingly, it is the *uncouth* pupils who soon begin to teach him the lessons. This is poignantly illustrated when the mother of one of the boys – the only mixed-race boy in the class – dies, and the pupils make it clear that although they are prepared to have a collection for a wreath, not one of them is able to deliver it, for to knock on the boy's door might be seen as fraternising with coloreds. 'Ricky' is quick to fall into a trough of judgemental despair.

It was a like a disease, and these children whom I loved without caring about their skins or their backgrounds, they were tainted with the hateful virus which attacked their vision, distorting everything that was not white or English.

I remembered a remark of Weston's: 'They're morons, cold as stone, nothing matters to them, nothing.'

I turned and walked out of the classroom sick at heart.

The following day, a still bitter Braithwaite turns up for the funeral.

And then I stopped, feeling suddenly washed clean, whole and alive again. Tears were in my eyes, unashamedly, for there, standing in a close, separate group on the pavement outside Seales' door was my class, my children, all or nearly all of them, smart and self-conscious in their best clothes. Oh God, forgive me for the hateful thoughts, because I love them, these brutal, disarming bastards, I love them . . .

Braithwaite also learns to be more tolerant of his fellow teachers, whose attitudes towards him vary from overt hostility to deep love. Navigating the choppy waters of the staffroom presents Braithwaite with almost as many problems as trying to control the pupils in the classroom, but he finally succeeds in creating a place for himself in the school, and by the end of the book 'Sir' is both respected and loved by pupils and teachers alike.

However, beyond the confines of the school, British society is rife with serious problems of prejudice and bigotry, and it is to Braithwaite's credit that he points clearly to these issues. Although he manages to charm the local Yiddish-speaking shopkeeper, and win the heart of a fellow teacher and the grudging respect of her highly suspicious parents, he *is* shunned in the streets, he *is* often insulted by strangers, and he *is* made fully aware of the painful paradox of being 'British, but not being a Briton'. To Braithwaite's eyes, post-war British society is in trouble, and already he can see the profound difficulties that must be overcome before a truly multiracial modern Britain can evolve, difficulties that, as it transpired, continued to plague the country for the whole second half of the twentieth century.

They had been reared in a neighbourhood as multiracial as anywhere in Britain, yet it had been of no significance to them. Some of them lived in the same street, the same block of flats, as Indians or Negroes, without ever even speaking to them, in obedience to the parental taboo. Others had known and grown up with colored children through the Infant and Junior stages, but when the tensions and pretensions of puberty had intervened the relationship had ended.

Fifty years on, *To Sir With Love* can be read as a narrative of triumph over adversity concerning one highly unusual man's eight-month-long experience of an inner-city school that enables him to grow and occasions some of the people he comes into contact with to put their prejudices on hold. But it is obviously more than this. The author is keen for us to understand that the Ricky Braithwaites of this world cannot, by themselves, uproot prejudice, but they can point to its existence. And this, after all, is the beginning of change; one must first identify the location of the problem before one can set about addressing it.

The author is also keen to remind us that in this post-war Britain, as in our own contemporary Britain, one wrong step and teacher 'Ricky' is just another nigger on the street. *To Sir With Love* leaves the reader in no doubt about the degree to which British society has, for centuries, been wedded to prejudice. *To Sir With Love* reminds us that in the early fifties, as tens of thousands of easily identifiable 'others' were beginning to enter the country in an attempt to rebuild Britain after the ravages of the Second World War, this deep-seated problem of unquestioned hereditary prejudice was waiting to greet them in the streets, in the workplace, and in institutions of learning.

After the publication of *To Sir With Love*, E.R. Braithwaite left teaching and pursued a successful career as a social worker and then a diplomat. Reading this book it is easy to discern how well suited he was to both careers. He also continued to produce books, including a memoir about his time as a social worker, *Paid Servant* (1962) and another about his time in South Africa,

Honorary White (1975). Yet, partly because of the success of the filmed version of the book, *To Sir With Love* remains his best-known work. This fine, and genuinely touching, portrait of a post-war English working-class community coming face to face with a decidedly atypical West Indian man, has much to tell us about race, class, and the education system in Britain. It also speaks eloquently to the individual courage of a Cambridge-educated West Indian who is prepared to share with us his own prejudices and fears as he trips cautiously across the rubble of the East End of London in those bleak, austere years following the end of the Second World War.

John La Rose (2007)

In 1982, shortly after the conclusion to the First International Black and Third World Book Fair, Errol Lloyd interviewed John La Rose and asked him to describe the opening ceremony to the Book Fair. John replied as follows:

'I introduced the person we had asked to open the Book Fair. C.L.R. James, political theorist, novelist, critic, political activist ... for us C.L.R. James had become a symbol for the continuity between the past and the present in Britain. Between an earlier intellectual presence and political presence here: [represented by figures such as] Olaudah Equiano: Paul Robeson: the revolutionary Pan-Africanist ... George Padmore: C.L.R. James himself: Kwame Nkrumah: and what they had been able to do and what foundations they had laid in Britain at an earlier period ... [and] what we were about to begin in the International Book Fair on the 1st April.'

Even before John La Rose arrived in Britain in 1961, he intuitively understood the wisdom which informs the statement of another Trinidadian, the scholar and former Prime Minister Eric Williams, who said that 'History is the basic science.' John knew something about 'foundations'; he knew that unless you first understand who has preceded you, and respect the sacrifices and difficulties that have bedevilled the journey of those people who have travelled before you, then you are almost certainly wandering in ignorance and unlikely to go much further. John La Rose knew that one has to look to, and respect, the past, and as he grappled with what one might call the front story of British life in the sixties, and seventies, and eighties, and nineties, and on into the present century, John La Rose was always subtly and carefully reminding us of the back story. There were precedents; this was not a unique occurrence; it could, if you like, be framed and understood, which, naturally enough, often made the problem appear to be much less intractable.

The International Book Fair, which took place from 1982 until 1995, was, of course, a perfect example of John La Rose's vision as a determined front-line combatant and as both a keeper of the flame of the past and a respecter of history. At the International Book Fair new young publishers set up their stalls side by side with older more established ones. The venerable literary lions read together with the younger cubs who were just lolloping into view and hoping to establish themselves on the scene. And the Book Fair gave John a space in which he could be furiously innovative. Music, dance, film — all these forms of artistic expression were encouraged and coexisted with litera-ture; the new, and often avant-garde, was ordered to take a seat next to more traditional work. Of course, this well-orchestrated hybridity, this lack of fealty to traditional decorum, or to a conservative notion of form and order, is all part of the heritage of the people and the region that produced John La Rose: the Caribbean, that creolised and creolising tract of the Americas where anything is possible because on closer inspection one soon finds that most things have already occurred.

John La Rose wore many public hats in his life, and he wore them all with distinction. Activist, educator, publisher — he invigorated and motivated others, and was always keen that the potential of those around him should be realised. He was a man with an unerring sense of when to step forward out of the half-light and declare himself, and when to retreat and watch whatever it was that he had encouraged take its own shape and form. This is a great gift; to know how to lead, but to know also when to gracefully withdraw. John La Rose knew how to dance around celebrity and fame, and he had no desire to clasp either of these false totems to his bosom and take a quick whirl with them. When he moved, he did so stealthily and with purpose. But movement involves expending energy, and John paid a price for his constant attention to projects, initiatives and ideas. He was a writer who in the end did not have much time to write. He was a writer who put effort behind the writing of others at the cost of his own work. He was a poet, a man of vision and insight, a sensitive man, who decided that rather than build the citadels around his life that would be necessary for him to concentrate on his own work, he would give to others. And John sought to do this in the most practical way possible: in 1966, together with Sarah White, he created a publishing house. New Beacon Books was named after the famous Trinidadian magazine, *The Beacon*, which although it lasted only for a few issues, between 1931 and 1932, had a huge cultural impact on early twentieth-century Caribbean intellectual thought. In the following year, 1967, John La Rose opened the New Beacon Bookshop as a specialist Caribbean bookseller making available works in English, French and Spanish. As the enterprise developed, the bookshop began to stock material from Africa, the United States, Britain and Europe. New Beacon Books, both the publishing house and the bookshop, eventually became the engine room out of which was launched the Caribbean Arts Movement, the Book Fair, the New Beacon Educational Trust, the George Padmore Institute and many other initiatives.

But all of this activity, this energetic service, grew out of John La Rose's feelings for literature, and his love of the word. For John La Rose it began with the word. And the words became a line, and the lines finally declared themselves to be a poem. John was a poet, who while never turning his back on his calling, found a way to be true to it by being true to others. John published volumes of poetry by Mervyn Morris, James Berry and Lorna Goodison. Novels by Erna Brodber and Andrew Salkey. Volumes of essays by Wilson Harris, Kamau Brathwaite and Ngugi wa Thiong'o. These were not reprints; he was the original publisher of works by these authors – authors who form the canonical bedrock of our literature. He made their books, and countless other key volumes of contemporary and historical significance, available to us for the first time. Our debt to New Beacon Books as readers, as scholars, as critics, as researchers is inestimable.

But a bookshop and a publishing house are not, and should not be, cold places which exist solely for the sake of commercial interaction. They should be places of intellectual energy and free-flowing ideas; the ideal bookshop should be a place of creativity in itself, and this is what John sought to achieve with New Beacon Books. John La Rose established a space where readers and writers could come together and engage with each other, for he valued not only writers but also those who wanted to read or listen to literature and he gave them the opportunity to meet the writers and to discuss the work. New Beacon Books threw its doors open to readers and writers alike. Today technology has affected the manner in which we are stimulated by literature, beginning with the very act of how we purchase a book. However, New Beacon Books endures, and its legacy lives on both in its absolutely essential backlist, and in its continued commitment to publishing important new work. Working together with the George Padmore Institute, the bookshop programmes lectures, readings and recordings, all of which serve to enhance the primacy of the word.

In 1982, John La Rose spoke eloquently to Errol Lloyd of the foundations that had been laid by C.L.R. James and others upon which he was building. He was referring to the Book Fair, and obviously before this to the publishing house, and the bookshop. He was a quintessentially modest man who would never say this of himself, but in the second half of the twentieth century in Britain, no Caribbean migrant to this country did more to secure and expand the foundations of the work of the earlier generation of intellectuals, and build securely upon them, than John La Rose. This brilliant man of steely determination could easily have made a career for himself in Westminster, or in the media, or in the academy, but he chose instead to give grassroots service. His passionate desire for sociocultural change and justice, and the vision and leadership that he gave us, place him firmly in a very distinguished tradition. He understood that those who came before him – Padmore, James and others – had been correct to see the struggle for liberation in an international context, but he also understood the importance of seeing the struggle not just through the narrow prism of race which, of course, enabled him to form powerful alliances where it often appeared that none existed.

John offered us his leadership during that turbulent period of British post-war history as the Powellism of the late sixties gave way to the skinheads, bootboys and Paki-bashers of the seventies, the rise of the fascists and neo-Nazis of the National Front, the riots of Brixton, Notting Hill, Toxteth, Bristol, Leeds and other urban centres, the New Cross Massacre, Broadwater Farm, and many more violent and non-violent insurrections. He organised in the wake of these, and the many other, social upheavals that were tearing this country apart as the first generation of Caribbean immigrants learned, like the rest of Britain, how to coexist with the emergence of a second generation who were clearly not going to accept the same kind of treatment, disdain and police-sanctioned violence which had been offered to their parents. While all of this was happening here in Britain, and while similar disturbances and crises were plaguing continental Europe, the United States, the Caribbean, the Indian subcontinent and Africa, John was always busy and productive working with a megaphone on the streets, and with pen and paper in his office, and creating a space for his comrades to articulate their passion and their frustration, especially those who chose to do so with words.

But I want to return to John La Rose's words. Some years ago, New Beacon Books published a reprint of C.L.R. James's 1936 novel, *Minty Alley*. Those who have read this novel, and who know of James's subsequent remarkable career in diverse fields, must have wondered what kind of a literary life James might have enjoyed had he locked the door to the other activities with which he occupied himself, and thrown away the key. However, James knew that a literary life is a demanding mistress. She will not tolerate much in the way of philandering in other areas, and *Minty Alley* proved to be his only novel. John La Rose also fully understood the demands of literature, and like C.L.R. James he made a choice to keep the door to an active public life propped wide open and to step through it with vigour knowing that this would prevent him from living the full literary life that was his for the taking. John La Rose understood the choice he was making, and what it would mean in terms of his future. Quite simply, he made a decision to be creative in other areas, not just literature, but he always maintained a great respect for those who did focus largely on their writing and let the door slam shut. When he spoke of his great friend Andrew Salkey on the day of his funeral, one felt the respect and affection.

'I'll always remember Andrew,' said John.

'He was a friend, a close friend, and a comrade. He was a novelist, a poet, a playwright, an indefatigable anthologist, a fabulist, a children's novelist, a film buff and a diarist. An extraordinary person, a great talent. I was with him in Havana when he wrote his *Havana Journal*; [and] we were together in Georgetown while he composed his *Georgetown Journal*.'

These are typically generous words, but as wonderful as Salkey's books on Havana and Georgetown are, what one also longs for are John La Rose's books about these journeys. The truth is, literature's loss is our gain.

Much of the poetry that John did produce is tender, lyrical and speaks clearly to those words of Eric Williams, 'History is the basic science.' John's poem 'Not from Here' which begins 'You were not born here / My Child / Not Here' is both a declaration of fact and a tender lament; a hard fist encased in the tenderest of crushed velvet gloves. He produced two volumes of poetry, the appropriately named *Foundations* (1966) and *Eyelets of Truth Within Me* (1992). His poetic gifts are an important part of his legacy, and his highly developed writer's sensibility accounts in part for his sure judgement as a publisher, his loyalty to those he took into his circle, and the great affection in which he is held by writers literally all over the world. Writers can be suspicious, competitive creatures, easily slighted and quick to take offence. Alliances can be tenuous, and friendships are often built upon shifting sand. But mention the name of John La Rose to any writer and their face lights up. He was above us. He understood. He enabled.

Some years ago I wrote an essay about C.L.R. James, the concluding few words of which I've always felt were equally applicable to this remarkable man who, like his fellow Trinidadian, strode on to an international stage and declared himself a man of the people, a man for all seasons, a man amongst men. John La Rose.

> His view of the world was fundamentally generous. While he wished to impress his opinions upon his readers and his listeners, he respected individuals whom he disagreed with, and saw virtue in work that ran counter to his political beliefs. He never lost sight of the autonomy of art and literature, and never sought to use either for crassly political purposes . . . He believed in ideas, but he had an even greater faith in people.

Claude McKay (2008)

In May 1948, in a depressed post-war Chicago, the death of a Jamaican-born writer named Claude McKay raised few eyebrows, and generated even fewer column inches. McKay died of congestive heart failure after many years of struggling with illness and poverty, and at the time of his death he was employed by the Chicago Catholic Youth Organization who had charitably extended a hand to help this newly converted, and avowedly devoted, man. To those who were familiar with the details of the fifty-nine-year-old writer's life, it would have come as little surprise to learn that he had embraced his new faith with great enthusiasm. A self-declared freethinker at the age of fourteen, McKay had spent many years searching for a structure that might give purpose and direction to a life that was full of insecurities, both personal and professional. At different points, McKay had sought to root his journey in what he liked to call the modern 'isms — communism, socialism, liberalism, conservatism, and finally Catholicism. However, behind the sad anonymity of his demise lay hidden a quite brilliant literary career which was characterised by border crossings of both a literary and geographical nature. In this new transnational age, McKay's life begins to look both familiar and exemplary.

Born in 1889, in the parish of Clarendon, Jamaica, Festus Claudius McKay was named for a Roman governor and an emperor who were both mentioned in the Book of Acts. He was the eleventh and youngest child of a middle-class black Jamaican family who, while not wealthy by any stretch of the imagination, believed firmly in the principles of the Bible and a good education. When he was seven Claude was sent to live with his oldest brother, a schoolteacher, so that he would receive the best possible instruction in how to read and write. By the age of ten he was composing poetry. By the time he reached his late teens Claude was apprenticed to a carriage and cabinet maker, but he had also met an English gentleman residing in Jamaica named Walter Jekyll who would soon become his literary mentor. Back in England, Jekyll had formed many literary acquaintances, including a friendship with Robert Louis Stevenson who, so it was claimed, had borrowed his friend's name and utilised it in the title of the short story, *The Strange Case of Dr Jekyll and Mr Hyde*. Jekyll encouraged his young protégé to immerse himself in English lyric poetry, particularly the work of Keats and Shelley, but he also wanted the young poet to recognise the folklore value and dignity of Jamaican dialect, and to celebrate the nobility of the lives of ordinary Jamaicans. Eventually, Jekyll helped McKay to publish his first two collections of verse, *Songs of Jamaica* (1912) and *Constab Ballads* (1912).

In 1912, the twenty-three-year-old McKay left Jamaica, never to return. He enrolled at Booker T. Washington's Tuskegee Institute in Alabama intending to study agronomy, but he soon transferred to Kansas State University. He left both institutions without completing a degree. In 1914 he moved to New York City, where he tried his hand as a restaurateur, but after the failure of this venture he resigned himself to a series of menial jobs and continued to write poetry. During this period McKay became outraged at the racism and discrimination that he witnessed in both the southern and northern United States, and he fell in with a group of communist intellectuals with whose opinions he sympathised. In 1920 a volume of verse in Standard English, *Spring in New Hampshire* was published, but McKay was spending increasing amounts of time as both a contributor and an editor on the left-wing periodical, *The Liberator*. He had also begun to travel. In 1919 he visited London, where he worked on Sylvia Pankhurst's Marxist publication *Workers' Dreadnought*, and in 1922 he made what he called the 'magic pilgrimage' to Russia where he was enthusiastically received by Trotsky, Zinoviev and other leading revolutionaries, and invited to address the Third Communist International in Moscow.

McKay remained in Russia for over six months, during which time he came to understand that he had reached a professional crossroads. He had established a successful career as a black Communist radical, who was an influential theorist and organiser to the left during a period which had seen the establishment of the world's first modern socialist state, but it was literary fame that he desired. A return to Jamaica had never been seriously contemplated, but a return to the United States would most likely see his work as a party organiser, and magazine editor, intensify. Penniless, but determined to establish himself as a man of letters, McKay travelled from Russia to Germany, and then on to France. Between 1923 and 1934 he experienced great financial difficulty as he wandered in Europe and North Africa, but in terms of literature these were productive years in which he wrote the three novels that would cement his reputation. *Home to Harlem* (1928) was a popular success, but its uncensored portrayal of the seedier side of Harlem nightlife offended some of the more established African American critics, who felt that the novel crudely stereotyped the pretensions of the Negro middle classes while promoting the virtues of the common folk. W.E.B. Du Bois wrote that the novel only appealed to the 'prurient demand[s]' of white readers and publishers looking for portrayals of black 'licentiousness'. He went on: '*Home to Harlem* . . . for the most part nauseates me, and after the dirtier parts of its filth I feel distinctly like taking a bath.' But it was Langston Hughes who summed up the feeling of the younger set when he wrote, 'Undoubtedly, it is the finest thing we've done yet . . . Your novel ought to give a second youth to the Negro vogue . . . Everyone's talking about the book, and even those who dislike it say it's well written.'

Even before *Home to Harlem* was published, McKay had begun to plan his second novel *Banjo* (1929). A few months after leaving Moscow, he had travelled from Paris to Marseilles and found casual work among the dockers at this great European port which, like Hamburg or London or Cardiff, was considered by many to be a problematic gateway of racial and ethnic impurity. In Marseilles, McKay socialised with African, West Indian and African American drifters, all of whom were seeking a temporary shelter. The kinetic instability of their lives provided McKay with a perfect mirror in which he saw reflected the precarious nature of his own existence. McKay took as a central character an expatriate African American musician named Lincoln Agrippa Daily – 'a great vagabond of lowly life' – who was popularly known as Banjo because of his instrument of choice. Around this character he constructed a picaresque novel which he subtitled 'A Story Without Plot'. By chronicling Banjo's season of adventure and misadventure, and his exploits among the high and low, and black and white, in the hybrid turmoil of Marseilles's underworld of prostitution and criminality, McKay discovered a form that allowed him to share with his readers his thoughts on issues relating to race and politics during those turbulent interwar years.

Claude McKay was no stranger to offending people's sensibilities, and in *Banjo* he continued to be forthright. For instance, on interracial marriage. 'The successful Negro in Europe always marries a white woman, and I have noticed in almost every case that it is a white woman inferior to himself in brains and physique. The energy of such a Negro is lost to his race and goes to build up some decaying white family.' Or on the type of 'Negro' who might be described, behind closed doors or in a whispered voice, as an 'Uncle Tom'. 'You're a lost crowd, you educated Negroes, and you will only find yourself in the roots of your own people. You can't choose as your models the haughty-minded educated white youths of a society living solid on its imperial conquests. Such pampered youths can afford to despise the sweating white brutes of the lower orders.' Or in his description of Germany in the 1920s, a country that McKay had spent a fair amount of time in. 'Yet I never liked Germany. It was a country too highly organised for my temperament.

I felt something American about it, but without the dynamic confusion of America.'

On its publication, *Banjo* received a storm of negative criticism. Aubrey Bowser, in the black newspaper, the New York *Amsterdam News*, summed up the opinion of a great number of the African American establishment when he bluntly stated, 'He knows he is slurring his own people to please white readers.' However, there were others who realised that the diasporan novel had been born. Here was a man who originated in Jamaica, who was educated in a British tradition in the Caribbean and who had also studied in the United States; he had travelled all over Europe, and he was writing about these many different worlds using the cosmopolitan locale of Marseilles as a focal point. Like the former slave and abolitionist turned writer, Olaudah Equiano who, over a century earlier, had published *The Interesting Narrative of the Life of Olaudah Equiano, or Gustavus Vassa the African, Written by Himself,* McKay could best be summed up as a black man who seemed to hail from everywhere. In late 1929, a French translation of *Banjo* was published and was immediately championed by French colonial subjects for its courage in laying bare the duplicity of France's attitude to her colonial territories and peoples. The Martiniquan writer, Aimé Césaire, remembered: 'What struck me in this book is that for the first time Negroes were described truthfully, without inhibition or prejudice.' In fact, in contrast to the furore which greeted its American publication, a whole generation of French-speaking black writers, including Léopold Senghor, Léon Damas and Joseph Zobel, all paid tribute to the importance of the pan-African, diasporan vision and energy of *Banjo*.

McKay published a third novel, *Banana Bottom* (1933), which tells the story of a young woman who, having been schooled in England, returns to Jamaica and finds it impossible to reconcile the values and aesthetics of her English education with the reality of her feelings as a native Jamaican. McKay attempted to live and write in Morocco as well as Europe, but in 1934, after just over a decade of exile from the United States, his desperate financial situation forced him to return to New York and seek employment. He found a position with the Federal Writers' Project, which enabled him to complete and publish his autobiography, the appropriately named *A Long Way from Home* (1937), but although the remaining years of his life saw him produce the occasional essay, and a nonfiction work *Harlem: Negro Metropolis* (1940), his final decade was plagued by increasing difficulties with both his health and money.

At the time of his death, Claude McKay was probably best known for the poem, 'If We Must Die', which Winston Churchill quoted during the Second World War as a rallying cry against the Nazis. It is highly unlikely that the British Prime Minister knew that the author of the poem was a black Jamaican, or that McKay's poem was written and published in 1919 as a response to the Red Summer of race riots that took place throughout the urban centres of the United States. The poem begins:

> If we must die, let it not be like hogs
> Hunted and penned in an inglorious spot,
> While round us bark the mad and hungry dogs,
> Making their mock at our accursed lot.

'If We Must Die' is generally regarded as the clarion call of the movement that became known as the Harlem Renaissance, which places McKay at the head of an African American tradition in which post-First World War anger and frustration is laid bare, while Harlem is celebrated as the meeting place of creative souls from all corners of the diasporan world.

In the years since McKay's death in 1948, his reputation as a writer has grown considerably. In the Caribbean, his pioneering use of dialect, and his belief in the authenticity of a specifically Caribbean culture, have been built upon by writers as diverse as Louise Bennett and Derek Walcott. His work as a literary essayist with decidedly leftist leanings leads us directly to C.L.R. James, Frantz Fanon, George Padmore and Richard Wright. But it is his transatlantic, border-crossing sensibility, and his transgressive ability to rise up above labels and categories, that constitute his real legacy. This compulsively itinerant man is a true pioneer of literary transnationalism, and it is easy to see modern writers such as V.S. Naipaul, Salman Rushdie and Michael Ondaatje as his heirs, writers for whom the national label is unhelpful if we wish to see the full nature of their achievement. McKay is a writer who understood that for a great number of twentieth-century people 'imaginary homelands' are often more real than the places they presently inhabit. Nowhere is this engagement with 'home' and longing, and belonging, more dynamically demonstrated than in his great 'French' novel, *Banjo*.

Beginners

Water (1993)

Water. To a large extent my life has been determined by a journey across water. An actual journey. Across the Atlantic Ocean. I cannot remember the journey that I am speaking of. In all likelihood it occurred some time in the eighteenth century. Seventeen hundred and something. I was captured and sold into the custody of an Englishman. A slave ship captain, acting on behalf of a company whose headquarters were probably located in Liverpool, or Bristol, or London. And, thereafter, I began my long-forgotten journey. Chained and manacled in the hold of a ship. No longer a son, or a brother. A husband or a father. I was simply an object of commerce who, upon my arrival in the Americas, would be once again sold, this time into a life of unrewarded labour. I am not complaining. These are just facts. But, mercifully, as I said, I cannot remember the journey.

Three years ago I finished a novel called *Cambridge*. And, having shepherded it through to publication, I entered that valley of self-doubt which casts a deep shadow across the life of any writer who has just finished a large piece of work. What to write about now? I had plenty of ideas. But who doesn't? Most people are brimming with ideas that might be the subject matter of a good book. But most people do not write books. What a writer hopes is that one of his or her many ideas might rise up above the welter of competing ideas and declare itself. It is the ability to sift purposefully through ideas, to cultivate the necessary patience to wait for the one special idea and thereafter to pursue the idea with dogged determination that makes a writer different from the person who simply possesses ideas for a book.

A Yorkshire village during the Second World War. An English woman in her twenties is running the local shop. The American GIs arrive in England, and some of them are billeted in her village. Not the familiar gum-chewing, Glenn Miller, 'say, buddy can you spare a dime' wholesome all-American boys. These are black American GIs. During the last war the American army was segregated. In many ways the Americans brought two armies to Britain in 1942. One black, one white. The idea of an English woman in a village whose life is changed by the arrival of black American GIs had first occurred to me in the mid-eighties when I had conceived of it as a potential film. Three years ago, the idea declared itself again, this time more forcefully.

James Baldwin once began an answer to a question with the phrase: 'A funny thing happened on the way to the typewriter.' In my case two things happened on the way to the typewriter. First, it struck me that many English people's attitudes to race had, in all probability, been conditioned by this first encounter with black people during the last war. Particularly so as the majority of black American troops were stationed in East Anglia, Somerset, Devon, Yorkshire — parts of England that were removed from large urban centres, rural places in which many English people had probably never seen a black person before. The second realisation I stumbled upon was that the black American troops who returned to the United States after the war were part of the generation who began the Civil Rights Movement. In the main they had been treated with decency by the English people among whom they had lived, a decency which their fellow white soldiers had not extended to them. They returned home a different people, a people now fired with a determination to change the United States.

Novels are about characters. And at this stage I had only one character in mind. An English woman in her twenties, working in a village shop. Well, maybe two characters as I, or rather she, had already decided that she would fall in love with an American soldier. However, I now wanted to say something about the new ideas which had occurred to me on the way to the typewriter.

Either I would have to artificially open up the world of my young woman and her soldier and lead them by the nose down corridors and into conversations they would, in all likelihood, never have had, or I would have to cantilever the whole frame and structure of the novel in the direction of something which could hold both her and her soldier, and other people, new people, who might more honestly and naturally lend voice to the connections I was now making in my mind.

A young black man, a freed slave in nineteenth-century America, is sent back to Africa, to Liberia, as a Christian missionary. A black woman in the late-nineteenth-century American Wild West searches for her daughter. A twenty-six-year-old English slave ship captain is torn between the object of his passion, a young woman he has left behind in England, and the harsh brutality of his day-to-day life on the ship. A guilt-ridden father who has sold his children into slavery tries to talk to them across the years. And, of course, an English woman, who runs a shop in an English village during the Second World War, falls in love with an American soldier. All of these parts together make up my novel, *Crossing the River*.

Three years ago an idea declared itself. The idea became an obsession. I found two characters. But there were still more questions, which in turn led to a realisation that my village woman and her soldier could not, by themselves, bear the burden of all the issues that were now presenting themselves. Which led to a radical redevelopment of the form, and the problem of how to hold this rainbow coalition of people together.

Water. My life has been determined by a journey across water. Across the Atlantic Ocean. It was the people of the west coast of Africa who, looking out at the vastness of the ocean, first thought of it as a mighty river. Their journey — my journey — our journey, for if some were below, then others were on deck — our journey, back then in seventeen hundred and something, has changed for ever the nature of both British and American society. If I learned anything writing this novel, I certainly learned that. At the beginning, I said that I could not remember the journey across the Atlantic. Any more than I suspect you can. But trust me. It happened. It was not pleasant for anybody, but no matter. The fact is the journey is rooted deeply in my soul. And in your soul too. Water. Ribbons of water which ineluctably bind us together, one to the other.

Blood (1997)

In January of this year I found myself sitting in a hotel room in Bangkok working on a new novel. With the composition of each new novel I have become more aware of a pattern of work which repeats itself. It goes something like this: I have an idea. Which becomes an obsession. I begin to collect material. I am a detective. I search libraries for information. I photocopy material and I buy expensive books. I watch films. I make notes. And then, after perhaps eight to ten weeks, I realise that the obsession will not carry me much further than two dozen pages. And so I wait, for another obsession. And at last there is another flurry of activity, more note-making, and then the same sad conclusion. After two to three years of this behaviour, I suddenly find that I have enough writing to constitute a novel, the only problem being that the various parts are not stitched together in any coherent way.

Bangkok is not Europe. I like writing in Bangkok because it is highly unlikely that anything will happen on the street or in the hotel that will interfere with my line of thought. If I were to try this same exercise in Europe something would happen every day which would impinge upon my concentration, and perhaps eventually spill over and affect the book. I can write in Europe, but my writing is always in danger from my environment. This is not the case in Bangkok. Both culturally and physically, I have no connection to the country, or the people. I am a foreigner in the most radical sense, and this sense of alienation frees me to concentrate on my work.

However, earlier this year in Bangkok, I was temporarily undone.

The novel I was working on is about Europe. It is a novel about the Holocaust. But not just this. The primary obsession was the Holocaust, which is – at least in my mind – related to my secondary obsession: race and faith as seen through the prism of sixteenth-century Venice. Othello's Venice; Shylock's Venice. To write this book I needed to be in Bangkok. I needed to be far away from Europe. At first the writing appeared to be flowing, if not freely, then at least purposefully towards a conclusion. But there was a final piece to the puzzle that was clearly missing, and I could not identify where or, more importantly, when I might find it. And then one Bangkok morning I opened the *International Herald Tribune* and read the story of what had been occurring in Israel with the Ethiopian Jews, and I knew that these days, short of going to a desert island, my writing was always likely to be in danger from my environment.

According to the *International Herald Tribune* black Jews in Israel had been giving blood in the hope that it might be used to save somebody's life. However, the Israeli government, fearful of 'diseases' that might be contained in this blood, had instructed the medical teams to dump the 'black' blood. This 'secret' practice had now been exposed, and the black Jews were rioting and demanding that this racist policy be stopped. I could barely believe what I was reading. This, it turned out, was the story that would enable me to put the final piece of the narrative puzzle into place and finish my novel. I called my research assistant in the United States and asked her to immediately begin researching the background details to this story.

The novel is, both directly and indirectly, about blood. About Europe's obsession with homogeneity, and her inability to deal with the heterogeneity that is – in fact – her natural condition. The practice of using blood as a barometer of acceptability is very deeply ingrained in the European consciousness, and long before the present generation of non-white immigrants began to suffer because of this failure of European imagination, there were others – 'white', if you will – who had been identified as 'impure' and 'less' who suffered too. In other words, wherever one looks in European history, blood has been used as a pretext for the persecution of those whose faces do not fit on the canvas upon which the national portrait has been painted.

When I was fourteen I was very concerned with history. And, of course, the history we studied at school was European history. Colonial history was not taught. I like to think that even the teachers saw that in an increasingly multiracial Britain it might have been a little awkward, to say nothing of hypocritical, to continue to preach the glories of the Empire to a classroom peppered with brown and black faces. Whether this occurred to the teachers or not, I do not know. I do, however, know that European history still affords Britain great opportunities for gloating and sneering at the 'losers' across the Channel because, as everybody knows, Britain won both world wars.

One day I came home from school and, having finished my homework, I settled down to watch a television series called *The World at War*. This particular week the episode dealt with the Holocaust. I have a vague recollection of some footage of Dutch Jews in Amsterdam, and it is certainly possible that reference was made to Anne Frank. But my overwhelming response to the programme was shock. Utter, numbing shock. This did not make any sense. These were white people who were systematically rounding up and killing other white people. I could not understand it. Within the next few days I had written my first short story.

The story concerned a young Dutch boy. His parents informed him that he had to wear a Star of David on his coat. This was now the law. Naturally the boy was intensely upset to learn of this new decree, and saw no reason why he should obey. He was, after all, just the same as all the other boys. His parents tried to explain that it was not a mark to be ashamed of, and he should wear the star with pride. Reluctantly the young Dutch boy agreed. Soon after, while the boy and his parents were being transported to a camp in a cattle truck, the boy managed to prise open a small gap in the wall of the boxcar and leap from the speeding train. Unfortunately he struck his head on a rock as he fell, and knocked himself unconscious. Bleeding heavily, he was in danger of haemorrhaging to death. Luckily a farmer, who was out working in his fields, happened to see the sun catch his yellow Star of David. He found the boy, bandaged his head, and nursed him back to health. The boy survived.

The Dutch boy was, of course, me. A fourteen-year-old black boy in working-class Yorkshire in the North of England. I knew I was different from the other kids. I was reminded of it every day by the stares in the street, by the way in which shopkeepers dropped my change on to the counter rather than putting it into my hand, by the way in which I could suddenly find myself ostracised by people I had hitherto considered to be my friends. The last thing I wanted was to be reminded that I was different. I knew it, but I did not want to worry about it for I knew Britain did not celebrate, let alone encourage, difference. This was not the British way. As I watched the programme that evening, I became aware that around these issues of difference and visibility things could go horribly, horribly wrong.

Almost twenty-five years later I found myself sitting in a hotel room in Bangkok reading about the racism of Israeli Jews towards their own black people, a racism based solely upon visibility and difference. I was reminded again of how appallingly circular history can be, how replete with ironies, how chilling. I had, in the course of my research for this novel, visited Israel during the summer of 1995, and had clearly seen the problems which faced people who were visibly the 'other'. Blood. Always blood. Who are you? You are not us. Therefore we define ourselves, in part, by defining you. Questions that relate to blood can transcend national boundaries with laughable ease. After all, Hitler was not simply concerned with German Jews, and the black Jews, whose blood was officially dashed to the earth, were Israelis.

I left Bangkok with a reasonably coherent draft of the novel, and returned to London. I knew what the next step would be. Two weeks in which I would attempt to polish the prose, clean up the narrative line, and revise the choice of adjectives. Pedantic, painful work, but there was only one place I had in mind for this task. I needed to go to a city where my sense of security about what I had written would be vigorously challenged in the most radical and unnerving manner. In Bangkok I sought peace from the world. Now I actively needed my writing to be in danger from my environment. On 13 March, my thirty-eighth birthday, I flew from London to Amsterdam with my manuscript, my laptop computer and a portable printer.

Amsterdam was the location of my first story. I work with a large poster of Anne Frank above my desk. She has been with me for years. In fact, she is looking down at me right now. In Amsterdam I spent most days working in my hotel room, venturing out only to walk around the park in the misty rain, and then scampering back to my room to continue working. The room service guys, primarily Surinamese and Arubans, were puzzled by what the 'brother' was doing. I over-tipped in a panic-stricken attempt to staunch the flow of their questions. And then, after almost two weeks, I wandered out of the hotel and in the direction of the place that I knew I would have to revisit.

The Anne Frank House is becoming increasingly humbling and even more moving as the lines of people queuing outside get longer, and the crowds inside ever denser. I first visited fifteen years ago, and I remember being puzzled by the geographical relationship of the secret annexe to the house. Perhaps I wasn't really puzzled and this was just some elaborate way of avoiding the emotional train that I was sure was about to run me down. This time, as I walked around the house, the emotional train ran me down, yet it left me feeling strangely serene. Stronger, even. I left the Anne Frank House and went next door to the Rum Runners Caribbean bar and restaurant. I ordered a beer and sat on a stool and simply looked around. Next to Anne Frank's house there is now an establishment that is a monument to difference and otherness. And both serving and being served there are faces of all colors, races and ethnicities. Did this constitute progress? Was Europe finally beginning to deal with 'difference'? And why the serene feeling in Anne Frank's house?

Sitting in the Rum Runners bar, I thought about blood. No. No, Europe is not finally beginning to deal with 'difference'. The Netherlands tolerated 'difference' back in the 1930s, which is why Otto Frank removed his family from Germany and settled in Amsterdam. But it did not help them. And today? I know it would only take one madman somewhere in Europe to trigger a chain of events that would leave Rum Runners a charred heap of rubble. Then why the serenity? To understand this I had to turn my mind back twenty-five years.

My response to seeing the *World at War* documentary was to write. A private, annealing act. Writing helps to build a bridge across the space between one's own private world and the external world in which we all have to continue to live. In the Anne Frank House there was a moment of peace, for I knew that I had finally understood something. And sitting in the warm Caribbean bar on a damp Amsterdam afternoon, I felt grateful that I had undertaken the fragmented, obsessional task of writing about 'the nature of blood'. Doing so had enabled me to achieve a moment of temporary reconciliation with the young Dutch boy of my story of twenty-five years ago, and I also felt that I had repaid a small part of the personal debt that I owed to the remarkable young girl who used to live next door to Rum Runners bar and restaurant. If I could define what it was that I finally understood, or why exactly I felt serene, then I would not be a writer. A large part of being a writer does, after all, involve one's own acceptance of the fact that the journey is intuitive, the destination often a mystery. All I knew was that a particular journey had finally come to an end on a damp Saturday afternoon in Amsterdam, almost a quarter of a century after I had first watched 'that' episode of *The World at War*, and I was grateful.

Fire (2000)

1. *Why I write fiction*

In her essay 'Professions for Women' (1931), Virginia Woolf talks about the necessity of killing what she terms 'the Angel in the House' before a woman can begin to write. She describes the soon-to-be-murdered 'Angel' in the following manner: 'She was intensely sympathetic. She was immensely charming. She was utterly unselfish. She excelled in the difficult arts of family life. She sacrificed herself daily.' Eventually Virginia Woolf defeats 'the Angel', although she confesses that 'she died hard', partly because 'she was always creeping back when I thought I had dispatched her'.

It seems to me that every writer has to begin by slaying a phantom of some kind. In my case I had to struggle with a phantom named 'Caution'. When, aged twenty-one, I declared that I wanted to be a writer, I was made aware of a number of facts. First, I was an immigrant. Second, I was a graduate of an important university. Third, I was the eldest of four. In other words, I had to be grateful for whatever success had already come my way and I had to set a good example for those who would follow. I was expected to be cautious. However, it is impossible to embark 'cautiously' upon the journey of becoming a writer. Immigrant, graduate, eldest son; it mattered little me how others wished to define me, for I had every intention of kicking 'Caution' into touch and getting on with the business of becoming a writer.

Why do I write? This is a question with which I am familiar.

How do I write? is a far trickier question and one which I will come to in a moment. But first, why do I write? Having dealt with the phantom of 'Caution', I found this question being put to me in a variety of forms by, among others, journalists, bank managers and anxious girlfriends. Why? What's the point? Mercifully, somebody else had already produced the perfect answer. George Orwell identified 'four great motives': sheer egoism, aesthetic enthusiasm, historical impulse and political purpose. He also suggested the following:

> All writers are vain, selfish and lazy, and at the very bottom of their motives there lies a mystery. Writing a book is a horrible, exhausting struggle, like a long bout of some painful illness. One would never undertake such a thing if one were not driven on by some demon whom one can neither resist nor understand. For all one knows that demon is simply the same instinct that makes a baby squall for attention.

He might well be right. But enough of this. The subject before us is, 'How do I write?' As I suggested, a far trickier question.

2. On Breaching The Security System

Where to begin? Most of the time the last thing I need is an 'idea' for a novel. Usually I am already working on a project, and if another idea begins to scale the security fence that I've constructed around my present task, and demands to be taken seriously, I regard it as an unwelcome intrusion. Sadly, from time to time the security system will be breached and on such occasions, irrespective of what I may currently be dealing with, I have to pay attention.

It may simply be a phrase that enters my mind, and for some reason the phrase begins to suggest a book. This happened in the case of my first novel, *The Final Passage*. The notion of 'the Middle Passage', the journey on the slave ships which took countless millions from Africa across the Atlantic Ocean to the

Americas had, understandably enough, always haunted me. Twentieth-century migration from the Caribbean to Britain involved a reverse crossing of the wide expanse of the Atlantic, and this seemed to me to suggest a 'final passage' of some kind. This phrase became lodged in the forefront of my mind and refused to retreat to a convenient corner.

On other occasions I have 'found' the idea for a book while rummaging around in the library. This happened to me with the novel *Cambridge*. I was sitting in the British Library when I decided to look up eighteenth- and nineteenth-century references to St Kitts, in the hope that I might unearth material which would enable me to unravel the mystery surrounding the history of an old plantation house on the island. At last I did find references to this now abandoned house. I realised that I wanted to embark upon the task of reconstructing the proud colonial history of this house which was once known throughout the Caribbean islands as a place of unparalleled grandeur.

With both *The Final Passage* and *Cambridge*, the idea for the novels interrupted other work that I was engaged upon. However, I did not stop working on my other projects, I simply logged the fact that an idea had shown up and it would eventually have to be dealt with. In the case of *The Nature of Blood*, I *did* stop working on my other projects for a few weeks. This was due in part to the strange manner in which the idea presented itself. One day I suddenly found myself writing down the following words, with no understanding of where they were coming from. This time, the security system was not so much breached as disengaged, dismantled, and packed away for a while.

> Between us a sheet-thin gauze of fire that a sudden gust
> might extinguish. But there is no wind. In the distance
> the low grinding of a river as it slithers across smooth,
> warm stones. Night sits easily on our shoulders.
> The scene is familiar.
> Why you insist on speaking with me, I do not know.

Through the fire
Why you seem prepared to trust me with your story,
I do not know.
Through the fire
As ever you stand before me, your eyes bright, your
arms outstretched, your palms upturned. You watch me.
I imagine you have been with me my whole life.
Watching. And waiting.
Through the fire
Many years have passed since I first discovered you. You
troubled me then. You trouble me now. But mortality,
like thunder, rumbles its dull way toward me.
It is I who must take the step.
Through the fire
And come unto you.

3. Are you going to read all of those books?

Having stumbled across an idea (soon to become an obsession)
which I intuitively feel will become a novel, I then begin to
think seriously about how I might further acquaint myself with
the subject. This involves research. For instance, in the case of
The Nature of Blood, I was reasonably sure that the novel was going
to be principally concerned with the Holocaust, but armed only
with a general knowledge of the subject I felt that I had to
become more familiar with the history. This proved to be no
easy task for the number of books, films and other materials
on this subject is quite overwhelming. For some reason I decided
to catalogue just how many books and films I read and watched
during the three-year period in which I was 'researching', and
the number was a little excessive. In retrospect I am not sure
that all of this research was strictly necessary, but at the time
it felt as though it was a process that I had to pass through.

Research is for me deeply tied up with two things. First, and
most obvious, a desire to immerse myself in the subject matter

in order that the imaginative act that is to come might be more substantially grounded in 'fact'. This seems to me very important when one is dealing with 'sensitive' material such as the Holocaust, or the African slave trade. There is a great desire on my part to simply get it as 'right' as possible. Not only for reasons of factual accuracy. There exists a group of people known as 'revisionist' historians who would seek to convince the world that such events did not happen or that, if they did happen, the 'facts' as we know them have been greatly exaggerated.

Second, and just as important, the act of research also involves my remaining alert to the possibility that some character, or characters, will emerge out of the many hours of research, and present themselves as the people who will eventually 'drive' the narrative. I am not a novelist in the postmodern tradition who makes himself visible to the reader and orchestrates the narrative from the centre of the stage. I like to hide in the wings and turn the stage over to my characters. An occasional whispered prompt is all that I permit myself. Therefore, without characters all I have is an idea and an ever-growing pile of 'research'. I cannot build a novel out of this flimsy material. I need people. And patience.

4. Strangers and other unusual guests who show up to the party

So, there's a party going on. But either no people, or the wrong people, have shown up. The party is in trouble. Having recognised the problem the anxiety-racked writer will naturally enough ask himself, when are the right people going to show up? Who knows? I spend much of my time in this 'gestation' period reassuring myself that I have the right music, the right drinks, the right food, and that in the end everything will be fine. But when? Meanwhile, I simply wait for the uninvited guests to leave and the *real* characters to show themselves. The hero of Thomas Mann's short novel *Tonio Kröger* was peering at these welcome, but elusive, characters when he observed the following: 'As I write, the sea whispers to me and I close my eyes. I am looking into a world unborn and formless, that needs to be ordered and shaped; I see a whirl of shadows of human figures who beckon me to weave spells to redeem them: tragic and laughable figures and some that are both together – and to these I am drawn.' If he is lucky, the writer may find himself drawn to certain characters and, like Thomas Mann's hero, he may even be able to see them as shadows; but will they show up to the party, sit down, and take part? Or will the uninvited guests continue to dominate the scene?

It is the quality of the guest list which largely distinguishes literary fiction from pulp fiction. Two-dimensional, flat characters – a type that we know from situation comedies, romances and thrillers – are easy to locate. Writers who utilise such people are generally able to produce at a prodigious rate, for everybody who turns up is invited to sit down and put on a funny hat. The literary novelist has to learn to distinguish between the important guest and the gauche gate-crasher. This is no easy task, and for young writers eager to get their careers off to a flying start, the cultivation of patience and the exercising of vigilance cause them no end of heartache and frustration.

5. How long will you be staying with us, sir?

Perhaps I have spent too long working on films and television scripts, but I always find myself describing the next two stages as pre-production and production. Pre-production lasts anywhere from four to eight weeks, and involves sorting out my files, reordering the research, writing whenever the mood takes me, and trying out the narrative voice or voices. This stage begins only when I am sure that I have located my characters, and it ends when I am 'pregnant'. In other words, when I cannot hang on any longer and I have to start writing in earnest. At this point – the onset of production – I invariably have to go away somewhere.

I like to write in hotels. I love the control that I have over the space. The 'Do Not Disturb' sign that I can hang up whenever I please. The towels in the bathroom that are replaced every day. Somebody to come in and change the bed linen and make up the bed. The phone that I can pick up and order food or drink. Outside is the city, preferably one that I'm already somewhat familiar with. A city that I can step into and go for a walk, or go to the movies, safe in the knowledge that I am unlikely to see anybody that I know. Then back to the hotel. If I want to work through the night I can. Or, time zones being what they are, I can simply call whomever I please in some far-flung part of the globe and say 'Hi, how are you doing?' Or alternatively, I can just ignore everybody and get on with whatever I am doing. Nobody knows where I am. Nobody can get hold of me.

I usually last about two to four weeks in a hotel, then I go back 'home' for a few weeks. Time to answer mail, sort out my life, catch up with whatever has been going on in my absence. It is true to say that I generally need a break from the work. Eight to ten hours a day, seven days a week, is a lot of writing and rewriting. A lot of concentration. However, after some time at 'home', I will once more leave, this time for a different hotel, in a different city, in a different country. And the process repeats itself. Two, three times. Maybe more.

Production lasts, for me, about six months. This may seem like a short time, but research, gestation and pre-production have taken anything from two to three years. The final six months is the hardest period, but if the rest of the work has been carried out properly, it is the most rewarding. The foundations of research have been established, I am sure about the characters, and they are now surprising me and twisting and turning the plot in unexpected directions. When I start to replace punctuation that only an hour previously I had removed, then I know I am closing in on the end. And when I finally realise that I am mentally and physically too exhausted to improve the manuscript any further, then that is the end.

6. *Still kicking 'Caution' into touch or, How I've started to get fancy in my middle years*

Computers: I came to these things relatively late. I wrote my first three novels in longhand and typed them up on a manual typewriter. In 1990 I paid a secretary to put the final drafts of my fourth novel *Cambridge* on to something called a disk. This turned out to be a smart move because it meant that I could make all the minor changes quickly and not have to bother with typing up the whole thing again. After the experience with *Cambridge*, I detected some virtue in this computer-gadget and so I decided that I should learn how to use one. I didn't. I engaged a research assistant for my next novel, *Crossing the River*, and she certainly knew about computers. My ignorance of, and admiration for, the gadget continued until 1993. It was only after the publication of *Crossing the River* that I bought a laptop, and enrolled on a computer course at a community college in Massachusetts. I had arrived: I was computer-literate, although I still write longhand and then transfer it on to the computer.

Assistants: To start with I did everything. I was broke, I had no choice. But then as the research started to get a little more complex I realised that I could save both time and energy if I put my hand in my pocket. Having somebody trustworthy to delve in libraries, deal with the intricacies of inter-library loan, do xeroxing, and find answers to questions of a factual nature is a blessing that I am grateful for. It is true to say that I could do most of it myself, but if I find myself sitting in a hotel room on the other side of the world, and I need some information immediately, it helps to have a capable and efficient person at the end of the phone. Also, writing is a lonely enough job as it is, and I confess to liking the teamwork involved in working with somebody else.

Hotels: To start with I would stay anywhere. In fact, during the writing of *The Final Passage* I slept in a rented Renault hatchback on a variety of beaches in Tenerife. I simply did not have the money for both a rental car and a hotel. After a while I traded in the car for a desk and bed, and I finished the novel in a Spanish 'flea-pit' that was masquerading as a hotel. A decade or so later I wrote *The Nature of Blood* while staying at more comfortable hotels in Toronto, Bangkok and Amsterdam. I now work on the basis that the fancier the hotel the quicker I will write. After all, the hotel bills will arrive before the advance for the book. I have to keep the gap between the two as short as possible. Twice I have turned up at hotels that have been perfectly acceptable, but I have shown up with *only* ideas and a little research, but no characters. Once in Spain in 1988 and once again in Cuba in 1993. I quickly learned that hotels are zones for production, not gestation. They are too expensive for mere head-scratching.

7. Waiting for a bus

You see, in the end it all boils down to this. Trying to write a novel is like waiting for a bus in the rain. A number of buses appear and pull up at the stop, but you have to know which is the one that you should climb aboard. In other words, which is the one that contains the *necessary* idea that will become an obsession. Once on board there is more waiting. A little anxiety as you flick open your research texts and begin to read and gather material. A little worry about paying for the ticket. Concern about how long this journey is going to take. Yet more anxiety as you look around at the other passengers and begin to wonder which one of them (if any) is 'it': a viable character. Finally somebody gets on board the bus and your eyes meet. You recognise the person and they recognise you. You gather up your texts and you stand before the person. They too stand, and one of you reaches up and sounds the bell. Together you step from the bus, and the two of you find yourselves alone on the pavement. You are clutching your research materials. You watch the bus trundle away into the distance and around the corner. You were on the right bus. You did your research. You waited patiently for the right character to appear. Now, as the bus passes out of sight, you are ready. But it is still raining.

Outside In

Belonging to Israel (2002)

I remember finding shelter some years ago beneath a flimsy tarpaulin tent on the outskirts of the town of Dimona in the Negev desert. My host was an African American from Washington, DC who, twenty years earlier, had uprooted himself from his New World 'exile' and 'returned' to Israel, the land that he imagined to be his historical place of origin. He had left behind a relatively comfortable life on the lower slopes of congressional politics and remade himself as a new man, which involved changing his name and his garb. My host, and the like-minded members of his exiled community, were clearly striving to make an economic and cultural contribution to the life of Israel, although the Israeli government were at best ambivalent, at worst hostile, to these 'returnees' who, despite their protestations of 'belonging', were not strictly classifiable as Jews.

My host gestured to the dusty, uninspiring landscape all around us and remarked on its beauty. To my eyes there was nothing attractive about the dustbowl that we were marooned in, and to undergo much hardship in order to migrate to such a place struck me as somewhat surprising. As far as he was concerned, the land could have been jungle, prairie or mountaintop: its topography mattered little, for its 'beauty' was more emblematic than physical. A 'return' to this land had given him the opportunity to close a historical circle and make himself 'whole'. Viewed through a diasporan lens, the land was not only beautiful, it was 'home'.

Hillel Halkin, an accomplished essayist on literary, cultural and political issues, and an admired translator of Hebrew and

Yiddish literature, is familiar with the multiple ironies and difficulties that surround a search for home. Born in New York City
in 1939, Halkin migrated to Israel three decades later as a
committed Zionist. He has subsequently served in the Israeli
army reserve, raised a family, and produced a distinguished body
of work, the vast majority of which speaks to a deep personal
and professional allegiance to his new country. Halkin's adult
passage from the Upper West Side of Manhattan to Israel has
greatly affected his subsequent writing. Sometimes it is the echo
of Halkin's own migratory feet that stirs him to write, as in
Letters to an American Jewish Friend: A Zionist's Polemic (1977), a series
of six carefully crafted letters that attempt to give form and
substance to Halkin's Zionist beliefs. More recently we find
Halkin listening across a thousand years of history as Shmuel
Hanagid, an eleventh-century Sephardic poet and Renaissance
man, arrives in Granada. Halkin's translations of Shmuel's verse
autobiography, *Grand Things to Write a Poem On: A Verse Autobiography
of Shmuel Hanagid*, have both fluency and passion. Yet it is Halkin's
desire to grapple with the complex issues of belonging and
membership that extend his political and literary meditations
beyond straightforward questions of migration into the deeper
mysteries of identity.

Halkin's impressive new book, *Across the Sabbath River: In Search
of a Lost Tribe of Israel*, finds him journeying out in search of the
truth behind the mystery of the Ten Lost Tribes of Israel, who
were driven out of their homeland by Assyrian conquerors and
have never been heard from since. The fate of this deported
and apparently vanished Jewish population has long fascinated
both Jews and Christians. Countless theories, some claiming to
be 'scientific', others admittedly speculative, the vast majority
of them highly implausible, have been put forward to account
for the approximately 27,000 people who 'disappeared'. On the
face of it, the loss of such a relatively small number of individuals might be considered to be of little consequence, certainly
by the cruel standard of modern wars and displacement; but
the subsequent diasporan wandering of the Jewish people, and

the fact that the 'loss' is included in biblical lore, has lent an almost feverish passion to the wish to understand what became of these original victims of exile.

If Halkin is the latest in a long line of those who have sought to solve this mystery, then we will undoubtedly better understand his quest if we know something about the Lost Tribes 'hunters' who preceded him. In the eighth century BCE the Assyrians overran and conquered both the northern kingdom of Israel and the southern kingdom of Judah in biblical Palestine. In the wake of their conquest the Assyrians deported many tribes of Israelites to different regions of Assyria, but the Bible says nothing about where they went, or what happened to them. Their eventual return was repeatedly predicted by the Hebrew prophets as being symbolic of God's future reconciliation with his chosen people. Jeremiah vividly imagined this final, blessed day:

'Behold, I will bring them from the north country, and gather them from the coasts of the earth, and with them the blind and the lame, the woman with child and her that travaileth with child together: a great company shall return thither . . . Hear the word of the Lord, O ye nations, and declare it in the isles afar off, and say, He that scattered Israel will gather him, and keep him, as a shepherd doth his flock.'

Across the years there have been numerous predictions about the imminent return of the Lost Tribes, including specific dates on which they were expected to arrive.

But still the Tribes have remained irredeemably 'lost' – somewhere beyond a great 'Sabbath River' which, according to the Roman historian Pliny the Elder, flows for six days a week and then, like the Jews, rests on the seventh day. Had a strange man who called himself Eldad the Danite not turned up in what is now Tunisia in or about 883 CE, the idea of the Lost Tribes might not have taken on its present-day significance. This man spoke a strange and ancient Hebrew, and he rekindled interest in the Lost Tribes by telling the local Jews many amazing 'facts' about his – and their – history, including the 'fact' that he knew himself to be a descendant of the Lost Tribe of Dan. Three hundred years later, in the middle of the twelfth century, Benjamin ben Jonah, a Jewish trader and explorer, left a record that has come to be known as *The Travels of Benjamin of Tudela* in which he catalogued the presence of Jews in Europe and beyond, and 'reported' that tens of thousands of the descendants of the Tribes were living in Kurdistan and other places in Central Asia.

By the seventeenth century these 'sightings' were getting a little out of hand. The Dutch rabbi and writer Manasseh ben Israel claimed that the Lost Tribes had been found in the Americas. It was a view that remained surprisingly popular until the twentieth century: in 1931, for example, Walter Hart Blumenthal published *In Old America*, a chapter of which is entitled 'The Red Hand Symbol in Aboriginal America and in Primitive Palestine'. (An even stranger chapter is entitled 'Circumcision in Red America'.) The fact that Halkin does not include Blumenthal's book in his exhaustive bibliography – Halkin is a learned man, and in this chronicle of his Eastern adventure he deploys his learning usefully while wearing it lightly – reflects the sheer number of published texts that expound this and other half-baked theories. According to Halkin, 'scholars' have at one time or another claimed the Lost Tribes to be, in their modern incarnation, the Welsh, or Dutch, Danes, Zulus, New Zealand Maoris, or even Eskimos.

When faced with a history of such quackery, what on earth would persuade an intelligent man like Halkin to join this long and undistinguished tradition? Halkin made three separate expeditions as a 'Lost Tribes hunter'. The first journey he makes in the company of veteran 'Tribesman' Rabbi Eliahu Avichail. 'Scholars and academics considered him a crackpot,' Halkin scrupulously reports, but he is himself fascinated by this modest man's conviction, and he accompanies Avichail to China and Thailand on what turns out to be a futile, if at times fitfully amusing, search for 'evidence'. Despite Halkin's healthy respect for the elder man, Avichail's patent lack of curiosity in people or places, as opposed to his deep belief in the authority of books, eventually frustrates Halkin.

Mercifully, things improve when they press on to Aizawl, the capital of the Indian state of Mizoram. In this small territory that is squeezed between Bangladesh to the west and Burma to the east, a great number of the Indian population seem to identify passionately with Jewish practice and history, and with the country of Israel. The people have organised themselves into congregations, they have synagogues, and they have even petitioned the United Nations, albeit unsuccessfully, requesting that they be formally recognised as a separate people (the Mizos) who have descended from the Lost Tribes. It happens that Avichail has been instrumental in helping the Mizos come to terms with their desire to embrace Judaism – but he has not discovered enough 'evidence' to 'accept' them as a Lost Tribe. What would count as evidence for the rabbi is determined by the definitions of Jewish law, and Halkin is frustrated by Avichail's inflexible orthodoxy. He accuses his elder of 'turning Judaism into an exclusive club' by not bending the rules a little to accommodate these Mizo people. Earlier in the week Halkin had received a visit from a Mizo man who spoke with a 'sudden, hard candor'. 'I want to know who I am. Show me I was once a Christian, and I'll be a Christian. Show me I was a Jew, and I'll be a Jew. Show me I was an idol worshipper, and I'll worship idols. *But show me who I am.*' It is a deeply affecting moment. Halkin is a writer, not a religious authority, and the human cry for help is what he most remembers. And it is this humanity that in the end will bring him back to Aizawl, this time without Rabbi Avichail.

But he is not stirred by this human cry alone. There are surprising empirical discoveries that demand to be investigated. During his first visit in the company of Avichail, Halkin had noticed many linguistic and cultural coincidences between Judaic and Mizo practice that deeply puzzled him. 'There were only two ways to think about it,' he remarks. 'Either a Tibeto-Burmese people in a remote corner of Southeast Asia had a mysterious connection with ancient Israel, or they were the victims of a mass delusion. Either way, there was a story to be written.' He resolves to return to Mizoram, and to the neighbouring state of Manipur, with two translators, one for each state. With his book contract in hand, Halkin tries to probe the mystery of why a small number of people in this otherwise Christian pocket of the world not only believe – without any real evidence – that they are descended from the 'Lost' Jews, but harbour a powerful desire to 'return' to their native land.

Free now of the double 'burden' of Avichail's religiosity and the narrative task of explaining the background to the quest, Halkin's prose gathers pace and becomes agreeably quirky as humour and irony bubble to the surface. The author writes in his notebook: 'The ultimate proof the Mizos are Jews: a small and never civilized people, they think they are better than everyone.' He makes a heartfelt speech in a local synagogue that is meant to reassure the people of his good intention: 'I do not know who my distant forefathers were. My more recent ones lived in Russia. The color of my eyes and complexion tells me that they probably did not all descend from an ancient tribe of Israel. And there are many descendants of Jews in the world today who have nothing Jewish about them.' He is, unsurprisingly, met with blank stares. Who then is he? More to the point, they still want to know, who are they? Why will he not give them the answer to their question?

As time passes Halkin reluctantly admits that his search for the 'evidence' of a Mizo connection to the Lost Tribes seems to be failing. He seems almost relieved. Under Avichail's guidance, a small number of Mizos had actually resettled and were studying in Israel; and Halkin casts his mind back and recalls attending a Mizo wedding in Gaza. He ruefully remembers noticing the evidence of 'Israelification' among these transplanted Mizos and he wonders about the folly of Avichail encouraging such people to think of themselves as 'belonging'.

They were eager to try on their new identity, on which they had made a large down payment. They were heady with the ease of slipping into it – and it was this that gave me pause. Once more an old life had been abandoned like a village in the jungle. When all was said and done, Avichail was not much different from the missionaries ... one wondered whether the children and grandchildren of the young couple beneath the wedding canopy would have to search for their identity again.

Halkin is not a sentimentalist about identity. He understands how brutal 'authenticity' can be, and he writes with compassion about the difficulties that await people with a hunger for it.

As Halkin's search for 'evidence' stumbles, his mood is not improved by a local man's deliberate, if somewhat convoluted, attempt to cheat him out of money by faking 'evidence' of a Mizo–Israel connection. Although the rational part of Halkin's mind is by now aware that he might well be wasting his time, he continues to encounter individuals who convince him that his instincts are correct. There are too many puzzling 'facts' that cannot be explained as mere coincidence. It is too simple to dismiss these 'facts' as the result of mass autosuggestion. He travels to Imphal, the capital of the state of Manipur, where he encounters an old man who unequivocally tells him that he is 'of the tribe of Manasseh'. The man continues:

'We Kukis do not belong to this place,' he said of Manipur. 'We have been here for hundreds of years, yet it is not ours. Have you ever heard of an entire people feeling out of place where their ancestors were born?'

Apart from the Jews, I confessed, I never had. 'There you are!' he said, vindicated. 'You see, we are not a happy people. We are always yearning.'

'Nostalgic.'

'Yes.'

'For someone else.'

'Exactly!' He was so happy that I understood.

But Halkin does not understand. He needs hard proof, and the absence of it is beginning to drive him to lethargy and despair. 'From the synagogue upstairs came the sound of the morning prayer. Too lazy to rise for it, I followed it from my bed.' Eventually he admits that his enquiries in both Mizoram and Manipur have reached their natural conclusion. 'There was nothing left for me to do in Imphal.' And then, as in all good dramas, just when we believe all is lost, that what seemed real was only imagined, the author makes the 'discovery' that leads to a breakthrough and prepares the way for the final act.

A local ethnographer named Dr Khuplam visits Halkin and shows him a manuscript. It is comprised of old chants, songs and tales that the doctor has spent thirty years putting together from material that he has collected from the old people in the hills. The manuscript astonishes Halkin, and he asks his readers not to 'prejudge the matter' that he is about to place before them. Halkin then unfolds his theory, based on the evidence of Khuplam's manuscript, as to why, having been previously filled with doubt, he is now convinced that the Mizo people are descended from the Lost Tribe of Manasseh.

What follows is a long and detailed chapter whose authority is bolstered both by the evidence of Khuplam and by discoveries that Halkin has been all the while making, but which have hitherto made little sense. Now almost everything makes sense to Halkin, and it is testimony to his superb grasp of storytelling that, as he makes his case, we not only listen to him, but we also want to believe him. At one point he uses the word 'suppose' ten times in the space of only two paragraphs, but he persuades us to accept this repetition as evidence of his painstaking process and caution, as opposed to the flimsiness of his argument. Halkin returns to Israel convinced of his theory, and then returns to India for a third time, specifically to see Dr Khuplam and other 'knowledgeable people' who might help him to further ground his ideas.

It is during this third and final visit that Halkin discovers that this obscure people 'in a little known corner of Southeast Asia had a holiday reminiscent of the biblical Passover' whose origin they did not comprehend. This discovery is made all the more remarkable by the fact that the Mizo are not bread eaters yet for some inexplicable reason know that they must sit down on this one day of the year and eat bread without yeast. When added to all the other discoveries, Halkin is now, as he tells the people, '107 per cent sure' of their origins as the Lost Tribe of Manasseh. In the passage that follows, which is as moving as it is scholarly and persuasive, Halkin addresses the people and gives to them their history. He is unsure about the chutzpah of his actions — 'A stranger who had spent only a few weeks among them, who didn't know their language, and had only a superficial knowledge of their culture, I was now expounding their own past to them' — but he justifies his presumption by relying on the authority of a 'Western education that enabled me to think about textual and historical problems in a way they were unaccustomed to'.

It is this same 'Western education' — fed as it is by the authority of books, and unmoved by the special appeals of the human heart — that, ironically enough after his admonitory words to Rabbi Avichail, now leads Halkin to fail the Mizo at the very moment when he is finally offering them hope. A local man asks the logical question of the Israeli who has proven to his own satisfaction that he has found descendants of ancient Jews: 'Will the government of Israel recognize us through the cooperation of your good self?' And his question is met with the following:

'All that matters,' I said, 'is who you are and want to be. You're not Jews. But you do go back, in one branch of your family, to the Israelites of the Bible. That's amazing. What you do with it is up to you.'

[The questioner objects and asks], 'does not this make you and us the same people?'

'No,' I answered. The word had rarely sounded so gross to me. 'Some of our ancestors were the same people. That was a long time ago.' It was the best I could do.

Halkin knows this is not good enough. He has a conscience about tribalism. But in the remaining two pages of his book he does little to repair or to explain his rejection of these people whom he has laboured so hard to find and to certify. His assertion that their discovery is of great importance for biblical scholarship falls on deaf ears: 'They listened without enthusiasm. They wanted fish or fowl, and kuki grub. I had given them cake.'

In fact, what he had given them was something far more difficult to digest. Halkin's rejection of them is based on blood. They are not Jews. On this point he is, of course, correct: if one uses blood and the existence of a Jewish genetic profile to determine membership of the tribe, then in all likelihood the Mizo will probably fail this test. Halkin apologises. 'I'm sorry I couldn't tell your people they're all full-blooded Israelites . . .' he candidly observes, 'I know that would have made them happier.' But surely this is not necessarily so. What would have made them happier, I expect, was to know that the 'fact' of their 'belonging' might now clear a path so that they could go 'home' and become 'whole' people in a land that might, in the fullness of time, embrace them, and their children, and finally their children's children. But as we know from the author's memories of the Mizo wedding in Gaza, he has little faith in such 'Israelification' for those who do not qualify by blood. By his own admission he is not a full-blooded Israelite, but he is quick to make his own case. 'There are plenty of us half-bloods, though. There's been a lot of research on the subject.'

Halkin is a Zionist, and also an extremely fine writer whose soul is in tune with the desires of the human heart. In this book, his ability to understand the desire of others to belong is strong and admirable. Yet it is not until he has found his 'evidence' that the real drama of Halkin's book unfolds. Will Halkin find a way to accept these 'lost' people – be they 'full bloods', 'half bloods,' or 'no bloods' – as his brothers, and welcome them as migrants into his world? In the end his answer is clear. He would prefer them not to attempt to integrate into his Israel. I understand that Halkin's preference is based on a realistic understanding of the hardships that would await these people if they acted upon their ancient identity – and yet it strikes me as oddly cruel. Would it hurt that much to allow them a chance to belong? After all, only 450 of them have migrated to Israel in the past decade, and in India only some 3,500 are living as practising Jews. Moreover, almost half of the recent migrants from the former Soviet Union are not, according to rabbinical standards, Jewish. Does Halkin really fear that an attempt at 'Israelification' in the wake of Mizo migration might somehow damage the Jewish character? Does this account for his bluntness?

Halkin calls the rejection of the Mizo people 'gross', and his word suggests an awareness of the conflict between his head and his heart. This would be a natural fissure in a writer who throughout the course of his book has proved himself to be an attractive mixture of assiduous detective and compassionate guide. But in the end, it appears, authority will prevail. Luckily for Halkin, when his own family left Russia for the United States there was no 'blood' impediment to bar their migration and subsequent assimilation. True, Israel is not the United States, and there are few writers today who understand this better than Halkin himself.

In May 1998, Halkin wrote persuasively in *Jewish World Review* about the increasing complexity of Jewish identity in a multi-cultural world of frequent migrations and interchangeable nationalities. He asked the pertinent question: 'Why is the Tel-Aviv-born-and-raised child of Thai parents who speaks Hebrew as his native language and relates to Israeli culture as his own not a Jew by nationality in the same sense that he would have been an American had he grown up in New York?' There is no easily packaged answer, of course; and as a result Halkin predicts a 'chaotic' opening up of Jewish identity in the near future, a kind of national affiliation that will militate against family ties that are defined by 'blood'.

And yet he laments this change. Describing himself as a 'secular Zionist,' he admits to liking the 'DNA' that creates the family bonding and he regrets that inevitably 'there will be a thinning out'. The conclusion of this new book suggests that Halkin remains somewhat conflicted about the desirability of a new, non-ethnic development of Jewish identity, although he knows, as he mentions in his essay, that 'the prospect of hundreds of thousands of native-born, non-Arab, Hebrew-speaking Israelis who are not Jews by halakhic standards is not merely a possibility; it is a near certainty'. One wishes that he could have shared these words with his Mizo hosts, however much they – the words, the hosts – might stick in his throat. Had he done so, he would have helped these good people in their quest to return to what they call home and become members of the new Israel that Halkin lucidly imagines.

Chinua Achebe: Out of Africa (2003)

Chinua Achebe leans forward to make his point. He raises a gentle finger in the manner of a benevolent schoolmaster.

'But you have to understand. Art is more than just good sentences, this is what makes this situation tragic. The man is a capable artist and as such I expect better from him. I mean, what is his point in that book? Art is not intended to put people down. If so, then art would ultimately discredit itself.'

Achebe does not take his eyes from me, and I stare back at him. The face is familiar and marked with the heavy lines of ageing that one would expect to find on a seventy-two-year-old man's face. But Achebe's lines are graceful, which suggest wisdom. He leans back now and looks beyond me and through the window at the snowy landscape.

We are sitting in his one-storey house in upstate New York, deep in the wooded campus of Bard College. For the past thirteen years, Achebe has been a professor at this well-known liberal arts college, which has had writers such as Mary McCarthy and Norman Mailer on the faculty. His house is decorated with African art and artefacts, but the landscape and the climate could not be further removed from Nigeria and the world of Achebe's fiction and non-fiction. As though tiring of the wintry landscape, Achebe turns and returns to our conversation.

'The man would appear to be obsessed with "that" word.'

'Nigger.'

Achebe nods.

'He has an admiration of the white skin. It is the whiteness that he likes, and he is obsessed with the physicality of the Negro.'

Again Achebe falls silent, but this time he lowers his eyes as though suddenly overcome with fatigue. I continue to look at him, the father of African Literature in the English language and one of the most important writers of the second half of the twentieth century. What I find difficult to fathom is just why Conrad's short novel, *Heart of Darkness* should exercise such a hold on him. Achebe has taught term-long university courses dedicated to this one slim volume that was first published in 1902. As long ago as February 1975, while a visiting professor at the University of Massachusetts in Amherst, Achebe delivered a public lecture entitled 'An Image of Africa: Racism in Conrad's *Heart of Darkness*'. The lecture has since come to be recognised as one of the most important and influential treatises in post-colonial literary discourse. The problem is I disagree with Achebe's response to the novel, and have never viewed Conrad – as Achebe states in his lecture – as simply 'a thoroughgoing racist'. At the same time, I hold Achebe in the highest possible esteem, and so a two-hour drive up the Hudson River Valley into deepest upstate New York seems a small price to pay to resolve this conundrum.

Achebe's lecture quickly establishes his belief that Conrad deliberately sets Africa up as 'the other world' so that he can examine Europe. According to Achebe, Africa is presented to the reader as 'the antithesis of Europe and therefore of civilisation, a place where man's vaunted intelligence and refinement are finally mocked by triumphant bestiality'. Achebe sees Conrad mocking both the African landscape and the African people. The story begins on the 'good' River Thames which, in the past, 'has been one of the dark places of the earth'. The story soon takes us to the 'bad' River Congo, which is presently one of those 'dark places'. It is a body of water upon which the steamer toils 'along slowly on the edge of a black and incomprehensible frenzy'. According to Achebe, Conrad's long and famously hypnotic sentences are mere 'trickery', designed to induce an entrancing stupor in the reader. Achebe drafts in the support of 'the eagle-eyed English critic F.R. Leavis' who many years ago noted Conrad's 'adjectival insistence upon inexpress-ible and incomprehensible mystery', the cumulative effect of which is to suggest that poor Africa is inexplicable.

But it is when Achebe turns to Conrad's treatment of African humanity that he is most disparaging of Conrad's vision. He quotes from the moment in the novel when the Europeans on the steamer encounter real live Africans in the flesh.

> 'We are accustomed to look upon the shackled form of a conquered monster, but there — there you could look at a thing monstrous and free. It was unearthly, and the men were — No, they were not inhuman. Well, you know, that was the worst of it — this suspicion of their not being inhuman. It would come slowly to one. They howled and leaped, and spun, and made horrid faces; but what thrilled you was just the thought of their humanity — like yours — the thought of your remote kinship with this wild and passionate uproar. Ugly. Yes, it was ugly enough; but if you were man enough you would admit to yourself that there was in you just the faintest trace of a response to the terrible frankness of that noise, a dim suspicion of there being a meaning in it which you — you so remote from the night of first ages — could comprehend.'

These people are 'ugly', but what is even more disturbing is that they are in some way also human. A half-page later, Conrad focuses in on one particular African who, according to Achebe, is rare, for he is not presented as 'just limbs or rolling eyes'. The problem is that the African man is, most disturbingly, not 'in his place'. 'And between whiles I had to look after the savage who was fireman. He was an improved specimen; he could fire up a vertical boiler. He was there below me, and, upon my word, to look at him was as edifying as seeing a dog in a parody of breeches and a feather hat, walking on his hind legs.'

Those critics who have defended *Heart of Darkness* against charges of racism have often pointed to both the methodology of narration and Conrad's anti-colonial purpose. The narrator of the novel is Marlow, who is simply retelling a story that was told to him by a shadowy second figure. However, in his lecture Achebe makes it clear that he is not fooled by this narrative gamesmanship, or the claims of those who would argue that the complex polyphony of the storytelling is Conrad's way of deliberately trying to distance himself from the views of his characters.

'. . . if Conrad's intention is to draw a cordon sanitaire between himself and the moral and psychological *malaise* of his narrator, his care seems to me to be totally wasted because he neglects to hint, clearly and adequately, at an alternative frame of reference by which we may judge the actions and opinions of his characters. It would not have been beyond Conrad's power to make that provision if he had thought it necessary. Conrad seems to me to approve of Marlow . . .'

Achebe is, however, aware of Conrad's ambivalence towards the colonising mission, and he concedes that the novel is, in part, an attempt to examine what happens when Europeans come into contact with this particular form of economic and social exploitation. In the lecture he remembers that a student in Scotland once informed him that Africa is 'merely a setting for the disintegration of the mind of Mr Kurtz', which is an argument that many teachers and critics, let alone students, have utilised to defend the novel. But to read the book in this way is to further stir Achebe's outrage.

'Africa as setting and backdrop which eliminates the African as human factor. Africa as a metaphysical battlefield devoid of all recognisable humanity, into which the wandering European enters at his peril. Can nobody see the preposterous and perverse arrogance in thus reducing Africa to the role of props for the break-up of one petty European mind?'

Achebe has no problem with a novel that seeks to question both Europe's ambivalence towards the colonising mission and her own 'system' of civilisation. What he has a huge problem with is a novelist – in fact, an artist – who attempts to resolve these important questions by denying Africa and Africans their full and complex humanity.

During the two-hour drive up the Hudson River Valley through a snowbound and icy landscape, I thought again of my own response to the novel. There are three journeys in *Heart of Darkness*. First, Marlow's actual journey upriver to Kurtz's inner station. Second, the larger journey that Marlow takes us on from civilised Europe back to the beginning of creation when nature reigned, and then back to civilised Europe. And finally, the journey that Kurtz undergoes as he sinks down through the many levels of the self to a place where he discovers unlawful and repressed ambiguities of civilisation. In all three journeys, Conrad's restless narrative circles back on itself as though trapped in the complexity of the situation. The overarching question is, what happens when one group of people, supposedly more humane and civilised than another group, attempts to impose themselves upon their 'inferiors'? In such circumstances will there always be an individual who, removed from the shackles of 'civilised' behaviour, feels compelled to push at the margins of conventional 'morality'? What happens to this one individual who imagines himself to be released from the moral order of society and therefore free to behave as 'savagely' or as 'decently' as he deems fit? How does this man respond to chaos?

Conrad uses colonisation, and the trading intercourse that flourished in its wake, to explore these universal questions about man's capacity for evil. The end of European colonisation has not rendered *Heart of Darkness* any less relevant, for Conrad was interested in the making of a modern world in which colonisation was simply one facet. The uprootedness of people, and their often disquieting encounter with the 'other', is a constant theme in his work, and particularly so in this novel. Conrad's writing prepares us for a new world in which modern man has had to endure the psychic and physical pain of displacement, and all the concomitant confusion of watching imagined concrete standards become mutable. Modern descriptions of twentieth-century famines, war and genocide seem to be eerily prefigured by Conrad, and *Heart of Darkness* abounds with passages that seem terrifyingly contemporary in their descriptive accuracy.

> Near the same tree two more bundles of acute angles sat with their legs drawn up. One, with his chin propped on his knees, stared at nothing, in an intolerable and appalling manner: his brother phantom rested its forehead, as if overcome with a great weariness; and all about others were scattered in every pose of contorted collapse, as in some picture of a massacre or a pestilence.

As my car moved ever closer to Bard College, I constantly asked myself, was Conrad really a racist? If so, how did I miss this? Written in the wake of the 1884 Berlin Conference, which saw the continent of Africa carved into a 'magnificent cake' and divided among European nations, *Heart of Darkness* offers its readers an insight into the 'dark' world of Africa. The European world produced the narrator, produced Marlow, and certainly produced the half-French, half-English Kurtz ('All Europe contributed to the making of Kurtz'), but against the glittering 'humanity' of Europe, Conrad presents us with a late-nineteenth-century view of a primitive African world that has produced very little, and is obviously doomed to irredeemable savagery. This world picture would have troubled few of Conrad's original readers, for Conrad was merely providing them with the descriptive 'evidence' of the bestial people and the fetid world that they 'knew' lay beyond Europe. Yet by the beginning of the twenty-first century, Conrad's readers are living in a decolonised – indeed postcolonial – world, and Conrad's brutal depiction of African humanity, as a 'savage' mirror into which the European could gaze and measure his own tenuous grip on civilisation, is now regarded by some, including Achebe, as deeply problematic.

But is it not ridiculous to demand of Conrad that he imagine an African humanity that is totally out of line with both the times in which he was living and the larger purpose of his novel? In his lecture, even Achebe wistfully concedes that the novel reflects 'the dominant image of Africa in the Western imagination'. And the novel does assert European infamy, for there are countless examples throughout the text which point to Conrad's recognition of the illegitimacy of this trading mission and the brutalising effect it is having on the Africans. However, the main focus of the novel is the Europeans, and the effect upon them of their encountering another, less 'civilised', world. The novel proposes no programme for dismantling European racism or imperialistic exploitation, and as a reader I have never had any desire to confuse it with an equal opportunity pamphlet. I have always believed that Conrad's only programme is doubt; in this case, doubt about the supremacy of European humanity, and the ability of this supposed humanity to maintain its imagined status beyond the high streets of Europe. As I pull my car up outside Achebe's house, I already sense that I had better shore up my argument with something more resilient.

For a moment Achebe has me fooled. He looks as though he has nodded off, but he has just been thinking. This mild-mannered man looks up now and smiles. He returns to the subject we were talking about as though he has merely paused to draw breath.

'Conrad didn't like black people. Great artists manage to be bigger than their times. In the case of Conrad you can actually show that there were people at the same time as him, and before him, who were not racists with regard to Africa.'

'Who?' I ask. Achebe says nothing for a moment, and so I continue. 'I find it difficult to think of any European writers who have had a benevolent view of Africa. Surely they've all used Africa as a foil.'

'Well, Livingstone,' suggests Achebe. 'He is not a writer, but he is an explorer and Conrad admired explorers. When asked what he thought of Africans, Livingstone replied that he found them "infuriating". In other words, they were just like everybody else.'

We both fall silent and I think back to Achebe's lecture. That Conrad had some 'issues' with black people is beyond doubt. Achebe quotes Conrad who, when recalling his first encounter with a black person, remembers it thus: 'A certain enormous buck nigger encountered in Haiti fixed my conception of blind, furious, unreasoning rage, as manifested in the human animal to the end of my days. Of the nigger I used to dream for years afterwards.'

Conversely, when the sixteen-year-old Conrad encounters his first Englishman in Europe, he calls him 'my unforgettable Englishman' and describes him in the following manner:

[His] calves exposed to the public gaze . . . dazzled the beholder by the splendour of their marble-like condition and their rich tone of young ivory . . . The light of a headlong, exalted satisfaction with the world of men . . . illumined his face . . . and triumphant eyes. In passing he cast a glance of kindly curiosity and a friendly gleam of big, sound, shiny teeth . . . his white calves twinkled sturdily.

Yet despite Achebe's compelling 'evidence', I am still finding it difficult to dismiss this man and his short novel. Are we to throw all racists out of the canon? Are we, as Achebe suggests, to ignore the period in which novels are written and demand that the artist rise above the prejudices of his times? As much as I respect the man sitting before me, something does not ring true. We both agree that Conrad was not the originator of this disturbing image of Africa and Africans. And we both appear to agree that Conrad had the perception to see that this encounter with Africa exposed the fissures and instabilities in so-called European civilisation. Further, we both agree that in order to expose European fragility Conrad pandered to a certain stereotype of African barbarity that, at the time, was accepted as the norm. Finally, we both agree that this stereotype is still with us today. Achebe speaks quickly, as though a thought has suddenly struck him.

'You see, those who say that Conrad is on my side because he is against colonial rule do not understand that I know who is on my side. And where is the proof that he is on my side? A few statements about it not being a very nice thing to exploit people who have flat noses? This is his defence against imperial control? If so, it is not enough. It is simply not enough. If you are going to be on my side what is required is a better argument. Ultimately you have to admit that Africans are people. You cannot diminish a people's humanity and defend them.'

I feel as though I am walking around an impregnable fortress. However, I am losing interest in the problem of breaching the ramparts and becoming more concerned with the aesthetics of its construction.

'Which European or American writers do you feel have best represented the continent of Africa and African people?'

Achebe looks at me for a long while and then slowly begins to shake his head.

'This is difficult. Not many.'

I suggest Graham Greene.

'Yes, perhaps. Graham Greene would be one because he knew his limitations. He didn't want to explain Africans to the world. He made limited claims and wasn't attempting to be too profound. After all, we can't be too profound about somebody whose history and language and culture is beyond our own.'

'But you're not suggesting that outsiders should not write about other cultures?'

'No, no. This identification with the other is what a great writer brings to the art of story-making. We should welcome the rendering of our stories by others, because a visitor can sometimes see what the owner of the house has ignored. But they must visit with respect and not be concerned with the color of skin, or the shape of nose, or the condition of the technology in the house.'

It is now my turn to stare out of the window at the six-foot snowdrifts and the bare, rickety arms of the trees. The light is beginning to fade and soon I will have to leave. I avert my eyes and turn to face my host.

'Chinua, I think Conrad offends you because he was a disrespectful visitor.'

'I am an African. What interests me is what I learn in Conrad about myself. To use me as a symbol may be bright or clever, but if it reduces my humanity by the smallest fraction I don't like it.'

'Conrad does present Africans as having "rudimentary" souls.'

Achebe draws himself upright.

'Yes, you will notice that the European traders have "tainted" souls, Marlow has a "pure" soul, but I am to accept that mine is "rudimentary?"' He shakes his head. 'Towards the end of the nineteenth century there was a very short-lived period of ambivalence about the certainty of this colonising mission, and *Heart of Darkness* falls into this period. But you cannot compromise my humanity in order to explore your own ambiguity. I cannot accept that. My humanity is not to be debated, nor is it to be used simply to illustrate European problems.'

The realisation hits me with force. I am not an African. Were I an African I suspect that I would feel the same way as my host. But I was raised in Europe, and although I have learned to reject the stereotypically reductive images of Africa and Africans, I am undeniably interested in the break-up of a European mind and the health of European civilisation. I feel momentarily ashamed that I might have become caught up with this theme and subsequently overlooked how offensive this novel might be to a man such as Chinua Achebe and to millions of other Africans. Achebe is right: to the African reader the price of Conrad's eloquent denunciation of colonisation is the recycling of racist notions of the 'dark' continent and her people. Those of us who are not from Africa may be prepared to pay this price, but this price is far too high for Achebe. However lofty Conrad's mission, he has, in keeping with times past and present, compromised African humanity in order to examine the European psyche. Achebe's response is understandably personal.

'Conrad's presentation of me is my problem and I have a responsibility to deal with it, you understand?' I nod. 'I don't come from a "half-made" society as your "friend" Naipaul would say. We're not "half-made" people, we're a very old people. We've seen lots of problems in the past. We've dealt with these problems in Africa, and we're older than the problems. Drought, famine, disease — this is not the first time that we're dealing with these things in Africa.'

He takes a deep breath and for the first time I can see that Achebe is tiring. Beyond him, and through the window, the blanket of night is beginning to descend over the woods.

'You know,' he continues, 'I think that to some extent it is how you must feel about your "friend". You take it to heart because a man with such talent should not behave in this way. My people, we say one palm nut does not get lost in the fire, for you must know where it is. But if you have twenty you may lose sight of some and they will get burned, but you have others. Well, as you know, we have very few who have the talent and who are in the right place, and to lose even one is a tragedy. We cannot afford to lose such artists. It is sheer cussedness to wilfully turn and walk away from the truth, and for what? Really, for what? I expect a great artist, a man who has explored, a man who is interested in Africa, not to make life more difficult for us. Why do this? Why make our lives more difficult? In this sense Conrad is a disappointment.'

Shusaku Endo: Confessions of a
True Believer (2003)

Muneya Kato is puzzled. He adjusts his glasses, then nervously threads and unthreads his fingers. A dapper-looking man in his early fifties, he looks more like a bank executive than the editor-in-chief of *Mitabungkaku*, one of Japan's most distinguished literary magazines. 'But why?' he asks again. He pauses and smiles quickly, as though to reassure me that he does not mean to be rude or intrusive. And then he changes tack. 'Endo Shusaku' – he uses the traditional Japanese way of placing the family name first – 'he would have enjoyed today. I am sorry he is not able to meet you.' I too am sorry, but meeting Muneya Kato is the next-best thing. All enquiries about the late Mr Endo have been met with the 'news' that I should speak with Mr Muneya Kato. And now we are seated together in the coffee lounge of a large hotel in the Shibuya district of central Tokyo.

Mr Kato's question still hangs in the air. Why, he wants to know, does a Caribbean-born British writer consider Shusaku Endo a great personal influence upon his own work? I have travelled all the way to Japan to, in part, seek out an answer to this very question. I have already told Mr Kato that the gentle intimacy of Endo's narrative style, with his deeply reflective first-person voices, has always appealed to me. Despite the intrusive 'barrier' of translation, Endo's novels have provided me with valuable instruction in how to locate character. Understandably, this technical and somewhat convoluted explanation of my connection to Endo has failed to satisfy Mr Kato. He continues to look at me with a puzzled expression. Mr Kato is still trying to understand how I have made a personal connection across race, nationality, religion and generation with his 'master', the man to whom he has dedicated the greater part of his life. As the waitress places two more cups of coffee in front of us I am beginning to flush with embarrassment, unsure if I can answer his question.

Shusaku Endo was born in Tokyo in 1923. He spent his early years in Manchuria, but after his parents separated, he and his mother returned to Japan and moved in with an aunt who persuaded Endo's mother to convert to Catholicism. Soon after, the mother convinced her young son that he should be baptised and Endo found himself part of the tiny minority group of Catholics in Japan. The religion did not sit easily on Endo's shoulders, and his shallow commitment caused him to suffer great feelings of guilt for he felt sure that he was disappointing his mother. In 1950, Endo became the first Japanese student after the Second World War to leave the country and study abroad. He travelled to France, where he enrolled in the University of Lyon to pursue his burgeoning interest in twentieth-century Catholic fiction.

These two events – the thrusting upon him of Catholicism, and his being exposed to the world beyond Japan – created a peculiar prism through which Endo peered at Japanese society. When the young author returned home to Japan and began to embark upon his career as a writer, he was immediately fascinated by questions of guilt and responsibility in Japanese society and history. These questions were all the more problematic for him because he continued to feel uncomfortable with certain aspects of his faith. His first great book, *The Sea and Poison* (1958), concerns the illegal vivisection of American soldiers by Japanese doctors during the Second World War, and it is based on historical fact. The lack of conscience of the doctors is set against the agonising predicament of a young intern, Dr Suguro, who feels compelled to obey orders despite his harbouring profound reservations about the actions of his superiors.

The novel *Silence* (1966), which most critics consider to be

Endo's masterpiece, is an austere historical drama which deals more directly with the religious concerns that plagued Endo's entire life. The novel centres on Rodrigues, a young Jesuit evangelist who travels to seventeenth-century Japan from Portugal in order to discover why his mentor has apostatised rather than suffer martyrdom. Soon after his arrival the young missionary is himself captured and forced to witness the brutal torture of native Japanese converts, a process that will cease only if Rodrigues is prepared to trample on the image of Christ. Although he prepares himself for martyrdom, Rodrigues eventually capitulates and desecrates the image of Christ having decided that, in this instance, martyrdom would be unacceptably selfish.

The eleven stories in Endo's collection *Stained Glass Elegies* (1984) further explore the conundrum of Catholic faith, as the author presents us with a series of characters whose beliefs are fading and who cling precariously to inherited practices which can be easily stripped from them. Endo's 'moral weaklings' continually restage the problematic encounter between Japanese and Western understandings of self and God, an encounter which, as Endo's work develops, increasingly comes to be characterised by an ongoing interrogation of the word 'betrayal'. By the time Endo reached the second half of his career the defining theme of his *oeuvre* was the yawning chasm between the internal contradictions and pressures of Japanese life on the one hand, and the world of Christianity and Europe on the other.

How can one be both Japanese and Western? How can one be a Christian and Japanese? Faced with two seemingly essentialist and inflexible ideologies, Endo sought to synthesise where it appeared there was neither room, nor possibility, for fusion. Not only did Japanese society appear 'closed' and resistant to change, Christianity – in the form of Catholicism – appeared to him to be equally stubborn and insular. Endo worried that Christianity might be ill suited to the temperament of Japanese religious psychology, which he felt demanded a more forgiving and accommodating God than the God whose image was being propagated by the Catholic Church. In these circumstances Endo's task became clear to him. He would attempt to re-tailor Christianity into a suit of clothes that could sit comfortably upon the Japanese body. But, as he was endeavouring to do this, he would also be wrestling the face of Japanese society around and pointing it towards a mirror where it would have no choice but to stare at its own contradictions and hypocrisies.

I ask Mr Kato if I am right in thinking that the recurring image of the swamp in Endo's work implies that Endo believed Japan to be a swamp, or a sea of mud, in which it was impossible to plant Christianity and expect it to take root. He nods, but is quick to clarify the situation. 'Your European God,' he says, 'is male. A father who is hard and who likes to punish, but we Japanese prefer a female image of God who is warm-hearted and forgiving.' Mr Kato thinks for a moment, and then continues. 'However, towards the end of his life Endo did come to believe that there was only one God, that male or female it was the same person, and this is what we see in his final novel *Deep River* [1994] when the Japanese tourists travel to India and find their spiritual selves.'

I am slightly taken aback and suggest to Mr Kato that this must mean there was some kind of a shift in position by Endo, perhaps even an abandonment of his proclaimed quest to re-tailor Christianity for the Japanese. 'Perhaps,' begins Mr Kato. 'Japanese people have begun to travel outside of the country now and, as in the novel *Deep River*, their own encounters with life beyond this country are changing both them and this society. They are doing some of the re-tailoring for themselves now.' Mr Kato falls silent. I look at him and want to be sure that I understand. I ask him if he is saying that by the end of his life Endo had moved beyond his early attempts to marry the essentialist notion of Japanese identity to the essentialist notion of Catholic identity? Mr Kato drains his cup of coffee and then stares into the middle distance. 'Yes,' he says. He turns and looks at me. 'Endo witnessed many changes and developments in modern Japanese society.'

Today there is an Endo Museum in Nagasaki, the Japanese city that has the most profound connections with the West. Here one can discover Endo's papers, manuscripts, letters, books, pens, even his clothes, all housed in a building that faces west. In Japan Shusaku Endo is remembered as a deeply respected author who wished to bring about a coming together of Japanese manners with European ideas, but he has his critics. Soon after the opening of the museum in 1999, a memorial plate that had been set up to commemorate the novel *Silence* was defaced with paint by Japanese Catholics who objected to the fact that Rodrigues chose to step willingly on the image of Christ. During Endo's lifetime, Catholic groups successfully lobbied to block his being awarded the Nobel Prize for Literature, but since his death in 1996 a new generation of Japanese Catholic writers has emerged and, despite the controversies, Endo's influence remains considerable. In fact, Mr Kato is at pains to assure me that Japanese readers consider Endo one of the handful of great twentieth-century Japanese writers. 'Endo', he says, 'created space for change in our society. He is a bridge from the old to the new.'

Mr Kato and I fall quiet. Out of the corner of my eye I can see the waitress hovering expectantly, and I think about ordering another cup of coffee. And then it occurs to me. I regarded the Britain that I grew up in during the sixties and seventies as inflexible and not readily open to change. Listening to people telling me to 'go back to where you come from' suggested to me that I was, of course, the unwelcome evidence of change. How would I ever reconcile my world, my people, myself to a Britain that had a woefully narrow idea of national identity? My life has been peppered with betrayals, both small and large, both personal and national, and by the time I was ready to leave university I knew that attempting to make contemporary British society accepting of, and even comfortable with, the complex-ities of her past and present would be a large part of my life's work. In fact, as I decide to order yet another cup of coffee I realise that the inflexible rigidity of the Japanese society that Endo portrays does, in fact, strike a familiar chord in me.

The waitress places two more cups of coffee before us. I will soon be able to repair the awkward silence between Mr Kato and myself and give him an answer to his question, for I now understand that it is 'Endo's people' who provide me with conclusive evidence of a connection between Endo's world and my own. Dr Suguro, the man caught up in the vivisection scandal, reminds me of a young nineteenth-century Englishwoman who finds herself on her father's Caribbean plantation 'supporting' a system that she gradually comes to understand is 'unsupportable'. 'Endo's people' remind me of the slave ship captain who slowly realises that the trading intercourse that he is perpetuating is immoral. They remind me of the African man who sells his own children into slavery, or the racist Little Englander, angry because he doesn't understand why and how his society is changing. 'Weak' people caught up in historically conditioned moral situations in somnambulant societies that are reluctantly waking up to change. I may not share Endo's Catholicism, nor his difficult internal debate with the nature of his faith, but his social and moral vision, and the manner in which he has sought to turn his understanding of inflexible societies and ideologies into literature, has been an important influence on me.

Mr Kato smiles. Having listened to my long-winded answer to his question, he now seems pleased to 'understand' why Endo means so much to a writer from the other side of the world. As the bill arrives Mr Kato is concerned to stress that, despite the gravity of his subject matter, Endo was very humorous and he remained an optimist. From the little that I had read about Endo's life, I had already guessed as much. I reassure Mr Kato that to my mind Endo's great gift to his readers, Japanese or otherwise, is to dignify ambiguity. To celebrate the puzzling grey area, and remind us that those old loyalties and certainties are, in our modern world, subject to fluidity and transformation irrespective of what the authorities above us — religious or otherwise — might have us believe. And today, if we are to survive our twenty-first-century world, slippage, hybridity and change must be embraced and go unpunished. Endo's baptism, and his journey to France, rocked the foundation of his identity. The fact that he chose not to fearfully grasp a 'safe', reductive and uncomplicated identity, but chose instead to try and synthesise these new influences and shape a new form of Japanese identity for himself and his society, is his great achievement.

Mr Muneya Kato stands and gives me a small bow, which I — somewhat self-consciously — return in kind. Mr Kato clears his throat. 'Before Endo writes any book he always picks up Mr Graham Greene's *The End of the Affair* and reads it through. I think maybe you should know this.' I thank Mr Kato for his time, and smile. There is more bowing, and then I watch him thread his way through the crowded foyer of the hotel and disappear through the glass doors and out into the busy streets of the Shibuya shopping area. What I didn't tell Mr Kato is that before I write any book I always pick up the work of Mr Shusaku Endo — usually the novel *Silence*. This literary baton-passing continues to make some highly unlikely teams out of a rainbow coalition of writers.

England, Half English (2004)

In February 1954 Kingsley Amis published *Lucky Jim*, a novel that reinvigorated the English comic novel. His hero, Jim Dixon, is a junior lecturer at a provincial university, a lower-middle-class man of biting wit who is disenchanted with his life and environment. The object of his scorn is pretentious, stuffy, middle-class England, which continues to cling to values informed by hypocrisy. Jim Dixon desires change, both personal and social. He craves mobility, but he senses that both he and his country are stuck.

The same inertia clouds the life of the working-class hero of John Braine's *Room at the Top* (1957). Joe Lampton is dissatisfied, sarcastic and cynical. As is Jimmy Porter, the anti-hero of John Osborne's play *Look Back in Anger* (1956). Jimmy Porter snaps at England, his posh girlfriend, in fact anything and anybody in his purview. The soundtrack to the British 1950s may be Tommy Steele's jaunty skiffle music and the steamy roar of an Italian coffee machine, but this was also the decade of the decline of Empire, of cold-war paranoia, when Britain's sense of itself began to come unmoored.

In many ways the critical year was 1956. That year witnessed the first production of Osborne's *Look Back in Anger*, as well as the Suez crisis, a foreign catastrophe played out against the backdrop of serious discontent on the home front. By 1956 three-quarters of all university graduates in Britain were dependent upon state grants to complete their education. These were the children of the Butler Education Act of 1944, which, for the first time, made universities accessible for working-class and lower-middle-class children. During the 1950s an empire was receding, while the working and lower-middle classes were finding their voice. But something else – something equally remarkable – was happening in British society that the vast majority of writers appeared to be incapable of either seeing, or reflecting upon.

I am referring, of course, to immigration from Commonwealth countries, primarily those in Africa and the Caribbean. In the 1950s, Britain became a multiracial and, to some extent, a multicultural society. In the census of 1951 there were just 15,300 Caribbean people living in Britain. Ten years later there were 171,800 – a phenomenal wave of migration in just one decade. These statistics do not include migration from Africa or Asia, but to factor in these figures would give an idea of how radically the country changed its racial face during the fifties. The 'color problem' was debated in parliament, on television, in newspapers, magazines, and on the radio. It was the big story of the decade. Yet where is it represented in the literature?

Today, Britain remains the most multiracial of European countries, and London is Europe's most multicultural and racially diverse city. More than 300 different languages are spoken daily in London schools, yet if we look at contemporary British literature, some of the absences of the 1950s continue today. Then and now, black writers addressed British life, and naturally enough these writers included black characters in their work. Perhaps Samuel Selvon's *The Lonely Londoners* (1956) is the best example of a fifties novel that tackles the problems of race and class that bedevilled British society at the time. But writers such as George Lamming or V.S. Naipaul also wrote about race, class and British society, as did Africans, most memorably Wole Soyinka in his poem 'The Immigrant'. Like their successors in Britain today – Ben Okri, Hanif Kureishi – these writers wrote and write about contemporary Britain with eyes that take in not only black people, but white people, too. The lack of reciprocal imagining on the part of white British writers is puzzling. Although Amis and Osborne were writers, not social historians or journalists, the omission of black people from the literary landscape is so glaring it does beg questions about the politics of literary representation.

The work of Colin MacInnes is the great exception. MacInnes was born on 20 August 1914 in London, the second child of James Campbell MacInnes, an Australian singer and professor of music, and the novelist Angela Thirkell. His mother left her husband in 1917, met another Australian and migrated to Australia in 1920. Colin MacInnes was educated there, but between 1930 (aged only sixteen) and 1935 he pursued a business career in Brussels. He left Belgium for England, where he studied painting, but at the outbreak of war he joined the British Army as a sergeant in the Intelligence Corps and served in Germany during the Allied occupation. After the war he joined BBC Radio, for which he wrote scripts, but in the mid-1950s he left the BBC and for the next twenty years, until his death in April 1976, he pursued a freelance career writing scripts, essays and novels and making regular contributions to a variety of magazines. His reputation, although somewhat faded now, rests on his three 'London novels' of the fifties, all of which betray a great deal of sympathy for the underdog. *Absolute Beginners* (1959) suggests the turmoil of a decade that witnessed the rise of the teenager as a cultural force. *Mr Love and Justice* (1960) examines the glamorisation of crime and criminals and the hypocrisy of the police, especially when dealing with pimps and prostitutes. But it is the first of these novels, *City of Spades* (1957) that is in many ways the most unusual, in terms of both subject matter and form.

Montgomery Pew, a cautious and somewhat shy Englishman, is employed as a welfare officer among London's new black immigrants. He is told to expect trouble from these somewhat excitable and not always trustworthy West Indians and West Africans, but he does not heed his superior's words of warning. In the end he is perhaps too attracted to the invigorating, vibrant, and above all new world that these newcomers inhabit, and he subsequently loses his job. What he gains is entry into a world altogether different from Jimmy Porter's or Jim Dixon's or that of Keith Waterhouse's Billy Liar. It is a hidden, bohemian London of nightclubs, shebeens, West African late-night restaurants, squats, brothels, cafés, bent coppers, gay pick-up joints, Indian restaurants on the Thames, all operating with dizzying intensity behind the façade of the post-Edwardian respectability that fifties Britain tried desperately to affect.

City of Spades has an ingenious structure, being narrated in short episodic bursts first from Montgomery's 'white' point of view, and then from that of Johnny Fortune, a genial West African scoundrel who befriends him. The two streams of the narrative flow and ebb together, presenting the same scenes from differing points of view in a manner that I suspect is derived from MacInnes's reading of Faulkner, particularly, I would guess, *Light in August*.

The novel offers its reader a unique glimpse into the worlds of both the West African and the West Indian, and although at times we may feel as though the narrative is stooping to the level of sociological instruction, with occasional discourses on the lifestyles enjoyed by different groups, the framework of the novel is held together by compelling, restless action and by dialogue that is accurate, inventive and always witty. Until, that is, the final third, where it collapses in a staged and disappointingly unengaging courtroom drama, failing in much the same way as the African American writer Richard Wright failed in the third and final panel of his fictional triptych, *Native Son* (1940).

At its best, however, *City of Spades* is an astonishing feat of imagination by a writer tuned in to the radical changes taking place in British society. MacInnes understood that the country was furiously remaking itself and he set out to depict this transformation. Only he, among British writers, seemed to want to see what was happening on the streets of Britain and only he seemed prepared to imagine himself into the world and lives of these 'dark strangers' who were both of, and not of, the country.

The more one reads of MacInnes, however, the clearer it

becomes that it is the sexual frisson of the black newcomer that must have attracted him to the subject, and at times one wonders if MacInnes is capable of talking about black lives in Britain without recourse to sexuality. Very early in the novel, Montgomery Pew watches Johnny Fortune as he leaves the Welfare Office building.

> I watched him go out with an unexpected pang. And moving to the window, soon saw him walk across the courtyard and stop for a moment speaking to some others there. In the sunlight, his nylon shirt shone all the whiter against the smooth brown of his skin. His frame, from this distance, seemed shorter than it was, because of his broad shoulders – flat, though composed of two mounds of muscle arching from his spine. His buttocks sprang optimistically high up from the small of his back, and his long legs – a little bandy and with something of a backwards curve – were supported by two effective splayed-out feet; on which, just now, as he spoke, gesticulating too, he was executing a tracery of tentative dance steps to some soft inaudible music.

So we have a little hint of Johnny Fortune's 'natural rhythm' in Montgomery Pew's unapologetically exoticised description of his new acquaintance. But it would be wrong to deny the sexual anxiety that was part of the reaction to the new Commonwealth immigrants, thousands of whom arrived in Britain without wives or girlfriends. Much of the antipathy towards outsiders of all kinds in Britain has been framed in terms of purity and pollution. MacInnes not only squared up to this fact, but in *City of Spades* he explored it, especially in a remarkable seven-page sequence between Part One and Part Two of the novel entitled 'Idyll of miscegenation on the river' – the river, of course, being the Thames.

These were years of tremendous and radical change in every major city, and it was difficult for white British people of all ages not to have contact with the newcomers. If one believed that 'England' – or Scotland or Wales – was white then right before your very eyes England was becoming half-English. But why then were these new, non-white English people not represented in the literature, theatre and films of the period? MacInnes was widely praised for tackling this important subject, and received numerous offers to take part in BBC discussions. Eric Moon in the *Saturday Review* said of *City of Spades* that 'MacInnes's identification and sympathy with the new blacks and his understanding of them are little short of miraculous.' So why didn't other white writers tackle the subject?

A clue to the answer can be found by looking at Shelagh Delaney's play, *A Taste of Honey* (1958). Delaney was a nineteen-year-old working-class girl from Lancashire when her first play was produced at Joan Littlewood's Theatre Royal in Stratford East. The play is set in a Manchester maisonette where an Irish woman, Helen Smith, a single mother who likes a good time, lives with her teenage daughter Jo. Helen is obsessed with her 'fancy man' Peter, who wants to marry her, and Jo spends large periods of time by herself. Jo eventually meets, and is impregnated by, a twenty-two-year-old 'colored naval rating', who is known only as 'boy' in the stage directions, but as Jimmie in the play. He goes off to sea and, in the absence of Jimmie and Helen, Jo turns to her homosexual art student friend Geoffrey, who moves in and helps her prepare for the birth of the child.

Early in the play Jo discovers that Jimmie is not one of the newcomers to Britain.

> JO: Sometimes you look three thousand years old. Did your ancestors come from Africa?
> BOY: No. Cardiff. Disappointed? Were you hoping to marry a man whose father beat the tom-tom all night?
> JO: I don't care where you were born. There's still a bit of jungle in you somewhere.

A Taste of Honey, which Graham Greene reviewed and described as having 'all the freshness of Mr Osborne's *Look Back in Anger* and a greater maturity', is almost unique for its time in that it features a black face on stage. But even Shelagh Delaney found it difficult to see her black character as much more than an irresponsible, though admittedly charming, sexual outlaw. In this sense, her depiction of Jimmie is reminiscent of MacInnes. But in a golden age of naturalistic English drama, with plays by John Arden, Harold Pinter, Alun Owen and Willis Hall, in addition to those of Osborne and Arnold Wesker, all of which grappled with the problems of contemporary Britain, how is it possible that only a first-time, teenage dramatist from the North of England spotted what Britain really looked like?

In 1959, MacInnes reviewed Delaney's play for *Encounter*. He opened his review with the following statement: 'Shelagh Delaney's *A Taste of Honey* is the first English play I've seen in which a colored man, and a queer boy, are presented as natural characters, factually, without a nudge or shudder.' MacInnes expands upon the plot of the play, and then digresses:

> The play gives a great thirst for more authentic portraits of the mid twentieth-century English world. As one skips through contemporary novels, or scans the acreage of fish-and-chip shop dailies and the very square footage of the very predictable weeklies, as one blinks unbelievingly at 'British' films and stares boss-eyed at the frantic race against time that constitutes the telly, it is amazing – it really is – how very little one can learn about life in England here and now . . . This last decade [the 1950s] will be remembered as the one in which the biggest social changes happened and the very least was discovered about them by 'the arts'.

Of course, this is something of an overstatement. The arts did engage with some of the big social changes, but to MacInnes, one of the biggest – if not the biggest – was the immigration of black people from the West Indies and West Africa, and the formation of modern multiracial Britain. And in this sense MacInnes is right, for very little was discovered about this particular social change by the arts. Both he and Delaney made some attempt to rectify this myopia, but the degree to which the subject was ignored remains shocking.

MacInnes argued that writers,

> the chief absorbers of 'culture' above the pop level – are themselves prodigiously self-insulated against experience. In the popular phrase, they just 'don't want to know'. Around them seethes a great flux of bizarre new social groupings through which they proceed, like tourists traversing the casbah, unseeing and unaware . . . and the instinct not to want to know is powerfully reinforced by that blind universal faith so many educated English men and women have today – that if you don't look closely at what the world, near and far, is growing to be like, it somehow won't be like that at all.

But perhaps MacInnes's personal interests and preferences prevented him from answering his own question more fully. Reading MacInnes's work, and to some extent that of Delaney, one might conclude that it is difficult for a white English writer imaginatively to engage with a black character, particularly a male, without thinking sexually. In one of the more unbelievable sequences in *A Taste of Honey*, Jimmie, who is a nurse in the Navy, quotes Shakespeare (*Othello*) to Jo and it is an entirely predictable line: 'Do you object to the "gross clasps of the lascivious Moor"?' Such a line is entirely out of character and out of place in this working-class northern drama. Unless, of course, Delaney wishes to remind us, just as MacInnes does, of the helpless relationship between blackness and sexuality. When George Lamming, or Naipaul or Soyinka or Wilson Harris, or other Caribbean and African writers sat down to write about Britain in this period, they included white as well as black characters. And when they imagined white people, they did not think of them as trapped within the confines of a particular stereotype. In other words, they did not see white people as merely mean-spirited or racist or violent. These writers were generous, and responsible, enough to see them first and fore-most as people.

As the fifties gave way to the Swinging Sixties, and then to the seventies and eighties, things did not improve. White British writers have continued to write about Britain without seeing any black faces, and the responsibility to represent a multiracial Britain has continued to fall on the shoulders of non-white writers. The plays and novels of the vast majority of Britain's literary labourers are devoid of black faces and, until very recently, the same has been true of film and television. One notable exception to this is Alan Hollinghurst's novel *The Swimming-Pool Library* (1988) which examines the complex relationship between race, class and sexuality across two generations. But even here, while one is grateful to see black characters represented, the role of sexual outlaw has once again been set aside for the non-white player. To be fair, almost everybody in this novel, especially the narrator, Will Beckwith, is a sexual outlaw of some kind, but there is no getting away from the fact that, as in *City of Spades*, we are encouraged to view practically every black character through the prism of their sexuality.

It is, of course, possible that MacInnes was correct; that white British writers have avoided writing about race in the hope that the problem (in other words, the black people) might just go away. It is equally possible, given the evidence of the work of those white writers who have written about race, that it is difficult for white British writers to engage with black characters without rummaging through the baggage of their sexual identity. MacInnes and Hollinghurst, and for that matter Delaney, are serious and talented writers who have had the courage of their convictions and told it as they saw it, but if, when sitting at their desks, white writers can see black people as little more than players with trousers down entering the bedroom, or pants up sprinting for the door, then it is better that they should stay silent. I, for one, am quite happy to read Amis's *Lucky Jim* or Braine's *Room at the Top* without having a poorly imagined black Lothario merely making up the numbers.

In 1961, a collection of MacInnes's journalism was published under the title *England, Half English*. Reviewing it in *The Listener*, one can almost hear the sigh of relief in the words of a youthful V.S. Naipaul: 'He wants people to *see*...' Naipaul concludes his favourable review with a final flourish: '... Mr MacInnes is important to half-English England, and she is lucky in him.' I second that motion, and I leave the final word to Colin MacInnes, who in the radical 1950s saw what was happening, understood the moral necessity to record it, and, most importantly, did so. MacInnes knew that to stay alive, societies must continually reinvent themselves. The arrival of tens of thousands of West Indians and West Africans during the 1950s contributed to this most radical reinvention:

> The nineteen fifties were an astonishing decade: during which England, under the twin shadows of the *Bomb* and its own sharp imperial decline, has altered more radically than it did in the silly twenties, the dreadful thirties, or in the certainly heroic but, in essence, static nineteen forties. Some of the changes in our social climate have been negative, frivolous and mean; but others have brought life and hope and what, since the nineteenth century, was unknown in England – a realisation that tradition, by which we set such store, must, to have meaning, be constantly remade.

MacInnes might have added that such changes 'must also be recorded'.

The Pleasures of Exile (2005)

Twenty years ago I first visited Toronto. I was attending my first ever literary festival, and the invitation to the event had arrived by way of my London publishers. Initially, I was sure that my publishers had made some terrible mistake and that the invitation was intended for one of their more illustrious authors. Unless I was misreading the letter, the proposal was that I be presented with a free round-trip air ticket from London to Toronto, housed in a five-star hotel for a week, paid a generous daily stipend, taken on a variety of outings to places such as Niagara Falls, and furnished with invitations to various parties and dinners celebrating myself and my fellow authors. In exchange for this largesse, I would be expected to read from one of my two novels for a mere twenty minutes and, incredibly enough, for this reading I would be paid an additional fee. Such was my initiation into the world of literary festivals.

Although I now try to avoid such gatherings, I do look back at that first literary festival with great fondness. Many enduring friendships were forged in Toronto, but as one year leads to the next there is a single incident that occurred there that I find myself returning to time and time again. It concerns my late, and much lamented, friend, the writer Angela Carter. One morning we were walking down a street near Lake Ontario, either on our way to, or on our way back from some appointment, when a smartly dressed Japanese man approached us. Angela was a tall woman and he looked up at her as he asked for street directions. Angela dealt with the enquiry with characteristic grace, but I knew immediately that there was something strange about the encounter. As I watched the clearly charmed man set off purposefully in the right direction, I could not put my finger on what was amiss. Angela and I walked on and perhaps a minute or so passed by in silence before she turned to me and smiled. 'You know,' she said, 'around about now it will be occurring to him that I just spoke to him in Japanese.' I almost stopped walking for, of course, I too had missed this fact.

In 1969, Angela Carter won the Somerset Maugham Award which carried with it a stipend of £500 and a 'suggestion' that the winner, who had to be under thirty-five years of age, should use the money for travel. The twenty-nine-year-old Angela Carter promptly took off for Japan because, as she later stated, she wished to live in a place that was outside the Judaeo-Christian world in order to 'see what it was like'. She already felt that she was situated somewhat awkwardly on the periphery of English society as a part Yorkshire, part south London, lower-middle-class woman of obvious, and to some people irritating, brilliance, but having been awarded the prize she consciously chose to remove herself to a place that would encourage her to see herself anew. Years later she declared that it was her two years in Japan that radicalised her as a feminist thinker. But her two years in Japan also transformed her into the wilful, stubborn and outstanding writer that she subsequently became. Which is not to say that there was not already a precocious literary mind at work prior to her departure. When one looks back at her fiction and essays from the 1960s it is disconcerting to discover that a writer who was still only in her twenties could be so confident and sure-footed. In later years, she felt a little embarrassed by what she described as the 'over-written and over-literary' nature of her early writing, but there is nothing for her to feel embarrassed about. Over-writing is the *rite de passage* for most authors, and in her case the dazzling insight which informs her observations, and her deft verbal play, more than make up for any temporary gushing.

Back in 1969, five hundred pounds did not go a very long

way, especially in Tokyo. Angela Carter was forced to take on a variety of jobs to support herself, including bar hostess work, modelling and freelance journalism. If one looks to her literary journalism from this period – much of which was published in the now defunct *New Society* – one can chart the 'growth' of Carter's mind. She was fully aware of the fact that the very act of living in a country where she would be a complete outsider would bring her face to face with herself at a critical time in her literary development. Although she knew that, as an exceedingly smart and outspoken young woman, it was already somewhat problematic for her to feel fully at home in British society, she absolutely understood that in Japan it would be almost impossible for her ever to belong. In other words, by travelling to Japan she would be free to reinvent herself without having to wrestle with the multiple anxieties of belonging.

Angela Carter's writing about Japan is a joy to read. She is by turns sharply observant, witty, and when she feels the occasion demands it, she can be acerbic. Over the years, critics have tried to read and interpret her writing on Japan by focusing on what it tells us about Japan, but this writing should more properly be read for what it tells us about Angela Carter. Today, most of her essays read like period pieces, but behind the temporal façade one can sense Angela Carter, the writer, rising to her feet.

> I am the first colored family in this street. I moved in on the Emperor's birthday, so the children were all home from school. They were playing 'catch' around the back of the house and a little boy came to hide in the embrasure of the window. He glanced round and caught sight of me. He did not register shock but he vanished immediately. Then there was a silence and, shortly afterwards, a soft thunder of tiny footsteps. They groped round the windows, invisible, peering, and a rustle rose up, like the dry murmur of dead leaves in the wind, the rustle of innumerable small voices murmuring

the word: '*Gaijin, gaijin, gaijin*' (foreigner), in pure, repressed surprise. We spy strangers. *Asoka.*

After her time in Japan, Carter returned to Britain and continued to enjoy a peripatetic life in the twenty years that she had left. She taught at the University of Sheffield and at Brown University in the United States, and she continued to travel extensively. After Toronto I subsequently met up with her in Germany and then again in New Zealand, as well as on numerous occasions in London. By this stage she was both a dear friend and, to my mind, the outstanding British writer of her generation. Whatever it was that I recognised in her, or she in me, I am sure that it had something to do with her curiosity and fascination with issues of belonging, a preoccupation that was fed by her two years in Japan. Angela Carter was not only unafraid of being 'the only one in the room', she seemed to intimately understand that sometimes it is *necessary* to be this person if one is to begin to see clearly.

In 1900, almost exactly seventy years before Angela Carter travelled to Japan, the great Japanese writer Natsume Soseki arrived in late Victorian London to study for two years. His writing about this period is not so well known to English readers, perhaps because they feel they have had their fill of narratives about fog, chimney sweeps, maids, and the draughty misery of this period from countless numbers of English writers from Dickens to Conan Doyle. However, as with Carter, the real drama of Soseki's 'English' writing is not what it tells us about England, but what it tells us about Soseki himself.

Natsume Soseki returned to Japan after his two years in London and began a tragically short, but singular, literary career that was marked by a furious sense of independence. With regard to literary form he was an avid experimenter; in his academic career he shocked his contemporaries by turning down a very prestigious professorship. His public voice was loud, vocal and critical. He had many things to say about Japanese society that were uncomfortable for some Japanese people to hear. This said, the more I read of Soseki's work, and the more I discover about his literary life and career in Japan, the more convinced I am that his being an exotic Asian stranger in London at an early and critical stage of his intellectual and literary development helped him to develop into the fully mature and outstandingly gifted writer that he subsequently became.

In one startling passage in 'Letter from London' (1901) we see Soseki as he sees himself:

> In any case, I feel small. An unusually small person approaches. Eureka! I think. But when we brush past one another I see he is about two inches taller than me. A strangely complex-ioned Tom Thumb approaches, but now I realise this is my own image reflected in a mirror. There is nothing for it but to laugh bitterly, and, naturally, when I do so, the image laughs bitterly, too. When I go to the park, herds of women walk around like horned lionesses with nets on their heads. Amongst them are some men. And some tradesmen. I am struck by the fact that they are for the most part better dressed than many a high-ranking official in Japan. In this country one cannot work out someone's status by their dress. A butcher's boy, when Sunday rolls around, will proudly put on his silk hat and frock-coat.

These sometimes alarming English encounters continually throw Soseki back upon himself and down into deep wells of self-reflective contemplation. He finds both who and what he is being continually challenged in a profound manner, and one can sense in Soseki's writing a man who is becoming unmoored in a most fundamental way:

> When I was in Japan I knew I was not particularly white but regarded myself as being close to a regular human color, but in this country I have finally realised that I am three leagues away from a human color — a yellow person who saunters amongst the crowds going to watch plays and shows

. . . In one park I heard a couple arguing whether I was a Chinaman or a Japanese. Two or three days ago I was invited out somewhere and set off in my silk hat and frock-coat only for two men who seemed like workmen to pass by saying, 'A handsome Jap.' I do not know whether I should be flattered or offended.

The literary exchange between Japan and the West has been explored by other writers aside from Angela Carter and Natsume Soseki. One has to think no further than Shusaku Endo, the first Japanese to study in Europe after the Second World War, or the Swiss writer Nicolas Bouvier whose meditation on Japan (*The Japanese Chronicles*) is as brave and eloquent as any piece of modern non-fiction that I am aware of. There is a fascinating self-searching literary energy that is generated in these writers by their having suffered the discomforts of temporary literary exile, but what they seem to gain is an often extremely penetrating sociocultural vision that is the legacy of their often gloomy sojourns.

During my one brief visit to Japan in November 2002, I found myself constantly wondering about both Angela Carter and Natsume Soseki. And, of course, I began to speculate on what, if any, are the links — conscious or unconscious — between, on the one hand, the African diasporan world that I represent, and which has formed the bedrock of the subject matter I have written about for over twenty-five years, and, on the other hand, the world of contemporary Japan. My own visit to Japan was hardly 'exile' but being outside what Angela Carter describes as the 'Judaeo-Christian world' it did force me to look at myself in a new way and to scrutinise each day this country in which I was most certainly *Gaijin*. Evidently I was in a society that had some difficulties reconciling vigorous expressions of individual identity with national expectation, and I reminded myself that this same problem has plagued people of African origin as they try to make a life for themselves in a wide range of societies. Certainly the Britain I grew up in operated with a tacit understanding that some individuals, because of their class, gender, race or religion, should have the good grace to remain mute, obedient and simply know their place. Mercifully, this has, to some extent, changed. In fact, the great majority of people of African origin who live in the West now do so with a strong understanding that they should resist any attempt to encourage them to pursue their lives in an obedient vacuum of silence. This impulse to speak is important for it is often activated by a moral impulse to tell the truth and avoid the tyranny of silence. To my mind, Shusaku Endo is a great moral writer, a writer whose best-known work is called, appropriately enough, *Silence*. But Angela Carter and Natsume Soseki are also great writers whose own temporary exiles eventually led them back through the door of themselves, and towards the moral centre of the debates that were raging back 'home'. While travelling in Japan it became clear to me the extent to which their sojourns abroad, as strangers in strange lands, had inestimable significance for their development as writers. Now, having reread their work, I am sure of this fact. I also now understand that an umbilical cord often connects the pain of exile to the pleasure of literature. It takes a politically determined, clear-sighted and brave writer to purposefully embrace wilful exile. Carter and Soseki were such people.

A Familial Conversation (2006)

In the 1930s, in a Paris that most of us can best imagine in black and white, and with an acoustic soundtrack, two remarkable men sat down for a conversation – or more properly, a series of conversations. One was Léopold Senghor, a young student from Senegal, and the other was Aimé Césaire, a young student from the French Caribbean island of Martinique. One imagines that they had much to talk about: the weather, the food, the girls, their studies and, of course, how much they were missing home. Important as all of these topics were, the two young men had a more urgent topic on their agenda which was that of their relationship to this world that they were determined to change. They already saw themselves as artists, but they also felt that once they had completed their studies they would have a responsibility to help to shape the political direction of their respective countries. Eventually, Senghor would return to Senegal where, some years later, he became President, and Césaire would return to Martinique and be elected to the influential political post of mayor of the capital city, Fort-de-France.

One can assume that these two men – one African, one Caribbean – saw something in each other which they respected. And one can also assume that the very act of conversational engagement must have helped them to determine their individual positions with regard to both politics and the arts. Beyond their obvious like and trust for each other, what bound them together was their stern questioning of French colonial rule, and their conviction that colonialism was most vigorous and corrosive when it sought – as it inevitably did – to destroy something they understood to be 'black culture'. Neither man could conceive of a future for himself in which his artistic efforts achieved validation only when reflected through European eyes. There were some writers who seemed content with such a fate, but not these two.

As they spoke long into the night, each learned to see himself reflected in the eyes of the other writer. The African man looking at the Caribbean man, the Caribbean man looking at the African man. Their many conversations gained weight, grew more focused, and eventually spawned a movement that became known as 'Negritude', a movement whose underlying principles asserted that a common 'black culture' existed; a culture which united those of Africa with those of the African diaspora, and a culture whose strengths and positive attributes were such that if one could only recognise and promote it, then it would no longer be neces-sary to continually negotiate Europe's assumption of black infe-riority, artistic or otherwise.

Some years later, in fact in September 1956, both men once again found themselves in Paris, a city which, without irony, continued to be spoken of as the intellectual hub of French West Africa and the French Caribbean. Both writers were, as they had hoped to become, politically active, and as writers their reputations were secure and their influence extensive. The one-time students, now writer-politicians, were attending the Conference of Negro-African Writers and Artists that was being held in the Sorbonne's Amphitheatre Descartes. The writer Alioune Diop, one of the conveners of the conference, was in no doubt what bound this diverse group of delegates and atten-dees together. During his opening remarks he commented that 'the people gathered together here held in common the fact of their subjugation to Europe ... or [at the very least] to the European vision of the world'. Continuing, he asserted 'that European well-being had been, for centuries, [so] crucially dependent on this subjugation'.

As the conference unfolded it soon became evident that the

black writers and artists gathered there were continuing and developing the conversation that had begun two decades earlier between Senghor and Césaire. Most of those who spoke at, or who attended, the conference, took for granted that all black people possessed a common heritage that existed in opposition to Europe, and their task was now to define that culture. The American writer James Baldwin was in Paris and he reported on the conference for the magazine *Encounter*. Baldwin recognised three clearly expressed aims. First, to define, or assign responsibility for the state of black culture; second, to assess the state of black culture at the present time; and third, to open a 'new' dialogue with Europe.

The conference lasted from Wednesday, 19 September, until just before 7 p.m. on Saturday the 22nd, and underlying most of the debate was an unease which was triggered on the very first day. The African American writer W.E.B. Du Bois had sent a message stating that, much to his regret, his government had denied him a passport to attend the gathering. This resulted in applause from the hall for presumably Dr Du Bois was telling it like it was. But Baldwin detected, and rightly so, something else. A discomfort, in fact a broad gulf of unease, that exists between what he termed the American Negro and other men of color. While Dr Du Bois was being enthusiastically applauded for what people perceived to be his courageous and ongoing struggle with the US government, the five-man American delegation at the conference felt somewhat isolated.

Potentially, an African man and a Caribbean man have much in common, largely because for much of the nineteenth and twentieth centuries they were forged in the same crucible of colonial exploitation. But the African American has a somewhat different history. He has been shaped not by colonialism, but by American expansionism. Indeed he has not only been shaped by it, he has been a central participant in it. Remember, the Buffalo Soldiers had rifles. Of course, W.E.B. Du Bois knew this, which is why in the early autumn of his life he gave up on America and embraced the flawed socialism of the Soviet

Union and China, and then eventually began to take on board the African essentialisms of Nkrumah, albeit leavened with a strong dose of quasi-Marxism. Having both witnessed and endured the African American's contradictory role in the republic, and struggled for years as a writer, teacher and activist to change individual and collective minds, Du Bois felt that the hypocrisy of his country had left him both fatigued and backed into a corner. There were few places left to run. One of the places he wished to run to was Paris in 1956, but his government had a noose around his ankle. At last, Du Bois did flee to Ghana where, having renounced his US citizenship, he died at ninety-five years of age in Accra, a Ghanaian citizen.

There was no such noose around the ankle of Richard Wright or James Baldwin, both of whom were in the audience for all four days of the conference. Wright, in fact, spoke at length, and Baldwin made notes and later wrote at length. Although they agreed on hardly anything else both writers certainly agreed on the central divide between American Negroes and these colored colonial 'whiners' from the French- and English-speaking worlds. Wright and Baldwin felt that, despite their own chequered relationship with the United States, they had been born into, as Baldwin put it, a world with 'a greater number of possibilities', and this 'brave new world' freed them from colonial constrictions. Their entrance into the American world may have been undeniably painful, but if they could convince America of their indispensability to the formation and development of the country, then they would have very little reason to look to Africa for anything. Baldwin in particular felt very strongly that part of his struggle as a writer was to help and encourage Negro Americans to see themselves as Americans, and until they could do this then it was arguable that it would be futile for them to start thinking of themselves as Africans.

Today, almost fifty years after the Paris conference, we still have major migration, both temporary and permanent, from Africa and the Caribbean to Europe – principally to Paris or London or Brussels or Amsterdam – but without any doubt the United States is now the first choice for most Caribbean or African migrants. There is an economic pull which attracts people to the United States, but one also wonders about the attraction of potentially functioning in a society that is not freighted with a history which views people of African origin through a reductive colonial lens. Racism, the noxious residue of colonialism and imperialism, is certainly present in the United States, but to many would-be migrants, enduring American racism is preferable to the European double-act of racism delivered with a postcolonial scowl. In theory, the United States is a society of great reinvention, so that one can arrive in the United States and literally begin again. This notion of freedom makes sense to many would-be migrants, including those from former European colonies in Africa and the Caribbean who, if they choose to migrate might well prefer to move to a place where there is the possibility of growth, without having to continually negotiate the hypocrisies at the heart of the old colonial empires in Europe. In this sense, concerns with negritude might be seen to have been replaced by what somebody once called a desire for American 'migritude'.

I wonder, however, if the clues to this new American 'migritude' were not already present back in Paris in the thirties when the two students, Senghor and Césaire, sat down to talk to each other. Their mentors, the very people whose work and thought liberated them, were African American writers, colonials who had made their journey of growth by way of the United States. Claude McKay, Alain Locke, W.E.B. Du Bois, Langston Hughes: these were the men whom the two French-speaking students looked to. It was, in fact, the Harlem Renaissance that provided Senghor and Césaire with the impetus to search for an authentic sense of black culture. And, in later years, other colonials who had passed through the United States, including Marcus Garvey, George Padmore and C.L.R. James, helped to further enhance intellectual development in the African diasporan world.

Today, in the English-speaking world, a great number of

African and Caribbean writers, who two generations ago might have looked to Britain to study in and launch their careers, are now based outside Europe, primarily in the United States. There are many conversations taking place in America between writers from Africa and those from the Caribbean, and of course African American writers are included in the mix. Meanwhile, back in Europe, African writers, Caribbean writers, and those writers of African origin who are now increasingly identifying themselves as simply French, or British, or German, or Italian writers, are trying to begin new conversations with each other. However, the central question that disturbed the conference in 1956, and continues to undermine the familial conversation to this day, is this: How does one have a conversation between African writers and writers of the African diaspora and effectively and productively include African Americans? And if we do speak to each other, which is of course highly desirable, what should we talk about beyond the banalities of pigmentation?

Clearly colonialism cannot be on the agenda. Unless, of course, we're talking about the neocolonialism that is US imperialism. If so, one is then forced to look very closely at the racial make-up of the US military machine, and explain the presence of Condoleezza Rice and Colin Powell at the heart of American policy-making. The question on the table will not be so much about finding a common black culture, it will be a more complicated question about the nature of, and the quest for, power. And how this 'power' impacts on the social, political and artistic expression of a people. This is what our two students were talking about back in the Paris of the 1930s when the debate was neatly circumscribed by race. By 1956, that crucial year of decolonisation, the presence of an American delegation in the Amphitheatre Descartes at the Conference of Negro-African Writers and Artists meant that race was no longer enough to ensure that the conversation could be neatly centripetal, and paradoxically the very people who had inspired Senghor and Césaire – African Americans – were no longer comfortable with that conversation.

Today, in order to build fruitful communication that would fully include all of those in the extended family of Africa and the African diaspora, we probably need to be attempting to achieve some consensus around the word 'power'. The question on the table today would seem to be less about finding a common black culture, and more about addressing the lingering legacy of European colonialism and the ongoing, unacceptable, spectacle of imperialism in our world. The continued uses and abuses of power affect not only the masses; they also affect the artistic expression of the self-appointed few – the writers and artists – which is why, tongue-in-cheek, the always perceptive James Baldwin called his essay about the fractious and difficult conference back in the Paris of 1956, 'Princes and Power'.

James Baldwin: The Price of the Ticket (2007)

In July 1957, an ocean liner set sail from France to New York and on board was the almost thirty-three-year-old James Baldwin. Nine years earlier he had made the reverse journey and left his native New York City for Paris with $40 in his pocket and no knowledge of either France or the French language. He had chosen Paris because his mentor, Richard Wright, was living there, having sought refuge from the demeaning racial politics of his homeland. The young James Baldwin felt that if he was ever going to discover himself as a man and a writer then he would also have to flee the United States. His exile in France had often been difficult and was marked by poverty, a period in jail, and at least one suicide attempt, but in the end this opening act of Baldwin's literary life proved to be triumphantly productive. His first novel, *Go Tell it on the Mountain* (1953), established his name, and his collection of essays, *Notes of a Native Son* (1955), and his controversial second novel, *Giovanni's Room* (1956), secured his reputation as an important, and fast-rising, literary figure.

Baldwin's first books were written in hotel rooms, in borrowed houses or apartments, and eventually in his own cramped flat in Paris. During these early European years, the relatively unknown Baldwin was largely 'offstage' and beyond the scrutiny of media attention. Aside from the weight of his own ambition, and the practical difficulty of money, there was little pressure upon his slender shoulders. The young writer was focused, and engaging fearlessly with a wide range of difficult subjects, including the frustrations of adolescence, homosexuality, and the problematics of the father–son relationship. The literary tone he seemed to have perfected was a powerful fusion of African American oration and nineteenth-century moral romanticism in the tradition of Thoreau and Emerson. Baldwin's gracefully lilting sentences were informed by the cadences of the King James Bible, but the influence of Henry James was also evident. The young author's mutable words and elliptical phrases endlessly circled back on themselves in a self-questioning manner, weaving patterns of doubt while, paradoxically, achieving an overall effect of carefully attained certitude. James Baldwin's decision to return to the United States in July 1957 marked a turning point in the writer's career and signalled the end of this age of both innocence and discovery.

The man who stood on the deck of the ocean liner in 1957 and turned his face towards the western horizon knew that by ending his European apprenticeship and returning to the United States he would be stepping onstage and into visibility. In August 1957, soon after arriving back in New York City, Baldwin made his first journey south to North Carolina, Georgia and Alabama, in order that he might understand, in more intimate detail, the difficult realities of his country and write a piece for *Partisan Review*. In later years, Baldwin often insisted that he had returned home because, at this stage of his life, he had little choice but to be a witness to what was happening in his country during this early period of the Civil Rights Movement. However, his desire to observe and record the tempest of change blowing through the United States did not, by itself, motivate him to return. In 1941, the seventeen-year-old Baldwin had declared, in his high school yearbook, an ambition to be a 'Novelist-Playwright'. When asked to add a further comment, Baldwin wrote, 'Fame is the spur and – Ouch!' All journeys exact a price, but as James Baldwin sailed towards the second act of his writing career, there is no way he could have intuited just how difficult for him, physically and emotionally, the next decade or so would prove, and how the frenzy of these years would ultimately affect his stated ambition to be a 'Novelist-Playwright'.

The second act of Baldwin's literary life extended from 1957 until 1970, and in this time the author produced two novels, *Another Country* (1962) and *Tell Me How Long the Train's Been Gone* (1968). The rather plotless drama of *Another Country* finally holds together because of the passion and intensity of the prose, particularly evident in the bold opening section of the novel which concerns the jazz musician, Rufus Scott. Yet even here the tone occasionally topples over into rhetorical excess and melodrama, and by the time we reach *Tell Me How Long the Train's Been Gone*, Baldwin's understanding of the form of the novel seems to have abandoned him. The narrative is inert and rendered largely in flashback, the tone is often shrill, the characterisation sketchy, and the book insists on pounding us over the head as it makes its 'points'. It is difficult to believe that the author of this rambling fiction could be the same person who wrote the poised and understated *Go Tell it on the Mountain*. When E.L. Doctorow, Baldwin's then-editor at Dial Press, asked him to work on the manuscript, Baldwin told him to do with it whatever he wished. He was simply not interested. When galley proofs were sent to him for correction, Baldwin failed to return them.

Baldwin's non-fiction of the early 1960s seems better suited to the more declarative register in his voice. The sinewy, almost hesitant prose and the unstable syntax suggest a purposeful, intellectual questing, but in his fiction these deviations imply an incompleteness of characterisation and a structural formlessness which give rise to a suspicion that the author has simply taken both hands off the steering wheel. His non-fiction better accommodates his stylistic circumlocution, and the essays in *Nobody Knows My Name* (1961) successfully pick up where *Notes of a Native Son* left off, so much so that the publisher subtitled them, *More Notes of a Native Son*. *The Fire Next Time* (1963) is Baldwin's masterpiece, and it spectacularly captures the racial and sociocultural divisions in the United States on the eve of the Civil Rights Act of 1964. On its publication the book created a sensation, for here was a black man insisting that white

Americans might not care about their own salvation, or their moral corruption, but if they didn't shape up then they would be faced with potential disaster. All over the South, blacks were being beaten at lunch counters or at voter registration drives, or when peacefully protesting in the street or worshipping in their churches, but this finger-wagging, pop-eyed, diminutive Negro of reputedly questionable morals was warning white Americans that the same iniquities might well be visited on them unless they began to put their house in order. His high style embraced ambiguity and paradox at a time when nobody had heard a writer, let alone a black writer, speak of race in a manner that went beyond the crude vulgarities of a discourse rooted in binary oppositions: good/bad, black/white, right/wrong. To Baldwin, the drama of race involved the confession box and whispered narratives of guilt that might eventually give way to blessings of absolution and 'no charge' on the penance front. Acute social observation and personal autobiography come together dramatically in *The Fire Next Time*, and this grand lyrical assault upon his country's wilful myopia, and America's inability to confront the full implications of its own history, was published, appropriately enough, one hundred years after the emancipation of the slaves.

Much of Baldwin's other writing in this period, including the play *Blues for Mr Charlie* (1964), the screenplay based on the life and death of Malcolm X (later published as *One Day When I Was Lost*), and numerous uncollected essays, testify to a stylistic shift away from the nuanced ebb and flow of the first act of his literary career, and a new engagement with a more judgemental polemic. This was the age of political assassinations, prison riots at Attica and elsewhere, and the emergence of the Black Power movement; given the times, Baldwin's belief in the refining power of redemptive love was beginning to sound like a decidedly unhip narrative. As the sixties progressed, an increasingly vociferous Baldwin appeared keen to adopt a public position in all his writings, as though trying to defuse some of the criticism that was being elled against him, particularly by the African American community and writers such as Eldridge Cleaver and Amiri Baraka. He seems to have been stung into becoming not just a witness, but occasionally a mouthpiece, and he began to thunder like a preacher and declare his beliefs with a vigour which would leave nobody in doubt as to where he stood on just about everything. However, this anxious attempt to 'hustle' a politically strident voice felt false, including, one suspects, to Baldwin himself.

This second act of his literary life is notable, not only because of the uneven quality of the work, but also because of the degree of fame that Baldwin achieved. Here was a man on a mission. In the mid-sixties he was arguably the most photographed author in the world; on 17 May 1963 he was on the cover of *Time* magazine the week after John F. Kennedy, the editors of *Time* regarding him as an appropriate follow-up. He was in constant demand for lectures and readings all over the United States and around the world, and he was continually being interviewed on television, radio, and in print. His performances were often dazzling and they were generally delivered with an authority which overwhelmed the audience. With this level of fame came a daunting travel schedule, and it is astonishing that Baldwin managed to get *any* work done during this period. In fact, he was only able to do so by temporarily withdrawing from the glare of public attention and retreating to the MacDowell Colony in New Hampshire, or to various friends' homes in New England, or else travelling to Turkey and hiding away from this monster called fame. However, there could be no denying that this was a monster that he had chased down and fed, and he was fully aware that it was easier, and more profitable, both financially and in terms of his profile, to stride to the podium, as opposed to the desk. In a July 1965 televised BBC interview with the writer Colin MacInnes, Baldwin spoke openly of his predicament: 'The great terror of public speaking is that you begin to listen to yourself. By and by, since you are always telling people what to think, you begin to forget what you do think. And the moment that happens, of course, it's over. It's over.'

By 1970 it was too much, and forty-six-year-old James Baldwin, his health broken, and in need of rest and recuperation, returned to France, this time to the South, to Saint-Paul de Vence, where he began the third and final act of his literary life. While the work in the second act might not have entirely fulfilled the promise of the first, he had, during his thirteen years in America, developed a reputation as a courageous man and a brilliant orator who spoke out for moral change, and he was, indeed, regarded by many as a witness. By this stage of his life he was more famous for being a celebrity-spokesman, than for whatever it was he was doing with his pen. By leaving the relative 'obscurity' of Paris and stepping on to centre stage in the United States he had achieved 'fame', but it now seemed that he had done so at the cost of his writing.

Even the most trenchant supporter of James Baldwin's work will find it difficult to argue that the two novels of the seventies, *If Beale Street Could Talk* (1974) and *Just Above My Head* (1979) would, if they were not part of the Baldwin *oeuvre*, be much spoken of today. Both novels suffer from, and then further develop, the problems evident in *Tell Me How Long the Train's Been Gone*. They are excessively rhetorical, structurally confusing, and lacking in coherent characterisation. There are passages in both novels, especially in *Just Above My Head*, which soar with a familiar eloquence, but all too often such moments quickly give way to longueurs where one feels as though the impatient author, James Baldwin, has decided to elbow his way past the gallery of assembled characters and speak directly to us – witness to congregation. Baldwin's non-fiction of the seventies and early eighties is more successful than the fiction, because the form itself is more forgiving of Baldwin's rhetorical habits. However, while *No Name in the Street* (1972) and *The Devil Finds Work* (1976) have much of Baldwin's familiar perception and wit, the sinewy prose appears to have atrophied, and the liturgical rhythms have lost some of their skip and their beat. Sadly, *The Evidence of Things Not Seen* (1985), Baldwin's report on the Wayne Williams trial for the Atlanta child murders, is a book that appears to have been, from the beginning, badly conceived. As it proceeds it feels increasingly padded with irrelevant autobiographical asides which continually lead the reader away from, rather than towards, the central subject matter under consideration.

Baldwin's biographer, James Campbell, recalls Jimmy talking to him in the early 1980s about making his 'comeback'. I, too, remember similar late-night conversations with Jimmy in France. He would speak of his 'comeback' with some gravitas, and then crack a huge smile as though the very notion of what he had just said amused him. But a part of him was in earnest. He knew that some of the purpose and clarity that he possessed in his early writing career had been lost in those recklessly public thirteen years. When he told me, in the summer of 1984, that he would soon be publishing his collected essays and that he was going to call them *The Price of the Ticket*, he burst out laughing. Jimmy loved titles, and he often had the title of the book long before it was written. Sometimes the book was never written and he was simply left with the title; for instance, his unwritten novel of immigration, entitled *No Papers for Mohammed*. Or his unwritten slave novel, which was to be called *Talking at the Gates*. Or his unwritten book about Medger, Malcolm and Martin, which he had christened *Remember this House*. *The Price of the Ticket* was a wonderfully compelling title, but I never asked him directly, either on that night or subsequently, what the price of the ticket was, or what kind of a journey he had endured, or enjoyed, in return.

During that same visit, Jimmy handed me the manuscript for *The Evidence of Things Not Seen*. It was late at night, and he was about to go downstairs to sleep in the study/bedroom that he liked to call 'the torture chamber'. Before he did so, Jimmy shared with me the news that his publisher had rejected this latest book, and he appeared to be understandably hurt. He asked me if I would read the manuscript and let him know what I thought. Of course I would, I was deeply flattered, and so I stayed up all night and read it through in one sitting. I put the manuscript to one side as the sun was rising, and then I fell fast asleep. As usual, Jimmy emerged around noon and we sat outside for lunch. 'Well?' he asked. I couldn't bear to tell the truth and told him that I couldn't understand why it had been turned down. The truth was, I could fully understand why his publisher was disappointed. *The Evidence of Things Not Seen* had begun life as an essay in *Playboy* magazine, and at this length it worked, but beating and stretching it into a book made little sense. When I told him that I liked the book — I think I called it 'outstanding' — I sensed that Jimmy knew otherwise, but he was really too kind a man to force the issue.

It is impossible to know what would have happened to James Baldwin's writing career if he had not boarded that ship to New York in July 1957 and sailed towards fame and his role as a witness. It may well be that, instead of producing more sensitively nuanced work in the tradition of his first two novels and *Notes of a Native Son*, his imagination would have stumbled in France (or in Turkey, or in Switzerland). Simply reading about developments back home in the United States, as opposed to participating in them, would probably have driven Baldwin to distraction. Between 1957 and 1970, James Baldwin utilised his great strength of purpose, and his boundless energy, in an attempt to combine his role as a public intellectual and spokesperson with his vocation as a writer. However, as time passed, it became increasingly clear that exposing his private life — the wellspring of his creativity — to public scrutiny, and investing so heavily in his sense of himself as a celebrity-witness, was costing him dearly as a writer. After all, if you refuse to edit your own book then you have either lost faith in the book, or you have lost sight of the importance of writing. By returning to France in 1970, Baldwin effectively left centre stage, moved back to the wings, slipped into a chair behind his desk, and tried to refocus as a writer. But what to write about? The United States in 1970 bore little relationship to the United States in 1957, and his role as a witness no longer appeared to be crucial. In 1973, *Time* magazine decided not to run an exclusive interview

with James Baldwin and Josephine Baker in France, conducted by their European correspondent, Henry Louis Gates Jnr. They deemed Baldwin – to use their word – 'passé'. However, though Baldwin's celebrity status was declining, he could at least reapply himself to his writing. Or so he thought.

James Baldwin was a fiercely intelligent and perceptive man, and he knew the perils of neglecting the inner self and relinquishing so much of his privacy. He frequently claimed that he felt compelled to live such a furiously public life as part of his duty to be a witness, but there are many ways of bearing witness. To do so while exposing oneself to the full glare of the media spotlight is a particularly risky way of fulfilling one's obligation. I am sure that, as he mounted public platforms or once again submitted himself to the often banal questions of the interviewer, Baldwin understood that he was avoiding the inner meditation and reflection – the sitting in judgement on oneself – which is an essential part of a writer's development. He seemed to be forever onstage looking out, and part of his inner turmoil was fed by his understanding that the price of the ticket that he had purchased had necessitated mortgaging his life as a writer. When I first met Jimmy in the summer of 1983, in the main village square in Saint-Paul de Vence, the BBC producer who accompanied me asked Jimmy if he thought that he would ever win the Nobel Prize. I was embarrassed by this question but, as generous as ever, Jimmy laughed, then took a languorous draw on his cigarette, smiled and said, 'They'll probably get round to giving it to me someday.' But that smile was a knowing smile.

As James Baldwin sailed towards his destiny in July 1957, he knew that in the immediate future it would be very difficult for him to 'settle down' and enjoy a life of domestic tranquillity. Perhaps if somebody had appeared in Act Two of his literary career, and forced him to change his lifestyle, then Jimmy might have saved some of himself for Jimmy, and ultimately for his work. After all, to fall in love and achieve security is to find a kind of peace – a kind of invisibility. But

this person did not appear, and for those thirteen years his crazed, peripatetic schedule seemed to ensure that domestic stability, let alone tranquillity, was doomed to remain an impossible dream. Outside of his immediate family, Jimmy lacked a constantly close companion who, to put it simply, could be relied upon to love and protect him. So much of his work rehearses the great difficulty, yet the absolute necessity, of love, and Jimmy *was* a romantic, and he *did* crave the type of protective love that would be enduring. As is often the case with generous and gregarious people, his fierce independence and general bonhomie often obscured this deep desire to be looked after and feel safe, but fame introduces a particular desolation into the soul, a loneliness that no amount of partying, or travelling, or drinking can mask.

The day after James Baldwin died, I stood in the entrance hall to the house in Saint-Paul de Vence and looked at Jimmy's body as he lay in an open coffin. In the living room his Swiss friend of nearly forty years, Lucien Happersberger, his brother David Baldwin, and his friend and secretary, Bernard Hassell, were talking quietly. I sat down next to Jimmy and stared into his now peaceful face. I remembered that I had challenged him one snowy night in Amherst, Massachusetts and asked him why he was wasting his time in 'this dump of a town' instead of buckling down and producing another Jimmy Baldwin novel. The folly and stupidity of youth. Jimmy heard me out, then smiled gracefully and said, 'One day you'll understand, baby.' As I looked at him in his coffin, I wanted to apologise for not understanding that night in Amherst. He had given me friendship and warmth, and I had nothing to give back to him. Twenty years after his death, I still have nothing tangible to give back to him, except some increased understanding of the price that he paid to become the extraordinary man that he was. By returning to the United States in 1957 he found what he called a 'role', and he found fame, but to achieve these goals he had to live a life that in the end could only prove injurious to him as a writer. I now understand that

behind the clever title, *The Price of the Ticket*, there was courage, sorrow and pain. There was no self-pity. I now understand that the seventeen-year-old boy already knew something profound about the man that he would become. The boy had already intuited the price of the ticket. 'Fame is the spur and – Ouch!' As the talented youngster grew into the eminent man, he remained true to his dream, and he succeeded beyond anybody's wildest hopes, including his own; but every day the man wrestled hard with the frustration of knowing exactly what he had lost, and missed out on, as he made his determined, and wilful, way in the world.

According to another of Baldwin's biographers, David Leeming, in November 1987 in Saint-Paul de Vence, an ailing and bedridden Jimmy turned to Leeming and said, 'Sometimes I can't believe that I'm famous too.' The thought had suddenly struck Jimmy, as the two men were talking about Charlie Chaplin, Lena Horne, Bessie Smith and Simone Signoret. At this stage of his life, Jimmy's mind was beginning to wander, and his body was weakening. However, he was simply checking that he had *really* made, and completed, the journey towards fame. He knew that he had paid the price. He had been suffering the heartache of rejections from publishers, indifferent reviews and falling sales for years now, but he had borne these slights with dignity. There is a beautiful innocence, and characteristic modesty, to his words as he conjured with the fact that this boy, who was born in a Harlem hospital some sixty-three years earlier, had actually travelled this remarkable path, one that he had laid down with the brilliance of his own vision. He may not have had at his side the one loyal, loving person that he seemed to yearn for, but at this juncture of his life he was surrounded by Lucien, David and Bernard, all of whom were devoted to him and who loved him deeply. And the passion and purpose of his writing, his early work in particular, had long ago ensured the permanence of his place in the literary canon. And, of course, more than any other late-twentieth-century American writer, he had set the stage for the debate on

race that was needed then, and is still desperately needed today. The journey was complete. The price paid. The pain and frustration fully absorbed. 'Sometimes I just can't believe that I'm famous too.' Three days later, James Baldwin died.

Ha Jin: Exile on Main Street (2008)

In Ha Jin's last novel, *A Free Life* (2007), the acclaimed Chinese American writer finally crossed the Pacific Ocean and rooted a work of fiction in American soil. It appeared that Ha Jin's fiction had finally caught up with his own life. Born in Liaoning in 1956, he joined the People's Liberation Army as a teenager and later attended Heilongjiang University where he earned a Bachelor's degree in English, and then Shandong University where he graduated with a Master's degree in Anglo-American Literature. In 1985, Ha Jin left China and arrived at Brandeis University as a twenty-nine-year-old graduate student. He began a Ph.D. in English, but dreamed of one day returning to China as a teacher or translator and perhaps eventually becoming a writer. It was the Tiananmen Square massacre of 1989 that convinced Ha Jin, and many other Chinese students studying abroad, that a return to China was ill-advised, and so a decision was made to remain in the United States and pursue what was now an urgent desire to be a writer. Xuefi Jin took on the pen name Ha Jin (the 'Ha' coming from his favourite city, Harbin), and began the task of learning how to become a writer in the United States.

Nearly a quarter of a century on, it is clear that this migrant writer has succeeded. Now a Professor of English at Boston University, his short stories and novels have twice earned him the PEN/Faulkner Award, and in 1999 he received the National Book Award for his novel, *Waiting*. Until *A Free Life* the focus of his gaze was backwards, over his shoulder and in the direction of the land he left behind. His novels *Waiting* (1999) and *War*

Trash (2004), in particular, are redolent with loss, and the essential tone of his writing would suggest that a quiet lament informs his carefully modulated sentences. However, there is also anger and frustration in Ha Jin's fictional world for Chinese bureaucracy is rigid, sometimes dogmatic, and Ha Jin's work has powerfully explored how Chinese authority and tradition often stifle human dignity and individual identity. Until, that is, his latest novel.

A Free Life is an epic work, with a panoramic vision whose narrative form resembles a hefty, plot-driven, nineteenth-century English novel. Nan Wu, a student who is pursuing graduate work in political science at Brandeis University, and his wife Pingping, become disillusioned with the prospect of returning to their homeland in the wake of the Tiananmen Square massacre. Nan decides to abandon his studies and instead nurture his love of poetry, and to this end he takes a series of menial jobs while his wife remains a housekeeper and cook to a wealthy American widow. Nan and Pingping are reunited with their six-year-old son, Taotao, who travels from China to join them in the United States, and they are thereafter free to begin life afresh as a family in Massachusetts. Eventually they leave the Northeast for an unappealing suburb of Atlanta, where they buy a Chinese restaurant that is located in a strip mall in a largely white, blue-collar and conservative rural subdivision. As they try to establish themselves as freedom-loving Americans who are attempting to run a business and pay off their mortgage on a modest home, Nan is increasingly haunted by his memories of China, including a woman whom he believes he still loves. He is also consumed with his present struggle to understand how to compose poetry and begin to live the life of a writer. Naturally, as their son grows up and becomes more American in behaviour and language, the hinge of generation starts to turn and open up the door on to an American world which Nan Wu and Pingping often find baffling.

We soon learn that this United States can be a frightening place for Chinese immigrants. In an early scene in the novel,

Nan takes time off from his duties as a nightwatchman at a local factory and goes to a nearby supermarket to pick up some food. Walking back to his car he is accosted by an aggressive white couple who want to take him to get 'some young pussies'. They persist, so Nan hurries to his car and flees but the couple pursue him. It is apparent that his 'difference' has placed him, and by extension his family, in danger. A distraught Nan asks himself, 'Why were they so determined to hurt him? Just because they could? Just because his face was yellow, not as white as theirs?'

At various points in the novel, Nan, Pingping and Taotao encounter the problem of being migrants who are visibly different in skin color, accent and culture. They are singled out for discrimination, but this is not the vision of America that Nan wishes to believe in. Despite these setbacks, to his mind the United States still represents opportunity and hope, in the same way that the country did when he first arrived as a student. Nan remembers:

> Among some of his contemporaries at Brandeis, Nan had a nickname, Mr Wagon Man, because he had once quoted Emerson at a party – 'Hitch your wagon to a star' – in an attempt to dissuade a linguist from switching to the field of economics. A historian, an arch-browed man from Henan Province, admonished Nan not to 'parrot that so-called New England sage' who was a racist and always despised the Chinese.

Nan comes to understand much about prejudice and the perils of being the 'other', but he attempts to contextualise his condition by looking at how others are treated. The novel is littered with references to blacks, Hispanics and gay people, but Nan also understands that as a would-be writer he should set his course and navigate towards those, including 'racist' New England sages, who might help him come to terms with what it means to be a writer. And, as the novel unfolds, we discover that Nan

Wu wishes to be a writer at least as much as he wishes to be an American.

The novel is unashamedly autobiographical, following the path of the author's own journey from China to Brandeis University and on to a series of menial jobs, then to suburban Atlanta, and finally to publication. The dedication of the novel is to Ha Jin's own wife and child 'who lived this book', and the epilogue to the novel is a fictional extract from Nan Wu's poetry journal followed by a selection of his poems. Ha Jin has published three collections of poetry. Looking at the novel through this lens, far from diminishing the achievement, we see a novel that is a meditation on the development of a migrant writer's sensibility *and* an immigrant success story of how a Chinese family adjusts and gradually becomes a Chinese American family. However, as readers we already have some experience of this second 'how we got over' story: as well as the direct reference to the Chinese situation, we have been exposed to this narrative in the many other novels of immigrant life that exist in the literature. As *A Free Life* proceeds it soon becomes clear that the strength of the novel, and its originality, reside in its evocation of the growth of a writer who is also an immigrant. Behind the well-constructed façade of the family story, the real drama of the novel concerns Nan Wu's individual struggle to remain focused and nurture the impulse to write and to find his literary voice.

Early in the novel Nan Wu leaves the family in Boston and travels to New York where he tries to get a low-level administrative job at a Chinese cultural centre. The interview does not go too well, and on leaving the centre he begins to speculate:

> Nan came out of the building with a sinking heart. Questions, one after another, were arising in his mind. Why do they call that place a cultural museum? Why are there so few exhibits that can be called artwork? How come there's no Picasso or Faulkner or Mozart that emerged from the immigrants? Does this mean the first Chinese here were less creative and

less artistic? Maybe so, because the early immigrants were impoverished and many were illiterate, and because they all had to slave away to feed themselves and their families, and had to concentrate their energy on settling down in this unfamiliar, discriminatory, fearsome land. Just uprooting themselves from their native soil must have crippled their lives and drained their vitality, not to mention their creativity. How could it be possible for an unfettered genius to rise from a tribe of coolies who were frightened, exhausted, mistreated, wretched, and possessed by the instinct for survival? Without leisure, how can art thrive?

But Nan Wu knows full well that this isn't the whole story. Chinese migrants *have* been writing stories about themselves and their culture, and he makes reference to 'contemporary authors such as Maxine Hong Kingston, Amy Tan, and Gish Jen'. He understands that such stories are subject to distortion and commercial pressure, and he is fully aware that 'success' can bring with it serious problems of authenticity.

Nan Wu's friend, Danning Meng, who has recently returned to Beijing, is one such migrant author who is now experiencing the problems of representation, albeit from the Chinese side. He writes to Nan Wu about his life and his writing.

Dear Nan Wu,
    . . . To be honest, I am not satisfied with my Alaskan novella. The editor cut too much from the story, and as a result the prose feels choppy and crude. She also put in many sentences of her own, which are out of place. Some of them are plainly jarring. The magazine was eager to cater to the readers' interest in the exotic, so the editorial department demanded that all the stories be set in foreign countries, and we were supposed to make them as outlandish as possible. I had no choice but to concede, otherwise they would not have printed the piece . . . I have been working hard on two novels,

both set in the United States. Stories about American life are hot nowadays. Have you seen the book *Manhattan's China Lady*? It's a runaway best seller here. My publisher is eager to have a blockbuster like that and has pressed me for the manuscripts several times. I have to finish my books soon, but I don't know how to write popular stuff and may disappoint my publisher.

From reading *A Free Life*, with its artful, yet anxious, digressions on just what it means to be both a migrant and a would-be writer, one can see why Ha Jin's most recent publication is a collection of three essays with the unambiguous title, *The Writer as Migrant*.

The three essays which make up this slender volume were originally delivered as the Rice University Campbell lectures in 2007. One immediately feels the leaden weight of the academy's often baffling obfuscations in the author's one-page preface. He states, 'By placing the writer in the context of human migrations, we can investigate some of the metaphysical aspects of a "migrant writer's" life and work.' Ha Jin continues. 'I make references to many works of literature because I believe the usefulness and beauty of literature lies in its capacity to illuminate life.' Well, yes, but where are we going with this? He continues:

> I will speak at length about some exiled writers, not because I view myself only as an exile – I am also an immigrant – but mainly because the most significant literature dealing with human migration has been written on the experience of exile. By contrast, immigration is a minor theme, primarily American. Therefore, a major challenge for writers of the immigrant experience is how to treat this subject in response to the greater literary tradition.

The first essay, 'The Spokesman and the Tribe', deals with what the author calls the 'Aristotelian questions – to whom, as who, and in whose interest does he write?' At the beginning of his essay, Ha Jin makes a passing reference to his own work. 'My initial answers to those questions were quite simple. In the preface to *Between Silences*, my first book of poems, I wrote, "As a fortunate one I speak for those unfortunate people who suffered, endured or perished at the bottom of life and who created the history and at the same time were fooled or ruined by it."' To begin with, Ha Jin considered himself a writer who was speaking for the downtrodden masses of Chinese people whom he had left behind. He admits that his appropriation of such a position was partly motivated by guilt, but he realised that by taking up this self-appointed task he was opening himself up to accusations from those whom he claimed to serve. He never reveals if he was ever subjected to the scrutiny of those who might have asked him, 'Who gave you the right to speak for us?' for, having cracked open the door on to his own personal situation, he is quick to slam it shut again. He talks instead of what 'the people' might do to 'a writer' who seeks to claim such spokesmanship and, having firmly established the character of 'the writer', he liberates himself from any obligation to fulfil our expectations, or hope, that 'the writer' will be Ha Jin. This is disappointing for one cannot escape the feeling that, even at the inception of the volume, the most fascinating example of 'the writer as migrant' is Ha Jin himself.

The opening essay looks at two cases of spokesmanship: those of the Russian novelist Aleksandr Solzhenitsyn and the Chinese author Lin Yutang. According to Ha Jin, once they were outside their countries they both embraced the notion of speaking on behalf of their people and subsequently caused great damage to their work. In the case of Solzhenitsyn, the author believes that 'the books he wrote in Vermont are less literary than the novels he had written before his exile' largely due to the fact that once in exile he sought to bear witness and preserve the memory of the Russians who had no voice. While he champions *One Day in the Life of Ivan Denisovich*, *The First Circle* and *Cancer Ward* he is sure that 'his later books do not have a firm artistic order, and their relevance might fall to the erosion of historical change'. Of course, this may well be true, but is it not possible that even before he found himself in the backwoods of Vermont events within the Soviet Union had already caused Solzhenitsyn to reassess his purity of purpose as an artist? Surely, *The Gulag Archipelago*, a book whose first volume was published before his exile in 1974, already betrayed evidence that Solzhenitsyn's vision was being influenced by what Ha Jin calls 'nostalgia' as opposed to a firm resolve to craft novels in the realistic tradition. If this is the case, then it would seem to follow that Solzhenitsyn's exile was not the sole cause of the artistic atrophy that Ha Jin seems to detect.

The episode in Solzhenitsyn's life that appears to fascinate Ha Jin is the 'mystery' that surrounds the Russian writer's flirtation with naturalisation as a United States citizen. On 24 June, 1985, inside the courthouse in Rutland, Vermont, reporters and photographers waited for Solzhenitsyn to take the oath of United States citizenship. In the end, his wife showed up alone and received the certificate, having explained that her husband was 'not feeling well'. Clearly Solzhenitsyn had changed his mind at the last moment, and decided that he was not ready to give up on his native land. Ha Jin claims that, 'Fortunately, he was coolheaded enough to restrain himself from attending the naturalization ceremony.' But why 'fortunately'? Ha Jin has no faith in the position of writer as 'spokesman', and he feels that such a position causes damage to one's art, so why should he be so pleased that Solzhenitsyn maintained his 'loyalty' to the Soviet Union? One senses, without knowing exactly why, that this episode has a more personal meaning for the author, but while his retelling of the events is compelling, his conclusions feel hurried and unsatisfactory:

> This episode in Solzhenitsyn's life shows that despite the writer's careful construction of his relationship with his tribe, his role remains susceptible to change — any accidental, sometimes necessary, step might easily undermine the construction and force it to drastic revision. By writing about Solzhenitsyn's

attempted naturalization, I do not intend just to point out the folly this great man almost fell into. What I mean is to illustrate the fragility of his identity as a spokesman for his people.

Ha Jin looks at the case of the Chinese writer Lin Yutang in order to further demonstrate the perils of embracing the role of spokesman, although Lin faced the additional problem of having decided to write in English and, in some respects, become a cultural interpreter of his people for a Western audience. Ha Jin is sure about the adverse effect that this had on Lin's many works of fiction and non-fiction, including encouraging him to 'sweeten' the narrative so that some works read like popular romance. He also insists that Lin spread himself too 'thinly', producing many inferior books for money. He then spent five years (1967–72) compiling a large dictionary, the *Chinese–English Dictionary of Modern Usage* which Ha Jin describes as a 'mistake', for it was soon rendered insignificant by a similar project launched from within the state on the orders of Mao Zedong and boasting an editorial staff of over fifty people. Ha Jin is clear about what we should learn from this 'mistake', although once again his conclusion feels stilted. 'An established writer must avoid pitting his individual effort against any collective effort, because his principal asset is his creative talent and energy, which should be used primarily for creative work – great literature has never been produced by collectives.'

And it is great literature that Ha Jin is interested in, for only such literature 'can penetrate historical, political, and linguistic barriers and reach the readership that includes the people of the writer's native country'. Having shown us some of the dangers and pitfalls that face the migrant writer who, like himself in the early period of his writing life, seeks to cling to some sense of attachment to his people, Ha Jin leaves us wondering just how the migrant writer *should* comport himself with reference to his place of origin. One might have guessed where Ha Jin would find his answer. For a moment, he briefly opens a door again on to his life. 'I still remember vividly my first reading of Naipaul's novel *A Bend in the River*, a book that changed my life. It was in late December 1992, three years after I had declared in the preface to my first book that I would speak for the unfortunate Chinese . . .'

Book Two of Naipaul's novel begins with a passage about a column of ants who remain undisturbed by the loss of a single member of their tribe. There is no contract between the individual ant and the collective, and it is up to the unfortunate individual ant to fend for himself. The passage reminds Ha Jin that in China there is some notion of a relationship between oneself and one's country, but here in the West (in the United States), 'I saw that such a contract gave you a false sense of entitlement . . . Here you had to work like everyone else to put food on your table and had to learn to live as an independent man.' It is Naipaul who frees him from the claim of being a spokesman for the downtrodden Chinese and 'the silliness of that ambition'. Ha Jin comes to understand that a writer's first responsibility is to write well, and that the social role is secondary, 'mostly given by the forces around him, and it has little to do with his value as a writer'. He carefully rejects Nadine Gordimer's notion of the writer as having a social responsibility to make an 'essential gesture' and be more than just a writer; he uncouples himself from his former fealty to Derek Walcott's line in 'The Schooner *Flight*': 'either I'm nobody, or I'm a nation', and he declares that 'today literature is ineffective at social change. All the writer can strive for is a personal voice.'

Throughout this first, and most important, of the three essays, Ha Jin carefully reveals to us how he has changed position with respect to the notion of spokesmanship, but he lets us know this without putting himself at the centre of the narrative. One can argue with his conclusions; after all, what of those writers in the Middle East, Africa or Southeast Asia who continue to be harassed and jailed or killed because of their 'essential gestures'? Not all of them are naïve romantics hitching a ride on the coat-tails of their nations with inferior,

or sweetened, narratives. Is it really true to say that all literature is ineffective as social change? While nobody can argue
with the essential selfishness of a writer who chooses to abandon
loyalty to a people and make his art the thing, it does seem a
little presumptuous to suggest that this is the *only* way to produce
great literature. Yes, we know, as Ha Jin reminds us, that 'The
writer should enter history mainly through the avenue of his
art. If he serves a cause or a group or even a country, such
service must be a self-choice and not imposed by society. He
must serve on his own terms, in the manner and at the time
and place of his choosing.' But what we don't know is why,
beyond the brief hints that are given to us in this essay, this
matters so much to Ha Jin (although, again, we can guess).
We also remain frustrated by the digressions, both anecdotal
and professorial, which seem to result in conclusions that feel
imposed and often come across as truisms. One senses that
the thicket and undergrowth that we should be chopping our
way through to reach these conclusions should be the dense,
complicated, evidence of the author's own life.

The second essay, 'The Language of Betrayal', begins by
making a bold statement that ' . . . linguistic betrayal is the ultimate step the migrant writer dares to take; after this, any other
act of estrangement amounts to a trifle'. The essay then continues
with an extended consideration of both Conrad and Nabokov,
which is properly footnoted and carefully argued, before coming
to rest with the conclusion that a writer 'must be loyal only to
his art'. True, we learn something of the dangers that wrong-
footed both Conrad and Nabokov as they moved between
languages, and Ha Jin questions their motivations and looks at
what options they had, but this essay moves with the surety of
a well-worn lecture traversing familiar ground, and flickers to
life only briefly on the second page.

I have been asked why I write in English. I often reply, 'For
survival.' People tend to equate 'survival' with 'livelihood' and
praise my modest, also shabby, motivation. In fact, physical

survival is just one side of the picture, and there is the other side, namely, to exist — to live a meaningful life. To exist also means to make the best use of one's life, to pursue one's vision.

Again, just as the door opens up and the author teases us with the possibility of weaving his own experience into the narrative, he quickly slams it shut again and continues. 'Joseph Brodsky once observed . . .' He later claims that 'we writers who have adopted English — are all related to Conrad one way or another', but he says nothing about his own adoption of English. The truth is, by leaving out his own story he has not only reduced the potential impact of his argument, he has also created the opposite effect of what one assumes is a modest purpose. Far from praising his coy restraint, we are left wondering 'well, in what way are *you* related to Conrad?'

By the time one reaches the final essay, 'An Individual's Homeland', one can almost predict what the conclusion is going to be. 'Home' is nothing to do with a piece of land for one cannot return to the same place as the same person, and 'home' is contained in the art, and more specifically in the language which, for a migrant writer who has changed language, must be always subject to continued interrogation and modification. In this essay the key texts are the *Odyssey*, Milan Kundera's *Ignorance*, and once again Naipaul's *A Bend in the River*. Ha Jin is perhaps most original, and interesting, when discussing W.G. Sebald's *The Emigrants*, but even here, while considering what happens to the artist Ferber, the analysis collapses to a conclusion which feels somewhat flat. 'It is the intimate and inseverable connection with his past that keeps him sane and safe and provides for him the space in which he can practise his art. In other words, he has succeeded in constructing a kind of homeland for himself, to survive the violence and horror of history.'

There are two ways to read these essays. First, as the reflections of a professor who has thought seriously on these issues of migration, representation, language and homeland as academic spheres of enquiry, and whose reading and erudition are on display. Approaching the essays in this manner one might reach the conclusion that they are undoubtedly well researched and well constructed, but in the end they shed little new light on the subject at hand. One might be inclined to put this professorial volume to one side and reach instead for essays on the same subjects by Chinua Achebe, Octavio Paz, Salman Rushdie, Czeslaw Milosz, V.S. Naipaul, Mario Vargas Llosa, Wole Soyinka and others, writers who have seriously grappled with these issues in their work and who feel comfortable importing details of their own struggle, including autobiographical details, into their essays. These authors have, of course, in every case, written pointedly about other writers and left their own experience to one side, but when talking about issues which are so fundamental to their own journey and existence they have not distanced themselves, and their work, from these matters of migration, language and spokesmanship.

The second way to read these essays is to approach them as though they have been written by a distinguished author who has close personal experience of the subject matter at hand. One might then reasonably expect some elucidation of the author's own journey or opinions by direct reference back to his life and work. One is not expecting confession or memoir, but some synthesis of his artistic life as a migrant who has had to grapple with issues of spokesmanship, language and homeland, with the experiences of his contemporaries and predecessors. Instead, Ha Jin has closed off the personal avenue to us which, while not undermining the erudition of the essays, leaves us feeling that we have participated in a strange exercise of reticence, to what purpose the reader is unsure. If the hope is that we simply turn back to the fiction to find the tensions, ruptures, betrayals and difficulties of being 'the writer as migrant', then Ha Jin has succeeded, for *A Free Life* is a far more profound meditation upon this condition than these three lectures. Midway through the novel Nan Wu ponders the difference between himself and an older scholar, Mr Liu:

Here lay Mr Liu's tragedy — he couldn't possibly separate himself from the state's apparatus that could always control and torment him. Without the frame of reference already formed in his homeland, his life would have lost its meaning and bearings. That must be why so many exiles, wrecked with nostalgia, would eulogize suffering and patriotism. Physically they were here, but because of the yoke of their significant past, they couldn't adapt to the life in the new land. In contrast, Nan was an immigrant without a noteworthy and burdensome past. To the authorities, he was nobody, non-existent. He didn't even have a Chinese official to beg. Who would listen to a man like him, a mere immigrant or refugee? People of his kind, 'the weed people', survived or perished like insects and grass and wouldn't matter at all to those living in their native land. To the people in China, they were already counted as a loss . . . The more Nan thought about these issues, the more upset he became. On the other hand, he was willing to accept the immigrant life as the condition of his existence so as to become a self-sufficient man. He felt grateful to the American land that had taken in his family and given them an opportunity for a new beginning.

Passages like this serve to remind us of how much energy the risk of what feels like candid self-revelation provides for Ha Jin's fiction, and how much we miss this energy in the essays.

Lafcadio Hearn: The Wanderer (2009)

In 1854, Commodore Perry steamed into the port of Yokohama and opened Japan to international trade. The subsequent era of the Meiji Restoration, which lasted until 1912, saw Japan begin slowly to transform itself from an insular, somewhat feudal society into a modern nation. Western envoys sent back dispatches about this mysterious country, whose traditions aroused fascination and suspicion in equal quantities. In the West, Japanese art and culture became all the rage, a vogue that reached its apotheosis in 1885, when Gilbert and Sullivan's *The Mikado* became a huge hit on the London stage.

The few from Japan who travelled abroad sent back their own reports about Western traditions and ideas. Chief among them was the writer Natsume Soseki, who journeyed to Britain at the end of the nineteenth century, but found it difficult to understand these tall, gangly strangers. Soseki's stay in London was miserable. Upon returning to Japan in 1903, he was offered a position at Tokyo University. He was both pleased and perplexed: pleased, because it was a distinguished professorship which recognised his achievements as a scholar and teacher; perplexed, because the writer he was replacing, Lafcadio Hearn, was held in high regard as the chief reporter to the West of all things Japanese. Hearn was married to a local woman, and he was the father of four children born in Japan. The non-renewal of his contract was as much of a shock to Tokyo University's outraged students and faculty as it was to Hearn, who never really recovered. A little over a year later, the fifty-four-year-old author died in Japan, a broken man.

Patrick Lafcadio Hearn was born in 1850 on the Ionian island of Lefkas to a Greek mother, Rosa Cassimati, and an Anglo-Irish army doctor, Charles Hearn. When he was two the infant was sent to Ireland with his mother, and they took up residence in Dublin with a great-aunt, Sarah Brenane. Two years later his increasingly unstable mother left Ireland for Greece, and two years after that his parents divorced. After his mother's departure, Hearn never again laid eyes on her, and eventually she died in a mental asylum on Corfu. Hearn was now the ward of his sternly religious great-aunt, and his relationship with his peripatetic father was, in all senses of the word, distant. A small, shy boy, Hearn attended a series of rigorously disciplined Catholic boarding schools in Ireland and England, where his experiences were uniformly miserable. His unhappiness was compounded by a playground accident that resulted in loss of the sight in his left eye when he was sixteen. Soon after, Hearn's estranged father died, and a year later his great-aunt declared bankruptcy. The publicly shamed boy was forced to withdraw from school. No longer able to contemplate attending university, young Paddy Hearn lived for a short while in great poverty in Dickensian London before, at the age of nineteen, boarding a ship bound for the United States.

After some months as a semi-destitute waiter and dishwasher in New York, Hearn set out for Cincinnati, hoping to find a family contact in the great riverfront city. Instead he happened upon work in a printing shop that was run by an Englishman named Henry Watkin, who offered him a place to sleep in exchange for Hearn keeping the shop clean and running errands. Watkin was a great raconteur, and a lover of Eastern philosophy and the generally bizarre, and he discovered in Hearn a young man whose eccentric tastes matched his own. Hearn's profoundly unhappy memories of school, and then London's filthy underworld, had led the young immigrant to cultivate a sense of himself as an outsider. He adopted a new and somewhat Gothically inspired identity in which he imagined himself to be a maverick whose tastes were rooted in the culture, folklore and mysticism of the past, as opposed to the crass materialism of the contemporary world. He found inspiration in the work of Edgar Allan Poe; but his true spur to self-definition was not literature, it was his unhappy life experience. Society never seemed to recognise this small, dark, displaced boy, and if the world would not recognise him, then he saw no reason why he should recognise it.

In 1872, the twenty-two-year-old Hearn presented himself before the editor of the *Cincinnati Daily Enquirer* and asked to be paid for contributions that he intended to make to the newspaper. Hearn had decided that he would have to earn a living from journalism and translation until he transformed himself into a real writer. He proposed pieces not so much about the gentle antebellum world of Cincinnati, as about the people who made up the lurid underbelly of the city. He was particularly interested in the riverfront world of the Negroes with their songs, folk tales and superstitions, which suggested to him a genuine connection to an authentic past. The editor was unconvinced by the young man, whom he later described as a 'quaint dark skinned little fellow', but he gave the brash youngster a chance, and Hearn began to write with a pen that veered from sensationalism to romanticism, depending upon the subject to hand. His dramatic reports quickly won him a wide audience. In 1874, an exceptionally ghoulish article called, 'Violent Cremation', about the lynching of a supposed murderer, made him something of a local celebrity. He described the body of the cremated man as being reduced to

a hideous adhesion of half-molten flesh, boiled brains and jellied blood mingled with coal. The skull had burst like a shell in the fierce furnace-heat, and the whole upper portion seemed as though it had been blown out by the steam from the boiling and bubbling brains . . . The brain had all boiled away, save a small wasted lump at the base of the skull about the size of a lemon. It was crisped and still warm to the touch. On pushing the finger through, the crisp interior felt about the consistency of banana fruit and the yellow fibres seemed to writhe like worms in the Coroner's hands.

In the same year that Hearn published 'Violent Cremation', he extended his professional interest in Negro life into the personal sphere by marrying Alethea 'Mattie' Foley, an illiterate black teenager born into slavery in Kentucky who worked at the city boarding house in which Hearn lodged. The association was, of course, illegal, but in a newspaper article that he wrote about Foley in 1875 one can sense that beyond his physical attraction to her, he was also won over by her love of storytelling:

> She had never learned to read or write, but possessed naturally a wonderful wealth of verbal description, a more than ordinarily vivid memory, and a gift of conversation which would have charmed an Italian improvisatore. These things we learned during an idle half hour passed one summer's evening in her company on the kitchen stairs; while the boarders lounged on the porch in the moonlight, and the hall lamp created flickering shadows along the varnished corridors, and the hungry rats held squeaking carnival in the dark dining-room. To the weird earnestness of the story-teller, the melody of her low, soft voice, and the enthralling charm of her conversation, we cannot attempt to do justice.

When word of Hearn's irregular marriage leaked out, the *Enquirer* terminated his employment. But Hearn was by now too celebrated a journalist to find himself idle for long, and the rival newspaper, the *Cincinnati Commercial*, soon picked him up. By this time Hearn's controversial marriage had already begun to fall apart, and the aspiring young writer was starting to tire of Cincinnati, and of his notoriety as Paddy Hearn, sensationalist journalist. He was ready now to stop wallowing in the outlandish and make a concerted effort to become a literary man. A move to New Orleans would allow him the opportunity to look at the old French culture of the country, plus give him the chance to engage with the creolised Negro population who were steeped in a folklore tradition richer than that to be found on the banks of the Ohio River. In 1877, Paddy Hearn left for New Orleans, and somewhere along the way he reinvented himself as the more romantic-sounding Lafcadio Hearn.

At first Hearn was convinced that he had arrived in paradise. He loved the sedentary pace of life, and the sensual faded glory, of the humid South. He sent articles back to the *Cincinnati Commercial*, before eventually finding employment with the local *Times-Democrat*. But he still struggled with the idea that he was doing the lesser work of journalism as opposed to what he described as 'the sacred work of literature'. He persevered, finally publishing *Stray Leaves from Strange Literature* (1884) and *Some Chinese Ghosts* (1887), which were rough adaptations from foreign literature, and also translations of Gautier and Flaubert. But where was Hearn's own literary work? His journalism continued to bring him a steady, if somewhat erratic income, but his heart was not in it.

A restless soul, Hearn soon began to grow weary of the city of New Orleans, and he made the decision to explore the hinterlands and islands of the bayou, which lay adjacent to the Gulf of Mexico. Most of all he enjoyed Grand Isle, which he had first visited in 1883, and he imagined himself reclaiming a languorous island past that reminded him – it was a fantasy, of course – of his Mediterranean origins. Encouraged by his discoveries, Hearn decided that he should further explore the world of the tropics. And so, armed with a commission from *Harper's Monthly*, he set off in June 1887 for the West Indies. He spent two months there, and submitted a piece to *Harper's* called 'A Midsummer Trip to the Tropics'. He found himself intrigued by the supernatural and erotic elements of the region, and recorded his attraction to the place, and also his repulsion, in quick-fire notes that made up his travelogue style. Although he had to stay indoors much of the time to protect himself from the heat and the snakes, no sooner had he returned to the

United States than he began planning once more to travel south. This time his base was Saint-Pierre on the French island of Martinique.

Hearn's extensive notes were later published as *Two Years in the French West Indies*, and his sojourn also gave him time to collect material for a second piece of fiction, *Youma* (1890) which, like *Chita* (1889), purported to tell a fictionalised version of a real event. But Hearn soon tired of the West Indies too, and in April 1889 returned to the United States. Less than a year later he persuaded *Harper's* that he should set sail for Japan and submit articles from the mysterious Orient. The most important literary period of Hearn's life was about to begin: finally he would find a world – unlike the underworld of Cincinnati, or the Creole world of New Orleans, or the creolised world of the West Indies – about which he could romanticise, but whose sense of itself was such that it would be difficult for him to patronise either the place or the people.

The work collected in *American Writings* (2009) covers the fifteen-year period from Hearn's writing for the *Cincinnati Commercial* to his fiction and non-fiction about the West Indies on the eve of his departure for Japan. The selected early journalism demonstrates something of Hearn's talent for teasing out other people's stories and then conveying the essence of their lives sympathetically, and in often luminous prose. Yet in 'Levee Life', which concerns itself with the 'original songs and peculiar dances' of the predominantly Negro stevedores and longshoremen of the Ohio River, we see another tendency of Hearn's: he is all too often content simply to gaze raptly and somewhat anthropologically at the world about him, and there is occasionally a pedestrian superficiality to his observations, as though the writer is himself fed up with his assignment. For example:

Half of the colored 'longshoremen' used at one time to wear only a coat and pants, winter and summer; but now they are a little more careful of themselves, and fearful of being sent to the Work-house to be cleaned up. Consequently, when Officer Brazil finds a very ragged and dirty specimen of levee life on the Row, he has seldom occasion to warn him more than once to buy himself a shirt and a change of garments.

At moments such as this, Hearn's uncharacteristically flat prose seems to betray a weariness with the task at hand, and frustration with the kind of writer he has become.

'Gibbeted', which reports the botched execution of a young murderer, is stamped with the familiar sensationalism of Hearn's Cincinnati pieces, but it feels over-rehearsed. Hearn seems too easily to be pushing the right buttons in an attempt to outrage his readership, in the manner of the earlier piece, 'Violent Cremation'. Not long after arriving in New Orleans, however, it is clear that the newly created Lafcadio Hearn is determined to roll up his sleeves and present his readership with a more literary man. His observations remain acute, but his prose achieves a new mellifluousness – one which is forever in danger of becoming purple. He describes an unusual visitation of frost to his new city: 'At moments the December sun intensified the brilliancy of these coruscations of frost-fire: lance-rays of solar flame, shivered into myriad sparkles against the glittering mail of interwoven crystals, tinged all the scintillating work with a fairy-faint reflection of such iridescence as flames upon a humming bird's bosom.'

It is apparent that, at least to begin with, New Orleans seized Hearn's imagination. Few writers have ever written with more panache about an American city. Taken collectively, his New Orleans writings, which range from stern editorials attacking political misdeeds to impressionistic sketches depicting the mystery of creolised New Orleans, suggest that this distinctive city has more in common with the West Indies and Europe than the American mainland, and it would be fair to say that Hearn's articles helped to create the myth of voodoo New Orleans. Once Hearn stopped writing for newspapers and began to contribute to more literary publications such as *Harper's Monthly*, one senses a new ambition in his writing.

Chita, from 1889, Hearn's melodramatic adventure novel of the period, is a work at odds with itself. It is the plot-driven story of the strange female child of a respectable middle-class doctor who survives a hurricane on Grand Isle and is subsequently raised by a family of simple fishing people. Mixed uncomfortably into this narrative are numerous digressions exploring cultural and linguistic practices. Hearn attempts to inflate his flimsy story into literature by adopting a highly stylised voice, and tries also to dazzle his readers with short bursts of rich description which ultimately seem to deviate from the main narrative rather than drive it. The novel is replete with these poetic but static set pieces:

> Sometimes of autumn evenings there, when the hollow of heaven flames like the interior of a chalice, and waves and clouds are flying in one wild rout of broken gold, – you may see the tawny grasses all covered with something like husks, – wheat-colored husks, – large, flat, and disposed evenly along the lee-side of each swaying stalk, so as to present only their edges to the wind. But, if you approach, those pale husks all break open to display strange splendors of scarlet and seal-brown, with arabesque mottlings in white and black: they change into wondrous living blossoms, which detach themselves before your eyes and rise in air, and flutter away by thousands to settle down farther off, and turn into wheat-colored husks once more . . . a whirling flower-drift of sleepy butterflies!

For all its weaknesses, *Chita* proved to be something of a commercial success, combining as it did sentimentality, an exotic location, and often startling descriptions of seascapes and storms that remind one of Melville and anticipate Conrad. The money that Hearn received from *Harper's* for the serialisation of the novel encouraged him to travel further into the creolised world and head back down to the West Indies.

Hearn's West Indian writing reveals a strange fascination with the bodies of Negroes, which often crosses the line into an awkward voyeurism. Although the younger Hearn had identified with the black community of Cincinnati, there is a marked change of tone in his writings on racial matters once he reinvents himself in New Orleans. He suddenly appears to have imbibed the southern nostalgia for the passing of the institution of slavery, and it is in this frame of mind that he sets sail for the West Indies. His dispatches suggest a continued interest in folklore, music and dance, but his work does little more than preserve a record of a world past and fading, while his attitude to the people he encounters is too often one of undisguised superiority. He recaptures the delicacy of description that he achieved in *Chita*, but he now flaunts some newly acquired racial attitudes: 'There is a glorious sunset, — a fervid orange splendor, shading starward into delicate roses and greens. Then black boatmen come astern and quarrel furiously for the privilege of carrying one passenger ashore; and as they scream and gesticulate, half naked, their silhouettes against the sunset seem forms of great black apes.'

Hearn is fascinated and repulsed by the 'half-breeds' that he encounters, and obsessed with the relationship between the mingling of blood and the aesthetically acceptable (or unacceptable) appearance of various grades of people. Increasingly wedded to the notion of 'the dignity of a white skin', Hearn muses on what he sees as a conflict between black and mixed-race peoples, and he speculates as to what might happen should trouble break out:

And the true black element, more numerically powerful, more fertile, more cunning, better adapted to pyrogenic climate and tropical environment, would surely win. All these mixed races, all these beautiful fruit-colored populations, seem doomed to extinction: the future tendency must be to universal blackness, if existing conditions continue — perhaps to universal savagery.

Youma, Hearn's second West Indian novel, is less successful than *Chita*. Predictably enough, cultural observations and descriptive flourishes are thrown in to spice up the narrative, but it all feels tired, in the same way that Hearn's sojourn in the West Indies seems to fatigue and in the end disappoint him:

> One must send abroad to obtain even a review, and wait months for its coming. And this mental starvation gnaws at the brain more and more as one feels less inclination and less capacity for effort, and as that single enjoyment, which at first rendered a man indifferent to other pleasures, – the delight of being alone with tropical Nature, – becomes more difficult to indulge. When lethargy has totally mastered habit and purpose, and you must at last confess yourself resigned to view Nature from your chamber, or at best from a carriage window, – then, indeed, the want of all literature proves a positive torture. It is not a consolation to discover that you are an almost solitary sufferer, – from climate as well as from mental hunger.

In the end, what are we to make of these West Indian writings, which make up the vast majority of Hearn's *American Writings*? The appendix entitled 'Some Creole Melodies' may point to their real value: they were meticulous records of cultural practices that used to be commonplace but which are now in danger of being forgotten. Anthony Trollope and J.A. Froude, the great nineteenth-century Negrophobic chroniclers of the region, wrote with a dyspeptic sneer on their faces, but it is both surprising and disappointing to find that the same is true of Hearn. His may have been a more romantic vision, and he certainly captured the sunrises and sunsets of the West Indies with more literary panache than his English contemporaries; but like Trollope and Froude he looked down on the region and its 'childish' people. Instead of seeing a rich past seeping through and contributing to a delightful tropical present, he saw only chaos, disorder, and a place of intellectual torpor. The West Indies disappointed

him as the United States had disappointed him. He would need to journey again.

The almost one thousand pages of *American Writings*, including a short selection of Hearn's letters, end abruptly with the author's departure for Japan, which is where his reputation was eventually made. Unlike the West Indies, Japan did not bore Hearn with a lack of intellectual vitality, and it remained exotic enough to beguile him with the sensuality that he craved. Finally, Japan stimulated his senses and his mind; and it enabled him to focus on a single patch of earth rather than skipping in a seemingly erratic and disorderly fashion from one place to another. Between his arrival in 1890 and his death in 1904, Hearn produced more than a dozen books about the country and people, and found himself positioned as the man who was introducing the culture of Japan to the West. This last 'rebirth' suited Hearn, who had been more or less discarded at the beginning of his life, and thereafter remained suspicious of co-option into any group or category out of a fear of further rejection. As a child growing up in Ireland and England, he was always dark-skinned 'Paddy', and knew that he did not fit in. Although he tried to begin anew in the United States, his career never really took off. But things would be different in Japan. He had barely set foot in the country when he wrote to his friend Elizabeth Bisland, who would become his first biographer, that 'I only wish I could be reincarnated in some little Japanese baby, so that I could see and feel the world as beautifully as a Japanese brain does.'

American Writings concerns itself with the work that was produced as a result of Hearn's migration to the United States in 1869. Perhaps no other writer of the American world of the late nineteenth century demonstrated such a fascination with a wide range of eclectic material as Hearn, and his tastes and his interests are reflected in the idiosyncrasies of the people and the places about which he chose to write. Still, for all his protest-ation of detachment, and his cultivation of an identity as a misfit, from the beginning one senses in Hearn a desire to

belong – a desire that is always, and quickly, usurped by a growing unease, leading to a precipitous departure. Hearn possessed an understandable yearning to be rooted, and to that end was even moved to commit a socially suicidal marriage. But somehow the American world did not suit his temperament. All his life he had been made to feel offbeat and strange; and when he came to see that, despite his reinvention of himself as Lafcadio the literary man, he would never truly be comfortable in the United States, he headed south and further embraced the worlds of voodoo, myth, legend, rituals, and the oral tradition and song.

Predictably, he felt safest in the American world of the past, and this can be seen in his choice of cities – Cincinnati and New Orleans. In 1869, the western frontier had already moved far beyond Cincinnati; and the end of the Civil War, and the decline of a slave-based economy, had signalled a major slump in the fortunes of New Orleans. But the nostalgia that permeated both cities seemed to suit Hearn's spirit: he was a man who liked to look over his shoulder and report on how the past had contributed to the present, as opposed to looking up the road and figuring out how the present might contribute to the future. He chose not to write about Chicago or New York, the great capitals of modernity, or to head west to the new frontier lands, or to press on to California. In unfashionable Cincinnati and New Orleans, he was able to make good use of his talent for noticing and transcribing minutiae that spoke to an authenticity more primary and more mysterious than present-day modern American society.

So just what kind of a writer was the thirty-nine-year-old Lafcadio Hearn who, on St Patrick's Day 1890, set foot on board a ship bound for Japan? He was a writer who moved from one oddball subject or location to the next, and whose sense of prose was lyrical, and occasionally beautiful; but aside from his body of journalism on New Orleans, he had not yet produced anything truly original. Since his death, it is Hearn's reputation in Japan, as a dedicated interpreter of their country

to the West, which has kept his name before the public. And his *American Writings* – do they offer us anything beyond a sepia-tinted window through which we can take a peek at various peculiar corners of American and West Indian life in the late nineteenth century? *Some Chinese Ghosts* is a fairly uninspired retelling of stories already in the public domain. *Chita* lacks coherent characterisation, and the bizarre location and occasional poetic flourishes cannot compensate for the lack of real drama. *Two Years in the French West Indies* and *Youma* tread slump-shouldered across ground that had already been clumsily covered by writers with less literary talent than Hearn; but whatever fascination Hearn might have initially felt for the region was soon replaced by a lethargy that dulled not only his mind but also his pen. So the *American Writings* suggests a writer with a profound literary gift that flickered only from time to time, and a man who eventually allowed his cosmopolitan bent to become corrupted by the vulgar battle between the supposedly superior and the supposedly inferior, and who, in the West Indies, compromised his literary gift so that he might play the lesser role of judgemental cultural interpreter.

It is the journalistic pieces that are the most impressive legacy of Hearn's American period, allowing us to glimpse the post-Civil War country coming to terms with crime and punishment and entertainment. But Hearn was no Whitman or Twain; he had no desire to use his pen and his imagination to help usher the United States forward and encourage the nation to think of itself in a new and self-confident way. He was attracted to the exotic elements of American life, but he rejected American life in its broadest sense. In the end, he did not want to belong to a place that appeared not to recognise him. He peered down the alleys, he stole in through the back doors, and then he scrambled out again. For something more and better, we will have to await his *Japanese Writings*.

Distant Shores

France: Strangers in a Strange Land (2001)

He looks like a policeman. He wears a white shirt and tie, his shoes are well-shined, and his moustache is clipped and neat. As he leans against the bar he announces that he is from Runcorn in Cheshire, and that he has been here, in Sangatte, for two and a half years. Through the window of the Off Road café I can see groups of Afghans and Iraqis drifting by. It is early evening and they are moving in the direction of the Channel Tunnel. He sips at his beer and eyes the refugees. 'They are stinking and disgusting. They shit on our beaches. I don't go anywhere without a can of Mace, which is legal here.' He offers a short, theatrical, pause before he continues. 'I'm not a racist, but it has to be said. They are stinky, smelly people. Sometimes they come into the bar and we have to move away because they make us want to retch.' Again I look out of the window. The men continue to file by. They seem subdued and fatigued, marooned as they are on the north-east coast of France. Less than a mile away, in the Sangatte Red Cross centre, there are 1,600 men, women and children waiting for a chance to get into Britain. These few dozen are tonight's 'advance' party. Most will fail in their attempt, some will be injured, one or two might even be killed. Some time after midnight the French police will escort almost all of them back to the Red Cross centre.

Earlier in the day I had travelled from Paris to Calais-Fréthun. The modernist Eurostar terminal is located outside the town of Calais and is entirely surrounded by green fields. There is an Avis Rent-a-Car desk and one taxi. I ask the cab driver to take me to Sangatte Central. He laughs. I ask, 'Is there such a thing? He shrugs his shoulders and turns up the music. 'Well,' he shouts, 'they've got a big hotel there.' He laughs loudly at his own joke and then tears along the narrow country lanes. In the distance, beyond a freighter train that inches its way towards the tunnel, I can see two cross-Channel ferries sitting high on the horizon, moving with a ponderous certainty towards the clearly visible white cliffs of Dover.

Sangatte is a collection of homes strung out on both sides of a half-mile stretch of the D940, a main road that connects Calais to Boulogne. Situated three miles to the south-west of Calais, it is a small, predominantly middle-class commuter suburb by the sea. The cab driver drops me at Le Week End bar, which is tobacconist, newspaper shop, bar, amusement arcade and restaurant. Once inside I edge past the table football. At the bar, a pair of local old boys are downing their beers, seemingly oblivious to the loud French rock music that emanates from the tinny radio. The semi-shaven barman eyes me suspiciously as he makes me a coffee. Above the pool table, I see a picture of him resplendent in a bright red jacket standing beside a woman I assume to be his wife. They were contestants on the French version of *Who Wants to Be a Millionaire*. Apparently they lost. The wife catches me looking at the photograph. She nods a silent greeting and then moves through into the restaurant.

The barman makes me a second cup of coffee, but it is clear he doesn't want to talk. I ask one of the old boys if it is always this quiet. He nods. 'What about the refugees?' I ask. 'Do they come in here?' Again he nods. But he tells me that the barman will not serve them if they do not speak French or have French money. He tells me that they will be down later on. After lunch. They sleep until lunchtime, then come out at night, when they try to get through the tunnel. He has been here since 1987, when he came to work on the tunnel, but he is retired now. He takes a sip of beer. They don't bother him, but he seems momentarily puzzled. 'They tell us they are qualified people. Doctors and lawyers. They are supposed to have skills, but I don't think so. Eighteen months ago, when they first came to Sangatte, some of them asked for jobs, but now they have stopped. They just stay up there.' He points in the direction of the camp. 'But I don't care.'

I begin to walk towards the camp. I notice small groups of refugees, mainly Pakistanis and Iraqis, walking slowly towards the town. We politely make room for each other on the narrow pavement. I also notice the French National Front posters which decorate the lamp posts. 'Dégage! Tu Niques La France' (Clear off! You are fucking up France). I enter the small Catholic church, which boasts beautiful stained-glass windows and is obviously an object of great village pride with its impeccably obedient rows of chairs. I look in the visitors' book. The last entry speaks in part to the village's 'problem'. 'In Jesus Christ we fellow Christians pray for our brothers and sisters in Muslim lands who are being persecuted because they believe in the son of God who has been saved and cleansed for their sins. Elisabeth and Marie. Christian Pilgrims.'

The Red Cross centre sits on a small rise beyond a field in which cows graze. The huge steel warehouse was originally a storage shed for supplies used in the construction of the Channel Tunnel. Eighteen months ago it was requisitioned by the Red Cross to provide shelter for 400 refugees who were hoping to enter Britain illegally. That figure has now swelled to 1,600, with dozens of nationalities represented although Afghans, Iraqis and Iranians still comprise the majority. As I near the Red Cross centre I realise that I am being followed, so I deliberately slow down until I hear the voice. 'Please, two francs.' I turn and look at the tall, handsome man. He is shabbily dressed, but his thinning hair is brushed and swept back. He is making some effort to appear presentable.

I ask his name, and he tells me that he is called Hassan and that he is Egyptian. Hassan has lived in Europe for twenty-five years, mainly in Holland, Belgium, Luxembourg and Italy. 'Two francs please, for food in the supermarket.' I give him two francs but, pointing to the Red Cross centre, tell him I thought they fed you in the camp. He sneers. 'Camp no good. I live there one month, but now for one month I live in town in burned-out house. Every night I go seven kilometres to tunnel, but now it is very difficult. Two police cars, one on either side, and they bring me back.' Hassan holds out his hand again, but I temporarily ignore it and ask him why he wants to go to Britain. Why not just stay in France? He is indignant. 'France no good. In England plenty people of my country. Friends. France no good.' After a quarter of a century of migrant labour in Europe, this proud man in his late forties, in stained jeans and a thin, inadequate jacket, seems both lost and angry.

As I pass through the gates of the camp and begin to walk up the long driveway, I notice greater numbers of refugees now streaming out towards the village. For the first time I see women and children, all bundled up against the cold. At the entrance to the warehouse, men squat idly in a scene that rekindles memories of prisoner-of-war films. Washing is hung out to dry along the fencing, and in the middle of this confusion there is a French riot police van. There seems little need for riot police, for a more somnambulant group of people I cannot imagine. And then I remember. Journalists are not permitted to enter the camp, so I try to affect the demeanour of a resident. I walk purposefully towards the open door and past the men queuing up outside the phone booth clutching precious phone cards. I can feel eyes upon me, but I look neither left nor right.

Once inside the warehouse, I see long lines to use the Portaloos. Men are washing themselves at open sinks, while others stand bare-chested and wait their turn. The warehouse is a vast open space which contains both Portakabins and tents. They are all numbered, and I peek through open doors and see that there is not a single inch of space between the camp beds. Some Portakabins are marked with a sign that simply reads 'Family'. There are many families in each one. Privacy is a luxury that has no place here. In an empty corner of the washroom, I notice two dozen Muslims praying together. Then I realise that I am freezing. I look around and feel as though I have entered a vast exhibition hall where the tents and Portakabins are the exhibits and the refugees have been assigned the part of extras adopting poses of extreme boredom, misery and anxiety. And then two Red Cross men, who look like security officers, shout at me. The game is up. As they approach me, I explain that I am looking for a West African friend, but they insist that they will have to escort me back to the door and check my identity.

They place me in a chair and three Red Cross officials-cum-guards keep an eye on me while somebody goes to enquire about my 'friend'. While I wait, I read the signs in four languages warning people of the 'mortal danger' and 'squashing risk' of trying to board trains going through the tunnel. I notice a man who looks Iranian in a Bob Marley hooded sweat top. He scrutinises me as he walks by. The Red Cross man reappears and says that he cannot find my friend. I stand and thank them all, and then I notice that an African man has suddenly materialised. 'Excuse me, sir. Are you the one asking about West Africa?' I nod. 'Where are you from?' I ask. 'Cameroon, sir.' 'I think this man may know something about my friend,' I say. 'He will come with me for a walk.' The Red Cross officials seem displeased, but they say nothing, so my new friend follows me out of the warehouse.

We walk back towards the village, treading the worn path littered with crushed Coke cans and empty cigarette packets. Along the way, Manuel from Cameroon introduces me to Jacob from Benin. Once we reach the village I offer to buy them both lunch and a beer, and the three of us enter the Off Road café. The blonde French woman behind the bar insists that the kitchen is closed. She makes no attempt to offer the three strangers a drink and so, for a moment, we stand there. I suggest to Jacob and Manuel that there might be another place, and we leave and walk further up the street to Le Week End bar. My retired friend is no longer there, but the disgruntled barman studies us as we walk in. I usher the two men to a seat in the corner and then order three beers and some crisps. The barman says he will bring them over. As I take my seat, Jacob and Manuel visibly relax. When the beer arrives, they drink with enthusiasm and I wonder how long it has been since they last had a beer.

Manuel is the more articulate of the two. An English-speaking Cameroonian, he tells me he has been in the camp for three weeks. He fled his country after three of his colleagues were killed by hard-line secessionists who want English-speaking Cameroon to become independent of French-speaking Cameroon. A gradualist, Manuel's politics embrace compromise, so he knew that he would be the next to be killed. A lecturer in history in his home town of Bamenda, he arrived in Paris knowing nobody. He spent what money he had on a ticket to London, but was pulled off the train at the cross-Channel border and sent to the camp. I ask him, 'Why Britain? Why not claim asylum in France?' He smiles. 'Everybody says Britain is better. Sometimes I hear the BBC news and they say they need 300,000 workers. And English is my language. But I will not risk my life jumping on a train like the Muslims. They have no fear. They are crazy.' He pauses. 'It looks like I will have to claim asylum here in France.'

Jacob listens carefully. I ask him if he is also a political migrant. He laughs. 'I am hoping to be.' It transpires that Jacob is a classic economic migrant. A car mechanic, he is proud that back home he passed his City & Guilds and he is therefore 'qualified'. Like Manuel, this is his first time out of his country. He paid a 'fixer' to get him into Europe via Istanbul and Greece, and then he took a train from Italy to Paris. He was sleeping rough in the station until somebody told him that if he could get to Calais there was a place where he could eat and sleep and maybe eventually reach Britain. But now Jacob is disillusioned. 'It is difficult to go to Britain. It is just there,' he points, 'but so far. Maybe Holland,' he muses. 'They speak English. To get asylum here in France can take eighteen months, and I cannot stay in that camp for eighteen months. I have no money and nowhere to go. I know nobody.' He pauses. 'And it is cold. We have a Slovenian in our tent, and the rest are all Muslims. They talk all night, but there is no trouble between us.' Manuel

Sierra Leone: Distant Voices (2003)

This is no ordinary rain. The sky has opened and the rain has transformed the streets into small rivers, bringing what commercial life there is in Freetown to an abrupt halt. Mike Butscher and I braved the deluge to reach this restaurant, but having finished our meal and a second beer, we simply stare out of the window and resign ourselves to being temporarily marooned.

The restaurant is called Stop Press. It is a favourite hangout for local writers, journalists and any foreign press personnel passing through Sierra Leone. Mike Butscher is the secretary of the local branch of PEN, the international writers' organisation. We sit and watch a skeletal dog, its sores red raw, wander in off the street and take up residence under a table so that it too can shelter from the rain. It is going to be a long afternoon.

Butscher raises his hand and politely declines my offer of a third beer.

'You were asking about the war,' he says.

I nod. I had been quizzing him about how Sierra Leonean writers were addressing the horrors of their recent history. More to the point, I hoped Butscher might enlighten me as to what role he imagined writers might play in a country whose average annual income is a mere US$470 per person, making it the poorest country on earth, and in which life expectancy is 34.5 years according to the UN Human Development Report, 2003. Since my arrival in Sierra Leone I have been wondering about the relevance of writing and writers in a nation whose social and economic infrastructure appears to be permanently close to collapse. So far, Butscher has said precious little about the war or about writing, but he now appears to be ready to talk.

'I remember one morning looking out of my window. I was on the second floor of my guest house. In the street below, the rebels had captured three Nigerian soldiers. They had tied their elbows behind their backs and the Nigerians were pleading for their lives. Right there, with me watching, the rebels began to slit these men's throats as though they were slaughtering animals. The final Nigerian soldier was trembling with fear, but a rebel simply whispered, "Do not worry, it will soon be over." And then he held him and quickly cut open his neck.'

Mike's narrative grinds to a halt. The rain, however, shows no sign of abating.

Freetown can be a dangerous place. Graham Greene's 1948 classic, *The Heart of the Matter*, is set in Freetown and draws on Greene's experiences as a British intelligence officer during the Second World War. The novel's main character, Scobie, wanders down to the seafront after nightfall. He passes scuffling rats and then asks two policemen if they have seen anything worth reporting.

'No, sah' . . . He knew that they were lying: they would never go alone to that end of the wharf, the playground of the human rats, unless they had a white officer to guard them. The rats were cowards but dangerous – boys of sixteen or so, armed with razors or bits of broken bottle, they swarmed in groups around the warehouses, pilfering if they found an easily opened case, settling like flies around any drunken sailor who stumbled their way, occasionally slashing a policeman who had made himself unpopular with one of their innumerable relatives.

Modern-day Freetown remains populated by scuffling rats. Open drains, heaps of rotting garbage and a crippled sewer system ensure that after dark the rats emerge and scurry in all directions. But Greene's human rats rarely left Freetown. If they it open with his shoulder. We enter a box-like room which has the feel of a tiny waiting room. A fluorescent strip light hangs unconvincingly on the wooden wall, an illuminated exclamation point. There is a wooden bench, a desk on top of which sits an ancient Bakelite telephone, and a small anteroom with space enough for a second desk, two chairs, a fan, and a small trestle table upon which Butscher has neatly displayed a range of PEN pamphlets, old and faded copies of foreign magazines, and application forms for those who wish to join the organisation.

I sit with Butscher in the anteroom, and almost immediately the rain begins again. It clatters against the galvanised iron roof just above our heads. Butscher raises his voice.

'So, this is where I work, although I have no stipend or anything. I am trying to raise some funds so that we can pay the rent and get some supplies and expand a little.'

I sense him following my eyes as I look around and try to take in what is before me. Were I stuck in an English allotment shed on a wet Sunday afternoon, this would make sense. To be in the national headquarters of an internationally respected writers' organisation only drives home the stupidity of my having pestered Butscher to tell me why there was not more writing from Sierra Leone available to 'us'. That he has managed to found a chapter of PEN here in Freetown, find premises, paint and furnish this room-and-a-half, arrange some magazines and put a lock on the door is already beginning to look heroic. Butscher picks up a thin sheaf of papers from his desk and hands them to me.

'Please, for you to look at.'

I glance at the title. 'Mike Butscher's War Diary.'

'Perhaps, after you have met some of our writers, you will have time to scrutinise this.'

Osman Conteh is a stocky man built like a good middleweight boxer. He meets me exactly on time outside the British Council Library. We are high on Tower Hill, with an unrestricted view across Freetown below and the estuary and Atlantic Ocean in the distance. We find an empty room. A dozen chairs are arranged around a large wooden table, and Conteh carefully puts his brief-case on the chair next to the one he sits on. He looks as though he is ready to talk. In fact, he does not wait for a question.

'At first I did not know how to contact publishers, but I wanted to write. Then somebody told me that Macmillan had an office here from which they distributed educational books, so I asked them what to do. They said if you write a book give it to us then we will send it to London, and they will tell you whether the book is suitable.'

At this point Conteh nervously touches his briefcase.

'What happened is this. I sent it and they sent it back and said that it was absolutely not suitable for publication for I had too many author intrusions. And so I thought I should read some books on how to write and I managed to find some books. Eventually *Double Trouble* was published in 1991. It concerns the kidnapping of children for ritual murder. This was followed by two other novels, and my present one, *Unanswered Cries.*'

I hand Conteh a copy of his own book, having brought two copies with me from London. The book addresses the issue of female circumcision, and it won the Macmillan Writer's Prize for Africa, Children's Literature Award. I had been led to believe it would be difficult to find the novel in Sierra Leone, but I had not realised just how difficult. Aside from a small church bookshop specialising in Christian material, there are no book-shops in the country.

Conteh thanks me, and then explains that if the book were for sale, the price would be 10,000 leones (about £3) which places it beyond the pocket of most of the population. His face begins to cloud as he gently fingers the copy of his own book. 'Sometimes I think that the only way to become a proper writer is to go abroad. People read you and you can get paid. When I was starting to write, I read books by the Sierra Leonean writer Yulisa Amadu Maddy and I wanted to be like him. His novel, *No Past, No Present, No Future*, was a book that I enjoyed. But he is abroad.'

Actually, I had met 'Pat' Maddy the previous day in Stop

Press. In his late sixties now and somewhat frail, he held out his hand and I stared at his red, green and gold 'Jamaican' hat. Sliding easily from local Krio to Jamaican creole he laughed. 'Wha' you look 'pon, bway?' Maddy has been jailed, detained and harassed many times by Sierra Leonean and Nigerian authorities, but he has recently returned from the United States to mount a production of one of his plays. He was in a hurry to get to rehearsals. 'Welcome to Sierra Leone,' he said. Then he began to move off. 'It's a beautiful country. I wish I could say the same about the people.'

In the evening I began to read 'Mike Butscher's War Diary.'

January 8, 1999: . . . I slipped out of the guesthouse wearing shorts and slippers, with white cloth around my head to make me look like an RUF supporter. The rebels were everywhere but I chose a route through the quieter back streets. The city centre was destroyed and littered with corpses. At the entrance to Connaught Hospital, a rotting pile of corpses emitted an offensive smell. I held my nose and quietly walked through Kroo Bay, Kingtom, and Ascension Town. Finally I reached Congo Town, which is ECOMOG [West African peacekeeping mission] territory. Holding my hands in the air I walked over to some ECOMOG and Sierra Leone army soldiers . . .

January 11, 1999: . . . I crossed a bridge that had been a battleground 24 hours earlier, walking on spent shells with every step. I saw innumerable bodies under the bridge, and vultures hovering overhead. My legs felt shaky, but I tried to be a man as I passed bullet-ridden bodies and vehicles. One corpse had been hit in the head: his brains spilled all over the tarmac . . .

January 15, 1999: . . . I watched the big trucks dump bodies at the Ascension town cemetery. Five dogs hauled a rebel's body from his grave, growling over their catch.

The next day I hand Mike's diary back to him and thank him for letting me read it. It had made for compulsive, yet depressing, reading.

'You see, I am trying to write about the war in my own way. To turn my experiences into fiction or poetry, this will take time.'

Again we are sitting together in the cramped PEN offices, and I ask Mike about his years in England in the nineties.

'In 1990 I could see that Sierra Leone was heading for disaster, and so after some years working in Liberia and Sierra Leone in broadcast journalism, I joined the brain drain. I went to an International Organisation of Journalists conference in France. Rather than return to the massive corruption and turmoil of my country, I decided to go to London for I was fearful of government repression at home. I claimed political asylum in Britain in 1991. Eventually I was refused in 1995 and voluntarily returned to Sierra Leone where the situation was even worse than I could have imagined. But in England I learned a lot about writing and broadcasting, and that is where I first became aware of PEN and other organisations which help writers who are suffering trauma and oppression. By the time our own war was declared officially over in January 2002, twelve writers had been killed. For a country of our size, with a population of about five million, twelve writers is a lot.' He pauses. 'Of course, one dead writer is too many. That is one of the reasons why we have PEN. We have to come together now and as writers we must support each other.'

The rain has started again. It is thundering down on to the iron roof and flooding under the door and into the office.

'It is difficult to be a writer in Sierra Leone, but it is important that we start meeting and talking. Then, if nothing else, we can create our own readership and pass our work around.'

Back at Stop Press I am finally able to get Maddy's attention. He holds court, with a word for every passer-by, issuing invitations to some and instructions to others.

'I agree with and support this new PEN initiative, but the young people have to have mentors. They need models, otherwise they cannot succeed.'

'And if the models go away to Britain or to the United States?'

He smiles and taps his chest.

'I am here. I am trying. The role of the writer in society is a very dynamic one. But in this society it is difficult [because] our civil servants are really civil saboteurs and the country is full of moral and ethical corruption. We have no real writers, and no real interest in writing. In fact, we have created nothing in this country since independence for the writer or artist to be recognised.'

He seems both angry and defeated as he drinks from his bottle of Guinness. I suggest that at least Butscher and the PEN organisation are trying.

Maddy sighs. 'We are the same size as Denmark, where they have at least six large publishing houses. We have nothing. We are just not capable of helping each other. And who takes us seriously? Not even ourselves.'

On my final morning in Freetown I once again sit with Butscher in his cramped office. The rain has stopped and so there is no need for either of us to raise our voices. As organised as ever, Mike hands me a piece of paper with a list of equipment that the PEN office needs. Computers, printers, copying machine, reference books and stationery are the most expensive items. The total cost is US$25,000.

'Sierra Leone used to be called the Athens of Africa for we were the intellectual engine room of the region. We published books, we were readers, we had a university-educated elite. But history has not been kind to us.'

Holding Butscher's invoice in my hand, I ask him if there is any moral justification for spending a sum of this magnitude on making life easier for a small handful of people. While Maddy may think the writer is the social conscience of the country, the country is barely functioning. There is a dire need for basic medical supplies. Butscher thinks for a few moments. I feel guilty that I have put him on the spot, and find myself now wishing that the rain would come clattering down against the iron roof so that we might find it difficult to hear each other and therefore legitimately retreat into silence. But there is no rain.

'In a bad, bad situation like this,' says Butscher, 'we need to hear from writers. It is writers who remind people who they are and where they come from.'

Ghana: Border Crossings (2004)

And then, of course, it happens much as it always happens. The driver turns to me and says, 'Mr Caryl, please you can help me?' I wait for a beat and then he continues. 'I have a form for the visa lottery. I think it is for 2-0-0-5, but I don't know how to fill it. I would like to go out of this place.' Awuje has been driving me for four days now, and I have half expected this moment from the beginning. He certainly chose his location well. We are in the small town of Elmina on the west coast of Africa. It is the site of one of the largest and most impressive slave forts, those troubling edifices from whose dungeons millions of Africans were shipped in conditions of unspeakable misery, across the broad expanse of the Atlantic Ocean, and deposited into the new American world.

I smile somewhat helplessly at Awuje, who now pulls a form out of a battered manila folder and holds it out for my inspection. I glance at it and immediately see the problem. The form – which includes instructions for filing – has been downloaded from the internet, presumably by a friend of Awuje's. What Awuje does not realise is that this form has to be filled out online. Somewhere in the United States of America a Department of Homeland Security bureaucrat made the decision to switch from postal to online filing for visas and, by doing so, introduced another level of 'literacy' into the procedure, making it even more difficult for the 'huddled masses' to have access to the richest country on earth. I continue to stare at the form and then I see another problem. The online application has to be completed and submitted by 31 December.

We are now in late January. Awuje has missed the deadline by nearly four weeks, which renders the downloaded material doubly useless. I clutch the well-thumbed visa lottery form and tell Awuje that I will speak to him about it at an unspecified time called 'later on'.

Awuje wishes to do a little border crossing. In his case, from West Africa to the United States of America, where — incidentally — he knows absolutely nobody. And he is not a young man. Far from it. His mass of tightly curled white hair suggests early sixties. The sprightly manner in which he leaves the shade of a tree and runs to the car whenever he sees me coming, suggests late forties. At first I thought he was merely demonstrating his fitness, but I now understand that Awuje is keen to impress upon me just how alert he is to the details of the job. He knows that I will return and he assumes that there will be more employment. However, I have, on more than one occasion, told Awuje that while I appreciate his efficiency, his sprinting makes me feel a little uncomfortable. Really, there is no need to rush, but then again Awuje is rushing not only because he wishes to please me, but because he is also keenly aware that he is a man with a greater mass of life behind him than in front of him. In what time he has left he wishes to go to the United States of America to have a chance to better himself. In this sense, he is in a hurry.

He owns his own car, which in Ghana means that he is doing better than the vast majority of the population. And he keeps his car scrupulously clean, for it serves a double function as both status symbol and his sole means of income. I have already noticed that Awuje seems to have some difficulty reading, and he clearly has no understanding of the internet, yet he has worked assiduously over the years to purchase his second-hand blue saloon. The evidence of the car suggests a disciplined man who focused on a goal and is now reaping the benefits of having achieved it. What's more, he is a driver with foreign contacts, which places him among the elite of Ghanaian drivers. But Awuje wants more, and he is prepared to leave his relatively comfortable life in Accra and journey into the unknown in search of material reward.

Awuje's imagined border crossing will, so he hopes, allow him to prosper economically. If he is lucky enough to reach the Promised Land and get a job, then his border crossing will also help the United States of America, for Awuje brings with him a highly developed work ethic. His imagined migration will also allow his native country to prosper, for he plans to remit money to Ghana in order that he might prepare for his return 'home'. One thing Awuje is sure of is that he has no desire to die on American soil. He intends to undertake his border crossing with an imaginary return ticket, but even as he tells me these facts, I find myself wondering about the price of Awuje's ticket and I keep fastening hard on to one word which in itself seems somewhat innocuous, but on closer inspection is often freighted with frustration, confusion, and even despair. That word is, of course, displacement.

To be in Ghana musing on the word displacement is to force me to think of the life of one man in particular. William Edward Burghardt Du Bois was born in Great Barrington, in the rolling Berkshire Hills of south-western Massachusetts on 23 February, 1868, and he died ninety-five years later in Accra, Ghana. Du Bois was born in the year that Andrew Johnson was impeached, that Ulysses S. Grant was elected president of the United States, and at a time when African Americans were voting for the first time in the Reconstruction South. During Du Bois's childhood Mark Twain was writing *Huckleberry Finn*, and the newly formed Ku Klux Klan was beginning to make its ugly mark on American life. Du Bois graduated from high school in Great Barrington, the only black student in a class of thirteen, and he went south to Fisk University in Tennessee where he earned a Bachelor's degree in 1888. In the same year he was admitted as a junior into Harvard where he famously described his situation: 'I was in Harvard, but not of it.' In 1890 he graduated with a Bachelor of Arts degree, and thereafter entered Harvard's graduate school. Between 1892 and 1894 he studied at a university in Berlin, and in 1894 he returned to the United States where the following year he became the first African American to receive a Ph.D. from Harvard University. Du Bois subsequently set forth on an impressive career as a teacher, historian, sociologist, journalist, philosopher and political activist, a career which ultimately led to his being recognised as the quintessential American Renaissance man.

Du Bois died in Accra, Ghana, a country he had decided to make his own in 1961 when already ninety-three years of age. Disillusioned by the slow speed and nature of change in the United States of America, and increasingly attracted to the revolutionary principles of the Communist Party, in the very twilight of his life Du Bois determined that he would leave the United States and take up the offer of his friend Kwame Nkrumah, the charismatic president of the recently independent country of Ghana, to come 'home' to Africa. In 1961 a somewhat resigned Du Bois renounced his American citizenship and set sail for Ghana, where he intended to direct the Encyclopedia Africana, a project he had envisaged as early as 1909. Two years later, on 27 August 1963, the day before Martin Luther King's electrifying 'I Have a Dream' speech at the Lincoln Memorial in Washington, DC, the 'old man' slipped quietly from this world. The government of his newly adopted country afforded him a state funeral and condolences poured in from heads of state in all corners of the world, including China's Mao Zedong and Russia's Nikita Khrushchev. Sadly, the United States government did not acknowledge the passing of its esteemed, but now displaced, former citizen, despite his having served the country with distinction for the greater part of the century. The day after his state funeral the *Ghanaian Times* carried a front-page editorial under the banner heading 'NANTSEW YIE!' (which in Akan means 'Farewell!'). For the family of the recently departed Du Bois, the official unforgiving American silence must have deafened any expressions of appreciation from Ghanaians and others. Indeed, border crossings can be expensive and troubling.

I have made three migrations, all of which have brought me into close proximity to this troubling word 'displacement'. On 6 July 1958, after a tedious and often fearful journey across the Atlantic in the lower cabins of a cargo ship, my parents, both of whom were in their early twenties, stepped ashore at Newhaven and looked around them. They had arrived from the West Indies, and finally they were in Britain. I am sure that they both harboured different dreams of how they wished their new British lives to unfold, and the evidence of their acrimonious divorce a few years later would seem to confirm this. Nearly fifty years ago, on an English summer morning, they stepped ashore – my mother holding me in her arms, my father no doubt already scheming as to what mischief he might get up to. Ostensibly the pair of them had little reason to feel apprehensive about this new world. Tucked away in the inside pocket of my father's only jacket were the British passports which not only suggested, but confirmed, that they belonged.

But this was England in 1958, and within a few weeks of our arrival both Nottingham and London's Notting Hill exploded in scenes of racial violence the likes of which had never before been seen on the streets of Britain. My parents had already travelled north to Leeds, where they soon came face to face with the many difficulties that bedevilled West Indians in Britain during this period. Discrimination in housing and employment was openly practised and commonplace. Pubs and clubs were often segregated. For the first time in their lives my parents were called 'nigger', my mother was spat at in the streets, my father punched, they were short-changed in shops, offered accommodation that you wouldn't kennel your dog in, and constantly told to go back to the jungle. I was, of course, too young to know what they endured, or how they felt about their welcome in the motherland, but some few weeks ago I sat with my mother and watched a BBC documentary about the arrival of West Indians in Britain in the 1950s. As the programme progressed my mother gradually fell quiet and then she simply left the room. Before she did so she uttered her parting sentence with a quiet dignity that echoed long after her departure. 'I'd forgotten', she said, 'just how awful it was.' I sat for a few moments and then turned off the television.

But my parents were not totally naïve. Before embarking on the ship in St Kitts they *did* have some idea that the streets of Britain were not paved with gold. Letters from friends and relatives became the raw material of village gossip, and not every missive spoke with calypso warmth of Britain as the place to be. Not everybody sang the virtues of English fair play and decency of manners. Uncle Leslie complained that he was called 'Sambo' so often that he began to think it was his middle name. Aunt Monica wrote that the only thing colder than an English January was the look on an Englishman's face when you tried to get a job that involved using the intelligence that God had given to you. And speaking of God, Uncle Vincent could not for the life of him understand why, as he left the church, the vicar shook his hand and said it was nice to see him but please not to come again next week. These stories made their way back to St Kitts and so, in some sense, my parents *were* prepared for the possibility that, despite their British passports and shared cultural values, they might, on arrival, feel somewhat out of tune with Britain. And how right they were – yet they stayed.

Initially, they stayed because of me. In the years and months that followed, they had other children and so the pressure was off me a little because they were now staying because of *us*. But at least to begin with there was no doubt that these two extremely proud individuals stayed in Britain and took the abuse, the hostility, and at times the hatred, because of their son – me. They were English-speaking Christians who had been educated in the British system and who were, in more ways than one, coming home to Britain. But the truth was they had crossed the water and come to Britain not so they could feel at home, eat fish and chips, support a football team, go down to the boozer, and put money on the horses. They came to Britain to get ahead and grow, and to provide me with opportunities that I would never have had on the small twelve-mile by six-mile island that I was born on. This being the case, the anger, hurt and betrayal that they felt had to be accommodated; the social and cultural rejection had to be absorbed. They did not *feel* at home, but in the end it did not matter.

In 1990 I was invited to be the visiting writer at a private liberal arts college in western Massachusetts. As it turned out, the college was not too far from where W.E.B. Du Bois had been born over a century earlier. The appointment was for just one academic year. Eight years later, in 1998, I resigned and took up another academic post, which I still hold, in New York City. I may be a little slow, but only now am I coming to understand my time in the United States as a migration. It is only recently that I have felt comfortable answering the question 'Where do you live?' with the answer 'New York City', or writing 'USA' against country of domicile on forms that have been officially proffered. In many ways it was the events of September 11, 2001 that helped me understand the degree to which I had become involved with the United States. Like millions of other New Yorkers, I felt the impact of that day – and the bizarre days that followed – as a participant and not as a global observer. I was shocked to the core, but it was a response that was fed by proprietorial anxiety. What made my response all the more surprising to me is the fact that I have never really felt myself to be at home in the United States. I still prefer the pub to a bar; soccer as opposed to American football; cricket, not baseball. I still say 'tomahto' and not 'tomayto', spell theatre with an 're', tune into BBC news, avoid waffles, pancakes and doughnuts, and watch the *EastEnders* Omnibus on BBC America on a Saturday afternoon. But the United States does not punish me, or laugh at me, or belittle me for being who I am. I have been able to cross the Atlantic and enter into the society, and my sense of displacement is, in the context of my parents' experience, deeply designer in character.

But this is not, of course, the case for all migrants to the United States. I am a middle-class man, in a middle-class profession, who speaks English and who can navigate his way around the system. The land of the free and the home of the brave has always offered up 'freedom' and 'home' as extremely relative concepts depending upon who or what you are. I would not be waxing so lyrical about the United States were I a Native American, or Arab American, or Muslim American. In this instance my sense of displacement would not be designer; it would be deeply felt and painful. But I have been fortunate, and I have stayed in the United States for the same reason that my parents stayed in Britain: because the country has offered me the opportunity to grow. I used to think such opportunity was limitless in Britain, but soon after my arrival in the United States in 1990 I began to meet British writers, doctors, musicians, film-makers, newspaper editors, and others who were living in the United States precisely because of the opportunities to grow that the country was affording them. More often than not, these people's decision had little to do with their race, gender or religion, nor was it connected to prejudice or discrimination in Britain. The impulse to migrate, in nearly all cases, was connected to the individual's craving to better him- or herself, which is precisely why I left in 1990, and why I am still there. As long as growth remains a possibility then displacement, designer or otherwise, is a price that countless migrants, including my parents, are more than willing to pay.

I am also paying the price for my first migration, although I dearly wish that I did not have to. This was an act of forced migration: the Atlantic slave trade. I do not need to rehearse the iniquities of the trade, nor do I need to convince anybody of its fundamental immorality. However, the racial divide in Europe and the Americas between those of African origin and others – most commonly whites – is directly related to the vigour with which mythologies of racial difference were sown into the consciousness of people, black and white, during the seventeenth, eighteenth, and to some extent the nineteenth centuries. The involuntary migration of millions of Africans is the one border crossing – the one migration – that I regret having participated in.

In 1997 an African American journalist named Keith Richburg published a book entitled *Out of America: A Black Man Confronts Africa* in which, astonishingly enough, he wrote that he was delighted that the Atlantic slave trade had rescued him from an African future. In fact, he gave thanks for the slave trade, and others too have pointed to the diasporan achievement of those of African origin to support a claim that life in the diaspora is preferable to any kind of life in Africa. It is true enough that in music, sports, science, literature, in fact in many fields, people of African origin have made major contributions to Western civilisation. But it is pernicious to see such achievements as exempla of the benefits of the slave trade and slavery. A triumphant survival of the Middle Passage? I think not.

No African wanted to leave Africa. None. Including myself. Those of us in the diaspora are all involuntary migrants, people who were forced to leave our land, families, friends, languages, religions and cultures, and begin anew elsewhere. *Forced* to do so. Our displacement on arrival in the Americas was profound and it caused a psychic wound which, for countless millions of people of African origin, continues to fester. Today many diasporan people of African origin still feel, to borrow Claude McKay's title to his stirring autobiography, *A Long Way from Home*. Many diasporan Africans are unhappy, worried, even angry. In fact, a significant number are still trying to 'return' to the land that they were snatched and exiled from. I have sat in countries all over the world and talked with people of African origin who feel unmoored and displaced. And I have also sat in a half-dozen different African countries and 'reasoned' with those who have returned, many of whom, to my eyes, never look or feel as though they have truly closed the circle and, having undertaken their reverse 'Middle Passage', achieved peace. To *force* a people to migrate is to risk setting in motion decades or centuries of heartache. Whatever the *raison d'être* for a forced migration, the psychological and spiritual price of such an act is, in my opinion, almost always too high. In the case of the African diaspora, the combined cultural legacy of the Harlem Renaissance is worth nothing when balanced against the anguish of one single African in a dungeon deep in the bowels of Elmina Castle, chained to a now dead and putrefying friend, their mind racked with terror at the thought of what may lie ahead. Cab Calloway can keep singing 'Hi di hi de hi di hi', Duke Ellington can keep his band, and Claude McKay and Countee Cullen can hang up their pens. My sympathies are located on the west coast of Africa.

Yet human beings have a tremendous capacity to absorb the chaos and confusion that comes with migration, forced or voluntary. As I have tried to suggest, it is a natural human impulse to wish to cross borders in search of places that might enable one to fulfil one's potential; and a fear of feeling displaced is never going to be a serious obstacle to those who wish to voluntarily migrate. For such people it can take a few generations before the bewilderment and hurt of displacement begin to recede and are replaced by the warm glow of belonging. But not so for those who have been forced to migrate against their will.

Diasporan Africans are a long-memoried people. While driving in the hills beyond Accra, Awuje and I passed a large villa surrounded by a high concrete wall. Set atop the wall were imposing elaborate stone sculptures of lions. The wooden trim just below the roof was painted red, green and gold, and the signboard by the wall of the compound revealed exactly what was going on. 'Tuff Gong International Recording Studios'. On another board the simple slogan, 'Hit Me with Rhythm'. This property, high in the cool hills of Aburi, belonged to the widow of the Jamaican reggae superstar, Bob Marley. Rita Marley had, as her late husband always wished, found her way back to her roots in Africa. Later on this same day, Awuje dropped me off at the W.E.B. Du Bois Centre in Accra. Indeed, we are a long-memoried people.

In 1961, having arrived and taken up Ghanaian citizenship, W.E.B. Du Bois was presented with a large white villa in the residential cantonments area of Accra by President Kwame Nkrumah. Du Bois's second wife Shirley Graham Du Bois quickly set about transforming the grounds into a lush garden, while her husband busied himself with his writing. Today the house and grounds form the centrepiece of the Du Bois Centre, an arts complex that is managed by Sekou Nkrumah, son of the late president. A tall, serious man in his mid-thirties, he tells me that he was educated in communist Romania, which I decide must explain some of his gravity. Sekou escorts me from his office and the short distance to the main villa. Here I am able to see the personal library of W.E.B. Du Bois, his academic gowns, private photographs, first editions of his books, letters and papers, but all are in a terrible state of disrepair. The torn curtains in the villa are hanging sadly from the rails, and out in the grounds things are not much better, for the garden is largely denuded. In fact, the whole place is in dire need of paint and maintenance.

The government of Ghana own the building, and Du Bois's grave site and tomb, which are also on the land. However, Sekou tells me that it has been difficult to obtain funding to preserve the valuable evidence of one of the great American lives. I ask him about potential American help, but he smiles then sighs. He tells me that as long as the Ghanaian government claims ownership of the home, the contents and the grave site, then Americans have made it clear that they are reluctant to invest in the upkeep and preservation of the Du Bois Centre. The professional and personal turmoil which marked the displaced final two years of W.E.B. Du Bois's life, as he moved from the United States of America to Ghana, appears, some forty years later, to have escalated into a squabble over his actual possessions. The end result of this bitter stand-off is the sad, and continued, deterioration of the physical evidence of the legacy of a man who in the early winter of his life felt compelled to cross a border and go to a place where, even for somebody of his rare distinction and achievement, he still felt that he could grow.

Awuje stands outside Elmina Castle and tells me that he wishes to go to the United States of America, but despite the backdrop he speaks without any sense of irony. He views the Atlantic slave trade as neither good nor bad; he views it as history and therefore dead and somewhat irrelevant. To those in the diaspora, who remain long-memoried, the Atlantic slave trade is not only alive, it continues to be painful. The loss and confusion caused by the Atlantic crossing linger to this day, and only a few ever return in order to attempt to 'heal' themselves. However, Awuje has absolutely no interest in the psychological needs of displaced Africans in the diaspora. He wishes to go to America for the same reasons that my parents decided to come to Britain, and I decided to stay in the United States. To grow. And that's just fine. Awuje does not know anybody in the United States, and he has never come face to face with a US winter, but he is not afraid of any difficulties that such a move might cause him. Indeed, he has already factored in such difficulties as part of the price of the ticket.

Displacement, whatever. He just wants a chance, that is all, and who can blame him? Voluntary crossing of borders in an attempt to seize such opportunities is one of the oldest and most natural of human instincts; one that we should respect and, when necessary, one that we should vigorously encourage.

Belgium: The Silenced Minority (2004)

The puzzled Nigerian girl looks at me and asks, 'Are you a black man or a white man?' We are in a bar in Antwerp's red-light district where the girl's job is to sell her body to white men, many of whom are supporters of the far-right Vlaams Blok party. Her native Nigeria is far away. My accent and demeanour baffle her. The young girl does not fully understand the European world around her. She does, however, understand racism and I am prepared to pay her if she will share her thoughts with me on this subject.

To reach the bar I had walked past large windows which featured bored bottle-blondes from Moldova, Bulgaria and other Eastern European countries, girls who sat painting their nails or listening to music from portable CD players. Their pimps, hands jammed in pockets and faces decorated with large walrus-like moustaches, stood in the street and made no attempt to appear incongruous. They stamped their feet against the cold and scanned potential customers.

Chris de Stoop, a Belgian writer in his mid-forties, points to a window containing a black prostitute. 'She's from Ghana. They've been here for over ten years.' Slightly built, De Stoop looks a decade younger than his age. On these streets he is well known. His book about the trafficking of human beings for prostitution, *Ze Zijn Zo Lief, Meneer* (They Are So Sweet, Sir) (1992), was a succès de scandale in Belgium. He continues: 'The Nigerians can't afford to rent windows so they work out of the bar. They go with clients to cars, to cheap hotels, or to the bushes.' He pauses. 'It can be dangerous.'

A few months ago a Belgian friend of mine directed me to a website with the subtitle: 'Caryl Phillips: A New World Order'. The website was some kind of Dutch language think tank for the far right, and it featured chat room commentary on interviews I had given to Belgian newspapers about my collection of essays, *A New World Order* (2001). Among other things, I said that whether we liked it or not we were all, at the beginning of the twenty-first century, becoming multicultural individuals. This was not only inevitable, it was also highly desirable. Clearly not all my readers in Flanders felt the same way.

Some of the 'guests' who volunteered comments on the site tried to be reasonable, while others had little time for such niceties. The pithy comment, 'transport the darky' caught my eye, as did the logo of the Vlaams Blok party on the home page. In later visits to the site I noticed that the logo had been removed and replaced with a line drawing of Jacob van Artevelde, a fourteenth-century Flemish national hero, under the heading 'Heil Artevelde.' However, the link between the site and the Vlaams Blok party remained obvious.

Belgium is a small country, a little larger than Wales, with French-speaking Wallonia to the south and Flanders to the north. In Flanders the people speak Flemish, a language almost identical to Dutch. At the last election in Flanders the Vlaams Blok took 33 per cent of the popular vote in Antwerp. It is the largest elected right-wing party in Europe, and its policies are unashamedly racist. The other political parties in Flanders have constructed a cordon sanitaire around the Vlaams Blok and chosen not to deal with it, yet the party continues to attract popular support. In fact, the party's organisational power is becoming increasingly efficient, and has more in common with Jean-Marie Le Pen's National Front in France than with the transparently thuggish British National Party.

According to De Stoop, the growth of the Vlaams Blok has to be seen in the context of the history of Flanders. The main city of Antwerp was the Manhattan of the late medieval period, a restless, self-confident port of immense culture and vitality.

Then came the disaster of 1585 when the city fell to the Spanish; thereafter, the vast majority of the influential citizens fled to Amsterdam. For 250 years Flanders was kicked like a football between various European superpowers, and the Flemings were made to feel like second-class citizens. In 1830 Antwerp and Flanders once more became free and part of the new country of Belgium, but now the region laboured heavily under the double yoke of poverty and French influence. At this time Flanders, with Ireland, was the poorest country in Western Europe and many people chose to migrate to the United States. However, Flemish identity remained strong, even though Flemish socio-economic muscle continued to atrophy. After the Second World War Flanders began to revive, but it did so slowly as it continued to bear the baggage of insecure identity politics. Increased immigration in the late sixties and seventies, particularly from Morocco, served only to exacerbate anxiety.

Borgerhout (or 'Borgerocco' – as the right-wingers like to call it) is a part of the city that had been described to me as Antwerp's 'ghetto'. As I walk its streets I see a number of brown faces, but there is nothing about this tidy neighbourhood that is 'ghetto-like': 70 to 80 per cent of the immigrants in Antwerp are either Moroccan or Turkish, while Poles make up the largest contingent of Eastern Europeans. Black Africans from south of the Sahara are a small minority. Antwerp also possesses a sizeable Jewish population, about 20,000 of whom are Hasidic, many involved in the diamond trade. A long strip of diamond stores extends the full length of one side of Antwerp Central train station, but this hardly qualifies as a discernible Jewish 'ghetto'. In fact, as I walk around, I can see that, compared to Brussels or Liège, Antwerp seems to be a more or less 'white' city, which leads me to speculate that this electoral sympathy for the right might indeed be motivated by factors other than race and immigration.

De Stoop had explained to me that, in his opinion, the Vlaams Blok has always portrayed itself as a party which is struggling against Belgium and, to some extent, France, as it seeks to achieve

Flemish independence. In recent years its fortunes have risen, but only after it added an anti-immigration stance to its cause. By hijacking 'immigration', 'security' and 'crime' as party issues the Vlaams Blok has bolstered its carefully constructed position as the party of tough-minded mavericks and nationalist martyrs. If the questions on the street are — Can I keep my home? Can I keep my job? Can I speak my own language? Will I be safe at night? — then the Vlaams Blok has the answers. The party assures people it will make them secure in their own Flemish environment. It is a seductive promise made all the more enticing by the prospect of some degree of cultural purity.

I meet Mark Schaevers, the editor-in-chief of the leading Flemish weekly magazine, *Humo*, in a bar in Brussels. He says that it used to be the strategy to write off the Vlaams Blok as idiotic right-wingers, but he insists that these days its supporters are dangerous precisely because they have made great attempts to clean up their image. They like to position themselves as the reasonable voice of the people, but Schaevers's magazine recently exposed two members who have strong links to the violently aggressive neo-Nazi group, Blood and Honour. When I ask him why there has not been more overt racist violence in Flanders, he suggests that some of bloodiest battlefields of two world wars are located on Belgian soil. 'We've had enough bloodshed so if they were to take that route they would lose sympathy.'

Like many European capitals, Brussels is being transformed by postcolonial migrants who do not claim ownership of the city, who arrive with a fixed determination to make money, and only sometimes dream of returning 'home'. Of course many do stay, do claim ownership and make vital contributions, but either way this continued mobility encourages those on the right to retreat to old essentialisms that have no place in modern Europe. Contrary to what the Vlaams Blok or other European right-wing parties might think, Europe has long passed the stage where it can afford to imagine itself as a series of homogeneous, yet independent, societies. The newly interdependent Europe has little choice but to recognise and embrace multiculturalism. It could even be argued that coming to terms with the reality of this new vision of ourselves is the biggest social and cultural challenge that Europe has faced since the Renaissance, but in order to rethink ourselves and our societies we need to move beyond the double-speak of opportunistic politicians who think it legitimate to pose helplessly xenophobic questions such as: 'Why don't they like our values?'

De Stoop and I sit in a restaurant overlooking the River Scheldt. I stare through the full-length glass panes and watch huge barges floating by. Overhead seagulls lazily wheel on the stiff breeze, and in the distance the cranes of Europe's second-largest port dominate the skyline. I ask him what Flemish writers are doing to tackle the problem of the Vlaams Blok. I know that he and others, including Tom Lanoye, the city poet of Antwerp, have been vocal. 'But some writers,' says De Stoop, 'don't want to give attention to the Blokkers.'

As we wait for another beer, I can't help thinking of Joseph Conrad, who wrote about how European identity is shored up by identifying the outsider. He was a man who was avowedly political around issues of belonging and the plight of newcomers, being himself an itinerant. I think about his story 'Amy Foster', and how the stranger arrives in an English village and never quite fits in. And, of course, I think about *Heart of Darkness*. I think also of Hugo Claus, perhaps the best known of the Belgian writers, who when asked about the Vlaams Blok by *Le Monde* in 1997 replied, 'The fact that they exist and indulge in fascistic grousing puts the other parties under the obligation to set themselves apart from these ideas.' Sitting here in Antwerp, Claus's city, this seems a strangely coy response.

Lanoye, on the other hand, is not coy at all. A dapper man in his mid-forties, with greying hair and a hip full-length leather coat, he is immediately cordial and quick to share his views. In a crowded little café we struggle to make ourselves heard as we sip coffee and take shelter from the rain. Lanoye is clear about the role of his own writing and its relationship to activism, a clarity that has been sharpened by his spending a part of each year in Cape Town. 'In South Africa aesthetics and politics work together, despite the fact that politics works within the boundaries of compromise. However, in Flanders, politicians often try to use art by, for example, quoting me out of context.' As for the Vlaams Blok, he is quick to condemn them as anti-intellectuals. He laughs as he points out that none of them wear glasses. 'They don't want to appear to be weak.' However, he is definite about their role. 'They have a nationalist agenda to create a republic of Flanders, and it may well eventually happen. The truth is they are violent in speech and more racist than Pim Fortuyn was in the Netherlands, or Jörg Haider is in Austria.'

When I ask Lanoye why he continues to live in Antwerp, he defends his city. 'Antwerp is one of the most avant-garde cities in Europe in terms of fashion and music, and in a sense the Vlaams Blok has created a space for a counter-culture. The city has a register of gay marriage, and a powerful theatrical tradition.' But Lanoye believes that Antwerp is at a crossroads. He tells me that some gays vote for the Vlaams Blok if they have been gay-bashed by Moroccans. And some Jews vote for it because, although they know that the 'Blokkers' collaborated with the Nazis during the war, they also know that the Vlaams Blok will try to stop the building of mosques. 'The stupid logic is that the enemy of my enemy must be my friend. As the city poet of Antwerp I have felt opposition towards my adopting an activist role, but a writer must always take an individual stand.'

Later, in my hotel room, I wonder again if the rise of the right in Flanders can be so simply explained as an insecurity about the Flemish identity coupled with a more recent fear of immigration. I decide that even if these are the two principal reasons for the current malaise, the fact remains that until the victims of the far right start to construct their own narratives then very little will change in Flemish society. It is important that writers such as Chris de Stoop and Tom Lanoye speak out on these issues, but in the end the transformative and politically decisive narratives, particularly those that engage with racism, must also come from within the non-white Belgian community. But, as Lanoye pointed out to me: 'One of the devastating effects of the Vlaams Blok is that it has become more difficult to give money for education and language training to immigrant communities.' The truth is that non-white writers in Belgium have no visible role in society. In the Netherlands, second-generation Dutch voices such as Hafid Bouazza, Yasmine Allas and Moses Isegawa are strong and established. This is also the case in France and in Britain, but non-whites in Belgium have yet to find a literary voice. This is all the more disturbing given the fact that according to the recent EU-sponsored European Observation Centre for Racism and Xenophobia survey, Belgium was the second most 'actively intolerant' country in Europe with regard to minorities. Some narrative balance would appear to be in order.

I call De Stoop and ask him if he can arrange for me to meet some African prostitutes. If anybody can give me a measure of Belgian racism, they will. As we walk through the red-light district, De Stoop tells me that first we will visit Frank Cool and his 'Kettlepatrol', the Keteltje being the name of the bar where, according to De Stoop, the Nigerian prostitutes congregate. I look puzzled at the thought of this detour, but De Stoop reassures me. 'You'll see.' He stops and presses the buzzer to a nondescript door. De Stoop speaks Flemish, so I can follow only the essence of what he is saying. However, I understand that we will not be admitted. He waits a moment, says something else, and the door opens.

Frank Cool has a long grey ponytail and his face, body and clothes have all been well occupied. A former tug captain, he has spent most of his life on land living in Antwerp's red-light district. He leads us up a flight of rickety stairs to the first floor where De Stoop and I sit gingerly on a third-hand sofa in a cramped room that looks as though it might be the communal area of a squat. Which, I soon discover, is precisely what the place used to be until Frank persuaded the city government to give him the house so that he could look after Nigerian prostitutes. He and his 'Kettlepatrol', two of whom sit in the room with us, are white Belgian men with a 'special interest' in looking out for Nigerian girls. Some of the men have criminal records, but Frank insists that none is involved with the Vlaams Blok, which according to Frank is not true of the brothel owners, pimps, and a number of the local police. As he begins to explain how the girls are trafficked to Belgium, there is a loud scratching behind me. One of the 'patrol' men laughs out loud and says, 'Rats and mice everywhere.' He opens the door to what looks like an old gramophone and takes out a mousetrap from which hangs a bloodied dead mouse. 'Everywhere,' he says.

Having explained that the girls are aged between about sixteen and twenty-two, and that they are trafficked in on tourist visas with false names as maids or relatives, Frank invites me to look around their 'quarters'. Upstairs there are four 'bedrooms,' and the sullen girls are either coming in or preparing to go out to work. They sleep in shifts, continually rotating, and all of them will remain in a state of servitude for as long as it takes to pay back the debt to their trafficker. Frank's organisation makes sure the girls are screened for HIV, that they eat and that they have a place to sleep. However, when I see the deplorable sleeping conditions, I shudder to think what they would do without Frank. Although there are 300 Nigerian girls working as prostitutes in Antwerp, at Frank's there is only room for twenty at any one time.

The scene at the Keteltje is surreal: a hundred bored Nigerian girls are packed into this tunnel-like bar, and they outnumber their clients ten to one. They have arrived at a time of great recession and prospective clients are not as plentiful as they once were. Frank knows each girl by name, and he greets them warmly. He has, at some point, won them over with his gifts of chewing gum, bibles and condoms. As we make our way through the crush of girls, the barman hands Frank a present for his house: a jumbo-sized box of washing powder. Frank turns to me and confesses: 'Some of the girls stink.' I ask Frank if I can talk to one of the girls about racism in Belgium, and he says: 'Yes, I will arrange it.'

Once we have established that I am a black man and not a white man, the girl seems prepared to talk. She sits in a demure fashion, her hair neatly straightened, looking uncannily like a Sunday school teacher. 'I have been here four years, and things have got much worse,' she says. 'The people in the town don't want black people. Some of them use us and won't pay. But if I complain I am worried about being thrown out of the country.' I ask 'Cynthia' what the Vlaams Blok means to her. She looks at me with surprise. 'The Blok people hate us. They are not good people, and there are many, many of them.' When I suggest not all Belgian men are like this, she puckers her lips. Then, with a sense of cynical resignation, she turns to me and concedes. 'No, not all the men.' How, I wonder, would she know a Vlaams Blok man? She is firm now. 'I know a man who does not like black women.' I give her ten euros before signalling to De Stoop that it is time to leave.

Later that night I wake up and realise that I have been dreaming in the first-person voice of a black prostitute. But this is not my story to tell. Others in Belgium will have to tell it. I get out of bed, log on, and look again at the offending website. One man is trying to say something. 'Maybe I'm missing something,' he says, 'but what's wrong with Mr Phillips's view of a multicultural society?' I can answer his question. What is wrong with Mr Phillips's view of a multicultural society is that it presupposes that people like 'Cynthia' will be able to write, sing, paint or dance their stories, and that they will have an audience. Mr Phillips's multicultural society works only if there is a reciprocal exchange and, hopefully, one day a commingling, of narratives. Given the present-day absence of non-white narrative voices in Belgium, the situation is troubling. Having authority over our own story, and the means to tell it, is the most potent weapon that any of us are able to utilise against the corrupt vision of the far right. In Flanders there is much work to be done.

Kilimanjaro: The Height of Obsession (2005)

The hard, unrelenting light of Africa streamed through the windows of the minivan and caused us both to reach for our sunglasses. There was something satisfying about doing so, knowing that back home everybody else was caught up in the dark mornings and short days of deepest winter. Twenty-four hours earlier I had dashed frantically across a freezing London. At Heathrow airport I rendezvoused with my climbing partner, Russell Banks, who was reading a battered paperback copy of Hemingway's *Islands in the Stream*. Having flown overnight from New York, he looked as dishevelled and unprepared as I felt. The 19,343 feet of Mount Kilimanjaro was already beginning to feel like folly and we hadn't even left London.

Russell and I first talked about this climb in Saratoga Springs during the 2004 summer programme of the New York State Writers Institute. One night, in a bar called the Parting Glass, we found ourselves bragging to each other, and the assembled writing students, about how we had both climbed Kilimanjaro. I had done so three times, and Russell once, but it was some years now since either of us had been on the mountain. Also, Russell had gone up the easier Marangu route, and over drinks I was trying to introduce him to the idea that the more difficult Machame route was the way to go. Predictably, by the time the barman called last orders we had talked ourselves into an expedition.

I first met Russell Banks almost twenty years ago at the Harbourfront Writers Festival in Toronto. Late one night, Graham Swift and I were walking sheepishly across a car park, having missed the evening readings, when we were approached by the Swiss author, Nicolas Bouvier, who looked somewhat agitated. Had we heard Banks reading this evening from his novel, *Continental Drift*? We confessed our absence and an apoplectic Bouvier delivered his verdict. 'But he is a racist.' I burst out laughing, having correctly assumed that Russell had committed the 'crime' of daring to read in the vernacular of a West Indian, and had therefore set off all kinds of politically correct alarm bells.

Russell Banks's subsequent work has continued to step boldly into this minefield. In June 2000 he published a controversial piece in *Harper's Magazine* entitled 'Who Will Tell the People?', in which he argued that the vital American narrative was the African American story. In the autumn of 2004, his latest novel, *The Darling*, which is set partly in Liberia and explores the life of a middle-class white American woman who marries an African politician, was published to good, if somewhat puzzled, reviews. Traversing boundaries of class, race and gender is something that seems to come naturally to Russell, but as we settled in for the flight to Nairobi he admitted that he was burned out from all the feedback and debate that had surrounded the American publication of *The Darling*. He was looking forward to 'hitting the road', even though we were both a little concerned about the nature of the road we were hitting. After all, only about 50 per cent of those who attempt to climb Kilimanjaro ever make it to the summit, and my own memories of previous climbs included suffering a significant degree of physical pain and enduring the disturbing symptoms of Acute Mountain Sickness (AMS). The world's tallest free-standing mountain exercises a severe test, and while I knew I wasn't getting any younger, Russell was now sixty-four and nursing a 'bad' left knee.

Having fought its way through the downtown Nairobi traffic, the minivan deposited us both outside a restaurant called Carnivore, where we would have our final meal before flying to Tanzania and beginning the climb proper. Among the choice meats on the menu were crocodile and camel. As we waited for our order, Russell shared his own AMS stories from an earlier climb in Ecuador. This included an Albanian woman apparently walking into his tent at 19,000 feet and Russell sharing snacks and extensive conversation with her. Of course his colleagues didn't see her, and as I was digesting the full lunacy of his story, and exchanging his tale of the Albanian woman for my own memories of seeing luminous red rabbits the first time I went up Kilimanjaro, the waiter asked us if we were finished. 'Oh no,' said the intrepid Mr Banks. 'We'll both have a little more of the camel, please.'

Moshi, in northern Tanzania, is a quiet, dusty town, whose broad streets are decorated with bright red flamboyant trees and clumps of purple flowers. At the Keys Hotel, an elderly Tanzanian, whose manner suggested he had served in an earlier, colonial period, escorted me at a snail's pace up the solid wooden steps and into my room on the second floor. The open windows meant I could hear the raucous cacophony of the staff doing laundry and preparing food in the courtyard down below. I closed the windows and switched on the huge ceiling fan, but its rusty blades whirred and roared like those of a helicopter so I instantly turned it off.

Some years earlier I had stayed in a room with a glorious view of the snow-capped peak. Back then I only had to incline my head to see what Hemingway meant when he described the mountain as 'wide as the whole world, great, high and unbelievably white in the sun'. Today, I was swatting mosquitoes and listening to the discordant clatter of pots and pans. Eventually I went down to the restaurant for dinner and William, the head waiter, asked me where my 'Babu' ('grandfather' in Swahili) friend was. I said he would soon be down. William looked knowing. 'I will pray for you both,' he said.

The Machame route is reputedly the most beautiful, but it is difficult. According to the official literature, no crampons, axes or ropes are necessary, but good boots, huge determination, a knowledgeable guide, and a willing and able group of porters are all vital. The first day's climbing involves trudging uphill through the rainforest, the grey-green streamers of bearded lichen that decorate the trees rendering the whole scene ghostly. As we walked beneath the thick canopy, the silence was broken only by the shrieking roar of the black and white Colobus monkeys that were careful to stay out of sight, and Russell confirming that his knee was holding up. I looked around and marvelled at the fabulously twisted, moss- and fern-encrusted juniper trees, and then the sky began to weep gentle rain and the wind tugged a little at my T-shirt.

At last, at 9,776 feet, we burst clear of the rainforest and began to trip across a heather-clad moor, complete with drifting mist, in a landscape that was so reminiscent of the Scottish highlands that I half expected to discover a kilted bagpiper around the corner. Eventually we made camp and, as the porters began to pitch the tents and saunter off in search of fresh stream water, our guide, Arnold, approached and told my partner that tomorrow he should slow down. Arnold could have saved his words, for Russell's knee was now giving him trouble and he had already taken two painkillers. As we squatted in the cold Russell began to talk ominously of a knee brace.

In the morning we set off for Shira Camp (12,598 feet) knowing that our day would begin with a challenging uphill walk of about four and a half hours. And then the skies began to release a light rain, which soon stiffened into a downpour. As we trudged along, Russell declared: 'Climbing Kili is the only thing left in the world that reminds me of my first writing in that I'm doing it for myself and it makes no sense to anybody else.' I thought about Russell's words, but on this bleak windswept day, bent double into the wind and shivering with cold, it was difficult to concentrate.

By 6 p.m. it was getting dark and it had not stopped raining. I sat in the entrance to my tent and peered through the gloom at the huge white-necked ravens that hopped all around scavenging for handouts. Night had paused on the horizon and was simply waiting for the light to leave. Only then would the stars present themselves and night come hurrying towards us. I thought of the day's climb and realised that I wasn't sure why I had spent the past few hours clinging to icy rock in the driving rain, and tiptoeing along narrow ledges with sheer drops of up to 200 feet to one side. When I first started to write it didn't matter to me what other people thought: the fact was, writing made sense to me. For Russell, the selfish determination that was informing this ascent reminded him of his own writing, but I couldn't help feeling that our present predicament in the teeming rain suggested perverse wilfulness as opposed to admirable dedication.

That night I lay huddled in my sleeping bag, the wind howling all around, listening to Russell turning and tossing in his tent. The first two times I climbed Kilimanjaro, I did so alone and essentially to see if I could do it. The third time I did so to accompany a friend. But this ascent truly made no sense. I could talk to Russell about books at sea level in any number of restaurants in London or New York. Were we really so vain that once we had declared our intent in a bar in Saratoga Springs we felt obliged to follow through?

I woke up at 1.30 a.m. and reached for my torch. I could see my breath clouding, like that of a horse that has just won the Grand National, but at least the sound of slashing rain had stopped. Everything in the tent was wet: my bags, my books, and my clothes. Only my body, shivering inside the sleeping bag that was perched on a half-inch foam mattress, remained relatively dry. Water had seeped up through the groundsheet and this thin mattress was now functioning as a raft. The need to use the open-air 'toilet' meant I had to abandon the safety of my raft and pull on my boots. Once outside I could see that the wide sky looked as though somebody had taken a silver paintbrush and wiped it back and forth. Every available space was speckled with stars. Standing ankle-deep in mud, the cold cutting right through to my bones, I noticed that chunks of ice had formed on the outside of the tent and I began to cough.

At nearly 5 p.m. on the third day, Russell and I arrived at

the Barranco Camp (12,959 feet), both exhausted and somewhat worried. The Barranco Valley is celebrated for its teeming waterfalls, spectacular vegetation and abundant wildlife, but for most of the day visibility had been severely limited. There had been tantalising glimpses of the snow-capped summit, and occasionally I could see the long grass, the drooping boughs, and the unmanicured charm of the rugged valley, but the bigger problem was that I could now distinctly feel the lack of oxygen. For the first time I began to worry about AMS and I was closely monitoring my body for signs of nausea or lack of appetite. I remembered the crushing headaches and hallucinations that had plagued me in the past, and I kept reminding myself that the only way up this mountain is 'pole, pole', which in Swahili means 'slowly, slowly'. Sadly, each year AMS contributes to the deaths of a handful of climbers on Kilimanjaro.

The following lunchtime my headache seemed to have taken up permanent residence and Russell was clearly suffering with his knee. The clouds had lifted and in the distance I saw a flat parched earth that was sprinkled with tufts of green bush that looked like decorative sprigs of mint. The heath and moorland had gradually given way to this highland desert, a barren terrain of strong winds, thin air, and little bird or mammal life. Gone were the lumpish green hills and the valleys decorated with short, stumpy trees. Up here in the desert, I was no longer looking for kilted bagpipers, I was looking for camel trains. The previous days had seen us pass through three distinct climatic zones: equatorial, then moorland, and now desert. However, up ahead lay the arctic.

After two hours of fitful sleep at the Barafu Camp (14,927 feet) I woke up at 8 p.m. with a vicious stabbing pain in my stomach which I immediately knew to be the evening's stew impatiently re-announcing itself. I lay curled on my side, the howling wind beating the tent like a ragged sail, and I had the distinct feeling that at any moment the flimsy edifice would be ripped from its moorings. At 11 p.m. precisely, a porter appeared with tea and biscuits, and I forced down a few mouthfuls of tea and then listened as he smiled and said, 'Hopefully you'll summit at dawn.' Having introduced me to a new verb, he disappeared, and I stepped out into the bone-chilling night air and looked all around. Russell staggered out of his tent. 'What the fuck did we eat?' So it was not my imagination; on top of everything else, we were now suffering from food poisoning.

Other groups of climbers were already on their way to the summit, looking like a long line of coal miners with their lamps strapped neatly to their heads. I took up my place behind the guide, and in front of a visibly limping Russell, and began to breathe deeply as we stepped forward and commenced the long, arduous night-time ascent. Yet no matter how deeply I breathed it seemed to be impossible for me to get enough oxygen into my lungs and as a result my legs felt weak and unresponsive. I could hear Russell's footsteps behind me, and I tried to ignore the stabbing pains in my stomach and concentrate instead on the light from my headlamp that was shining on the back of the guide's woollen cap.

After three hours of climbing in the freezing dark I finally admitted to myself that I could see two black cats walking ahead of me. The cats suddenly transformed themselves into two dancing hobgoblins, and then a rock began to speak directly to me and gave me the GNER timetable for trains leaving London King's Cross. At about 18,000 feet I heard a horse neigh loudly, but there was no sign of a horse, and then I saw four men draped in white, carrying a white coffin, floating down the mountain towards me. I decided it was best not to mention any of my observations to Russell, whose indigestion system was now operating at full throttle, and whose breath had become worryingly short and laboured.

Some time later the batteries on Russell's headlamp gave out and he signalled to Arnold that he would have to stop and change them. I was relieved, and seized this opportunity to sit heavily on a rock, directly under Orion the Hunter. I felt so close to the constellation that I was sure I could reach up and pluck it out of the sky. And then I foolishly fell asleep. This is a place where if one sleeps for fifteen minutes, there is a very strong possibility of not waking up. When I heard Arnold say 'Ready', I snapped my head to attention and pretended I had not fallen asleep at all. And then, as we began to move off, the hallucinations began again, but this time I kept my eyes trained on my feet and mercifully all I saw were imaginary bright red flowers against the frozen scree.

As we inched our way towards Stella Point on the lip of the crater, I felt too physically weak to lift my head and look either left or right. I was also wary of listening or looking too closely at anything in case the rocks started to talk to me again or I saw those damn hobgoblins. Then, just as I thought this torture would never end, the sun began to rise on the horizon behind us and light quickly flooded the sky. The heavens turned from a silver-speckled black to the deepest blue, and away in the east the gentle curvature of the Earth was clearly discernible. Immediately I scrabbled in my pockets and pulled out my sunglasses, for the light reflecting off the snow and glacial ice was blinding. Then, towering above me I saw the huge peak that was now within striking distance.

The climb from Stella Point to Uhuru Peak was physically less demanding than the punishing six-hour ascent in the dark. As Russell and I edged our way along the narrow ridge, the sight of the snow-crusted volcanic crater to one side, and the wide glacial sea of the southern ice field to the other, was stunning. Forty-five minutes later we reached Uhuru Peak where a neat wooden sign informed us that we had now reached the highest point in Africa. Russell and I high-fived each other. 'Here's to the Parting Glass in Saratoga Springs,' he said. Then we both looked around at this most amazing sight. To be walking in the sky and see the sun rise over Africa is a precious gift. I contemplated the moment, but our shivering guide seemed keen that we should begin our descent. As we turned and began to walk away from Uhuru Peak, a newly ebullient Russell suggested that we climb together next in Ecuador. 'With the Albanian woman?' I asked, as innocently as I could.

It was nearly 10 a.m. when we finally returned to the Barafu Camp. I was tired and hungry, for the three-and-a-half-hour descent had been difficult. Skiing down the scree had provided me with the opportunity to do a reasonable impression of a two-legged Bambi, but it soon became clear that Russell's knee was giving him serious problems, as was his right foot. After some soup, Arnold insisted that we start yet another five-hour descent across a nondescript volcanic rock landscape that looked almost lunar, and try to make our final camp before sunset. At last, after six hours we limped into Mweka Camp, with Russell in considerable pain and needing not only to sit, but soak his injured foot in a bowl of water.

At five the following morning, the excited babble of porters, eager to return to friends and family, preceded the dawn chorus of birds. The Kilimanjaro wake-up call is a tinny blaring of porters' radios, cut with the incessant scraping and banging of pots and pans and the tented noises of snoring and the rustling of plastic bags. After breakfast, we set off through the dense vegetation of the rainforest, but Russell continued to walk slowly. The song of the birds and the howling of the monkeys, and the occasional flash of light that managed to penetrate the undergrowth, all seemed comforting after the arid terrain of the summit.

'I feel like I'm over the slog of the American book tour,' said Russell as he took a break and leaned against a tree. The sun caught the diamond stud in his ear, and suddenly the side of his face lit up. 'Climbing Kili has got me back again.' I looked at the rainforest surrounding us. More than a week had passed without either of us having seen a house, a car, a television set, a newspaper, or even another person going about their daily life. We walked on, but it was only when I saw the tracks where the four-wheel drive vehicles had passed that I truly understood that my re-entry into the 'real' world was almost complete.

At the gate we signed the book and received our certificates,

which confirmed that we had 'summitted'. As we did so, Russell scanned the pages to find out if, at sixty-four, he was the oldest man to reach the top in the past few months. On discovering a sixty-eight-year-old German only a week or so earlier, he laughed and shut the book. I watched his mind drift towards thoughts of Cuban cigars and doubles of whisky. My own mind drifted back to questions of what all of this had meant. Russell and I had not really talked about Africa, or about writing, or about race, which constituted the usual roster of subjects we kicked around whenever we met. Most of the time we were simply too exhausted to talk. I was happy for Russell that the climb had revived his spirits after his American publication, but for me it had been a lesson in understanding obsession.

After my three previous ascents I had learned to face down the question, 'Why do you do this?' with the same blank stare that I gave people who, many years ago, would ask me 'Why do you want to write?' It is difficult to explain obsession. However, on this particular ascent I rapidly discovered that there was no correlation between the selfish preoccupation of climbing Kilimanjaro and my writing. For the first time there was no obsession to alleviate the frustration of the task that lay ahead, and I very quickly found myself surrendering to the illogicality and pain of the journey. In response to 'Why do you do this?' I would now have to shrug my shoulders and say, 'I don't know', and really, that's not a good enough answer, either for climbing Kilimanjaro or for writing. A little obsession can go a long way towards assuaging hardship. Once we reached the Keys Hotel it was with a sense of relief that I offered my sleeping bag to Arnold. There would be no more Kilimanjaro ascents for me.

The following morning, while Russell slept, I took a beaten-up Peugeot into Moshi to try and find an internet café. The young, moon-faced boy of a driver was unsurprisingly proud of his third-hand vehicle with blacked-out windows. I found a café, but I could only receive and not send emails and so I quickly left. As we made our way back to the hotel, the clouds parted and suddenly there was a spectacular view of snow-

capped Kilimanjaro hovering right above the town. The driver pointed. 'Kili,' he said. 'Only crazy people go up there. It is too cold for us.' I asked him what was up there. He laughed and then slapped a thigh as he drove. 'Nothing,' he said. It was the best joke he had heard in years. 'They climb all that way and there's nothing there. No fruits to pick, no crops, no animals. Nothing.'

Sierra Leone: Bunce Island (2007)

I had been idling on the grounds of the Freetown Aqua Sports Club Ltd for nearly an hour and was now beginning to give up hope. A few minutes earlier a white South African had approached and assured me that he could 'fix things'. He claimed that he would 'see if it's possible' and then he sped off in his jeep throwing up a billowing cloud of dust in his wake. I did not expect to see him again. I watched two lethargic men stringing up a sign which read 'Happy Birthday' on the front façade of the building. To the side of the club a sagging electrical wire spanned the gap between two palm trees; it boasted a yellow bulb, a green bulb and an empty socket. Beneath the wire, permanently established stone tables and chairs were formally grouped, their dignity undermined by the presence of the odd plastic chair that had been carelessly tossed among them. The swimming pool was half full of filthy water, and near the steps which led down into the pool lay a pair of abandoned flip-flops. Up above, the buzzing of a helicopter competed with the tinny rhythms of hip hop that emanated from the inadequate speakers flanking the empty bar. Here, on a tranquil Sunday afternoon in Freetown harbour, in the shadow of high wooded hills which rose dramatically behind me, I too felt abandoned.

As I continued to wait, I wandered over to the Honours Board and noticed that the award for the Best Squash Player of the Year had last been given in 1996. Presumably the civil war had focused people's attention on more serious matters than club sport. It was now 2003, and although the war was over, the country remained visibly scarred by the physical evidence of

the recent conflict. Civic buildings were in a state of disrepair, the roads were full of craters, and even here, at a private and some-what privileged facility the air was redolent with the heavy scent of neglect. According to the Human Development Index Rating (which utilises longevity, literacy and income as its three criteria), Sierra Leone was officially 179th out of 179 countries; the poorest place on earth, with a life expectancy of thirty-six. These days, Best Squash Player of the Year was of little import-ance. As I ambled towards the jetty, I was careful to avoid the dog excrement on the grass. This club would once have been a splendid place for expatriate diplomats and businessmen to repair to and down gin and tonics and forget about the fact that a posting to Sierra Leone could legitimately be interpreted as evidence that their careers had already bumped up against a tin ceiling. But today I had little interest in reimagining a more palatable time before the horrific civil war; I was in search of a boat that might take me to a place whose brutal history was such that, in its heyday, it was known simply as the worst carbuncle on the face of Africa.

Twenty miles up the Sierra Leone River, and located at the furthest navigable point that could be reached by the ocean-going ships of the eighteenth-century slave trade, sits Bunce Island. One-third of a mile long, and only 400 feet wide, during the eighteenth century this small island was at the centre of a complex slave-trading network that stretched throughout the region of West Africa known as the Grain Coast. The trading island had considerable notoriety in Africa, in England, and also across the ocean in the Americas, and was known as a vibrant hub of commercial activity; the raw materials being traded were, of course, human beings. Bunce Island was a well-fortified holding place, a processing centre, and a place of dispatch from which tens of thousands of Africans were forcibly removed from their homeland and transported across the Atlantic Ocean and in the direction of the so-called New World.

Most of the slaves who were shipped out of Bunce Island had been specifically targeted because of their rice-growing skills.

Sierra Leone: Bunce Island

The American colonists of the eighteenth century, who culti-
vated rice on their southern plantations, yearned for this Grain
Coast labour and, after Bunce Island, the Africans' next port of
call would not be Brazil or the Caribbean, it would most likely
be Charleston, South Carolina or Savannah, Georgia. By the mid-
eighteenth century, slave labour had made South Carolina the
wealthiest of all English colonial holdings, and English slave ship
captains would sail from Liverpool, or Bristol, or London,
knowing that if they 'slaved' Bunce Island they would be hand-
somely rewarded in the American South should they arrive with
a 'full pack'. Many captains specialised in this small Sierra
Leonean island, including John Newton, who later wrote the
hymn 'Amazing Grace', but this area of Africa known as 'the
white man's grave' was replete with dangers, not least of which
were contagious diseases and potential native hostility.

Finally, I procured a small boat. The young man in charge
– I guessed him to be in his early twenties – stood erect and
bare-chested on the stern of the vessel and turned the rudder
by means of a long handle. The single engine purred as we
glided along, but the eerie stillness of the water made me feel
as though I was travelling across a vast lake as opposed to up
a river. Occasionally green mounds of vegetation appeared on
the flat horizon and presented themselves as islands, and men
and women stood perfectly still on these small protrusions of
terra firma and watched as we passed by. I tried hard to push
the word Conradian from my mind, for I understood it to be
imbued with all kinds of ambiguous connotations, but truly
this was a Conradian world that I was entering. We were moving
purposefully towards the past and, despite the overwhelming
beauty of the river, and the tranquillity of this West African
afternoon, I sensed a heavy, burdensome history beginning to
thicken the air.

On Bunce Island there was not much that had remained
intact. The place had been established in 1670 under the juris-
diction of the English Royal African Company, but had been
most active between 1750 and 1800. By 1830, the slave trade

335

having ended, the island began to fall into disrepair. To locals it was known as 'a place where history sleeps'. As I stepped ashore I reminded myself that history does not sleep; we just stop seeing and listening. The ruins that littered this small island included a well, two cemeteries, and the remains of a fortified estate house which included storehouses and a dormitory building. Many cannons were still visible, although some were overgrown with weeds and vines as though about to be claimed by nature. I was able to see the rubble of the Georgian Great House, where one could dine and gaze out on scores of chained Africans savouring their last glimpse of their homeland. As I wandered aimlessly, I soon discovered that the few muddy paths all seemed to quickly dead-end at the shoreline of this narrow, miserable place.

In a small hut I signed the visitors' book under the watchful eye of a barefoot local man who claimed to have a sure grasp of the island's history. There was another man in the hut, an American teacher from Ohio named Shaun, who announced that he would be my partner on the barefoot man's short tour. Shaun told me that he was a high school teacher with an interest in African American history, and that he had bribed a police launch to bring him out here. I looked through the open window at the launch as it bobbed playfully in the water next to my own small boat, which suddenly seemed to be lying perilously low in the water. I remembered that these had been crocodile-infested waters and there was no record of any slave having ever escaped. And then the skies opened and it started to rain heavily and, together with Shaun and the guide, I found myself marooned in the small hut on Bunce Island. There would be no tour.

The Europeans who sailed these waters in the eighteenth century were desperate men who were prepared to trade with anybody in exchange for a fast buck. There was never any pretence that their mission went beyond exploitation, or could in any way be perceived as civilising. These men of commerce often had no idea whether the natives on the islands in this huge estuary, who often sailed out to greet them in their canoes, would prove to be hostile or friendly. If challenged, the response of the slavers was often ruthless. Yet, towards the end of the eighteenth century, it was this heavily 'slaved' region of the Grain Coast that was chosen as the place in which to establish the first colony for repatriated slaves. Ironically enough, Freetown – the capital of this supposed Province of Freedom – was established just twenty miles from Bunce Island.

Some years earlier, I had read a moving volume of letters written by repatriated former slaves, in a collection edited by the historian, Christopher Fyfe. This stirred my curiosity about the formation of Sierra Leone and its deeply complex relationship to slavery and freedom. And then, two years ago, I picked up Simon Schama's book *Rough Crossings*. Here it was, all laid out in great historical detail, and peopled with vivid characters, finely drawn portraits of the minor players, and possessing a narrative flourish that enabled the author to tell this remarkable tri-continental story with panache and verve. My pilgrimage to Bunce Island was an attempt to further understand this period of history, and the stories of the men and women whose lives were rocked to their very foundations by the vagaries of the slave trade and the quest for individual human freedom.

Clearly it wasn't going to stop raining, and I could see that my pilot was growing impatient. I bade both Shaun and the local 'historian' farewell, then stepped out into the teeming rain and made my way to the shoreline and climbed back into the boat. The engine sputtered to life and we began to move slowly against the slant of the driving rain back in the direction of Freetown. The trip had given me a flavour of the isolation and misery of Bunce Island, but it had also allowed me to understand about the loneliness of what it means to sail upriver in Africa. I hoped that one day I would write something about the founding of Freetown, about the history that informs Sierra Leone, about slavery and freedom on the Grain Coast, but as yet I did not know what. As we passed gaudy-looking fishing boats whose bare-chested helmsmen, like my own, stood silently like Giacometti statues silhouetted on the horizon, with heavy sheets of rain washing across their image, I realised just how deeply I had been moved by this journey back in time. Silent and noble, these unhurried men seemed connected to an earlier epoch and I understood that this was the true gift of the day. The loitering at the Aqua Club, the desolation of Bunce Island, the thundering rain, all had been worth enduring in order to discover this serenely disturbing river where time seemed to stand still. And then I heard a phone ring, and I turned and watched as my pilot fished his mobile out of his trouser pocket. 'You will please call me later. Right now I am busy.'

Caryl Phillips was born in St Kitts and now lives in London and New York. He has written for television, radio, theatre and cinema and is the author of fourteen works of fiction and non-fiction. *Crossing the River* was shortlisted for the 1993 Booker Prize and Caryl Phillips has won the Martin Luther King Memorial Prize, a Guggenheim Fellowship and the James Tait Black Memorial Prize, as well as being named the *Sunday Times* Young Writer of the Year 1992 and one of the Best of Young British Writers 1993. *A Distant Shore* won the Commonwealth Writers' Prize in 2004 and *Dancing in the Dark* was shortlisted in 2006.